EXTREME
EVIL

EXTREME EVIL

Taking crime to the next level

PHIL CLARKE
KATE AND TOM BRIGGS

Futura

FUTURA

First published in Great Britain in 2011 by Futura

A CIP catalogue record for this book
is available from the British Library.

ISBN 978-0-7088-6695-5

Typeset in Great Britain by Omnipress Limited
Printed and bound in Great Britain

Futura
An imprint of
Little, Brown Book Group
100 Victoria Embankment
London EC4Y 0DY

An Hachette UK Company
www.hachette.co.uk

www.littlebrown.co.uk

Photo credits: Getty Images

The views expressed in this publication are those of the author.
The information and the interpretation of that information are
presented in good faith. Readers are advised that where ethical
issues are involved, and often highly controversial ethical issues
at that, they have a personal responsibility for making their own
assessments and their own ethical judgements.

CONTENTS

PART THREE: LADY KILLERS

PART FOUR: CULT KILLERS

PART FIVE: TYRANTS

PART SIX: CHILDREN OF EVIL

PART ONE
CANNIBALS

ALBERT FISH

*This modern-day Marquis de Sade resembled a
beloved grandfather, an innocuous, gentle-faced old
man to whom you would happily entrust your child's
care. The truth: Albert Fish was a sexually-depraved
sexagenarian earning the nicknames 'The Boogeyman'
and 'The Brooklyn Vampire' following a number of
cannibalistic acts that shocked pre-war America.*

AWFUL ORPHAN

From religious mania and hydrocephalus to visual
hallucinations, mental illness had always been rife
throughout the Fish family line, so when Hamilton
Howard entered the world on 19 May 1870 in
Washington DC, few would have been shocked to
learn he would later have problems. Yet nobody
could have foreseen the extent to which his afflictions
would play out to the detriment of so many lives.

His childhood was far from happy. His father,
Randall Fish, died when Albert (the name he later
took) was just five years old, forcing his mother to
pack him off to the St John's Orphanage. It was here
that he was subjected to incessant teasing, humiliation

and considerable physical harm. Beatings from the teachers became so commonplace he came to look forward to the pain, causing him to get sexually excited. And this brought yet more teasing.

Thankfully he escaped further torments, returning to his mother a few years later, but the damage was done. By the age of twelve, he had developed such perverse urges as coprophagia – the eating of excrement – and had begun to spend much of his time visiting public baths where he would watch other boys undress.

These predilections were however kept fairly private, hidden in the background while he endeavoured to lead a normal life. In 1898 he married Anna, a woman nine years his junior and they would have six children together. The happy family man travelled from state to state through his job as a house painter, all the while his abnormal sexual cravings bubbling under the surface.

SINS OF THE FLESH
His clandestine molestations of young children soon began and continued unabated, arousing in him deeper carnal pleasures as the new century progressed. However in January 1917 his wife left him for a simple-minded handyman named John

Straube, taking all the furniture but leaving behind all six children. It was this rejection that triggered a more outward display of perversion and mental illness.

Albert began acting like a madman. Hearing voices in his head and hallucinating, the forsaken husband turned fearsome father as his children witnessed him shaking his fist at the sky, exclaiming he was Christ. This led to serious self-harming episodes, abusing his own body with a nail-studded paddle in an attempt to atone for past sins. He even asked his own children to spank him with the device until blood ran down his legs.

When this religious self-punishment failed to provide satisfaction, Albert resorted to more obscene attacks on his person. He burned alcohol-soaked cotton pressed into his anus and embedded needles into his groin, many so deeply inserted he was unable to retrieve them. He then started to write obscene letters to lovelorn women, hoping to find a willing partner to share in his extreme self-cruelty. Surprisingly, he found no takers.

BUDD-ING EVIL

In the summer of 1928, during one of his regular searches through the classified ads, Albert Fish came upon the appeal of one Edward Budd, an eighteen-year-old from Manhattan, asking for work in the country to help out with his family's money worries. Three days after placing the ad an old grey-haired man with soft blue eyes arrived on the doorstep of the Budds' Chelsea apartment.

Introducing himself as Frank Howard, the meek old gentleman offered young Edward a job at $15 a week on his Long Island farm. It seemed too good to be true; it was. For this was Albert Fish on the hunt for a victim.

Over the course of a week Albert ingratiated himself further with the Budd family, bringing gifts for all the children. His attention had now turned from Edward to their oldest daughter, ten-year-old Grace, whom the benevolent benefactor invited to accompany him uptown to his niece's birthday party. Keen not to offend Edward's future employer, her trusting parents allowed little Grace to leave with 'Mister Howard'. It was the last time they would see her alive.

A six year long manhunt followed led by chief investigator, Detective William King; a tenacious veteran of the force nearing retirement. No sign of Grace or the old man could be found and, despite media involvement generating hundreds of leads, the case began to grow cold.

Then one autumnal November day in 1934 Mrs Budd received an anonymous letter. It told of a Captain John Davis who, while travelling in China during the great famine, had eaten human meat. The author continued, confessing he had also partaken of the flesh of a child, namely that of their lost daughter, Grace.

What followed was a lurid disclosure of what happened to her child. The morbid message explained how the writer had taken her by train up to Westchester County, Washington to an isolated house. Here, he choked her to death before chopping off her head and cutting her in half. He then proceeded to devour her over a period of nine days; each cannibalistic course served with vegetables. The letter finished with a poor consolation, that she died a virgin.

CATCHING A FISH

Immediately the distraught Budd family passed the murderous missive on to the police. After a dearth of recent clues this fresh evidence brought fresh hope. The search was back on. Using a spectroscope, the authorities discovered an almost invisible mark on the back of the envelope revealing the letters: N. Y. P. C. B. A. - an acronym for the New York Private Chauffeurs' Benevolent Association.

An appeal to its members resulted in a confession from one Lee Sicowski, who admitted to stealing some of the stationery and leaving some in a flophouse on 200 East 52nd Street, New York. Further investigation revealed an elderly gentleman fitting the description of the fictitious Frank Howard had recently stayed in the same room. When the signature in the doss house register was compared to the handwriting of the letter they matched.

Speaking to the landlady, Mrs Frieda Schneider, the police learnt their man was expected to return. Detective King rented a room at the top of the stairs and waited. Three weeks went by until Fish showed up. On 13 December the veteran cop came face to face with the killer, a seemingly harmless old fellow. However, before King could slap on the handcuffs, Albert lunged at him with a razor. One final attempt to avoid arrest. Thankfully, it failed.

Once in custody, Albert Fish delivered a never-ending flow of shocking tales and unforgivable acts, admitting to as many as fifteen child murders and up to four hundred sexual assaults over twenty-three states. He confessed how he was ordered by God to castrate as he travelled about the country, his grip-bag filled with knives, saws and a meat cleaver – his self-titled 'Implements of Hell' – used to carve up his victims. The authorities were further disturbed to learn that Fish had been arrested as many as eight times during their six-year search. Fish had even had two spells in Bellevue Psychiatric Hospital, but had been released after examination, perceived as no threat to society.

SUPREME THRILL

The jury at the White Plains trial of Albert Fish took a mere ten days to come to a collective decision. Charged with the first degree murder of Grace Budd, whose remains had been retrieved from Wysteria Lodge, the defendant sat motionless as grisly details of his sexual abnormalities and sadistic cannibalism were read out to the court.

These despicable acts left several expert witnesses under no illusion that Albert Fish was insane, supporting the official plea from his own defence. Described as a psychiatric phenomenon who associated his cannibalism with the holy communion, Albert Fish simply stated, 'I am not insane, I am just queer'. The jury agreed and found him suitably sane to be granted a guilty verdict.

On 25 March 1935 Albert Fish was sentenced to the electric chair. Far from fearful of his imminent death, Albert rather relished the method of his demise saying, 'It will be a supreme thrill – the only one I haven't tried!'

When he took his place in Sing Sing's hot-seat as the oldest inmate to be executed on 16 January 1936, the convicted cannibal appeared almost enthusiastic, assisting the guards with his own straps.

It took two jolts to deliver the state-appointed justice. Many still believe the rumour that the first one short-circuited thanks to the twenty-nine various needles later found embedded in his nether regions. His final words were: 'I don't know why I am here.' Those who had the misfortune of hearing the details of his crimes against children would not have been as confused.

ARMIN MEIWES

*To those who came into contact with him, he was just
an introverted computer repairman but the man – later
dubbed the 'Hannibal of Hesse' – held a shocking secret
of unrivalled savagery; a gruesome belief-defying pact of
sadomasochistic fantasy that was to shock the world.*

SMOTHERED BY MOTHER

Many a twisted mind is forged by an atypical
upbringing and in this tale of extreme evil it is no
different. Born on 1 December 1961 Armin Meiwes
was raised in the small central German village
of Wustefeld, where he spent most of his early
childhood inside the family home; a huge medieval
mansion dating back some seven hundred years.
However, at the tender age of eight, Armin's world
was to be thrown into turmoil when his father and,
soon after, his two brothers left the house leaving
him in the care of his mother.

Waltraud Meiwes was a domineering woman
who ruled the roost with an iron hand, stifling poor
Armin with an all-invasive love. She would intrude
all areas of his life, demanding to know where he

was and who he was with at all times. This resulted in Armin spending an unhealthy amount of time on the extensive premises and he soon began to lose touch with reality.

Longing for companionship the repressed child was forced to look inward and soon invented an imaginary younger brother named Frank. While not uncommon for lonely and imaginative youngsters to fabricate friends, this fictitious relationship soon went beyond the banal when Armin began to wish he could consume Frank's body in an attempt to absorb his soul. This quickly developed into fantasies of dismembering and devouring his fellow schoolmates. A disturbing perversion was now taking shape.

Then on 2 September 1999 Waltraud Meiwes died after a long illness. Armin was now all alone. Freed from his mother's claustrophobic attention Armin attempted to live a normal life. He took a job fixing computers and endeavoured to interact with the outside world, becoming the perfect neighbour, repairing the cars and mowing the lawns of his fellow villagers. But he could not shake off the urges.

FRANKY ONLINE

Armin soon lost himself once more inside the manor house, discovering whole new worlds via the internet. He quickly found that there were others out there whose passions matched his own and began to connect with these like-minded deviants online.

Within the imaginary walls of chatrooms dedicated to cannibalism, torture and sadomasochism, Armin fed his obsession using the alias: Franky – after his make-believe brother. In one of the forty rooms he constructed a 'Slaughter Room' in which he built a cage and a blood drainage system, uploading photos for his fellow freaks to see.

Unable to resist the craving to cannibalise, Armin then posted a morbid message calling for, 'a well-built eighteen- to thirty-year-old to be slaughtered then consumed'.

Shockingly, he received over two hundred replies from interested parties, some of whom made the trip to the big house in the tiny village. These willing participants in Armin's lust-filled amusement would allow him to draw lines on their naked bodies, marking out where he would cut them. Others he hauled up by their feet on the custom-built pulleys inside the Slaughter Room. For all of Armin's guests, though, this was all pure role-play. None would give their consent to go further.

BERND BRANDES

Then on 5 February 2001 during another session online he met Cator99 in the cannibal chatroom. Rather than wishing to merely pretend, this member appeared to share Armin's cannibalistic dream, bewitchingly replying: 'I am your meat.' The pair engaged in fetishistic talk over the coming weeks, exchanging naked photographs, whipping one another into an erotic frenzy. Within a month, they would meet.

Cator99 was, in fact, Bernd Jurgen Brandes, a software developer for Siemens in his early forties. He had worked for the telecommunications company for fifteen years and was known to his colleagues as a normal, sociable human being. They had no idea of the darker side that existed outside of work, hidden away from public scrutiny.

Bernd's mother had died in a car crash when he was just twelve years old, a tragic accident for which he blamed himself. Carrying this guilt through into adulthood, his mental frailty was exacerbated by confused feelings of bisexuality. Splitting from his long-time girlfriend and unable to stand being alone, Brandes threw himself into a number of relationships before moving in with his male lover Rene, a baker ten years his senior.

Sadly, this stable relationship failed to curb his burgeoning sexual desires and Brandes secretly began visiting male prostitutes for violent sex. He would plead for them to bite off his penis, for him the ultimate masochistic thrill. This perverted path of self-destruction stemmed from a need to belong. Finding Franky online was a godsend. He now had someone who wanted him in a way that would answer all his grotesque prayers.

DINNER AND A MOVIE

On the morning of 9 March 2001 Bernd Brandes was on a train bound for Berlin, his mind filled with thoughts of his impending mutilation, his stomach empty in order to improve his date's dining experience. On reaching the capital he bought a one-way ticket to Kassel some 150 kilometres from Armin Meiwes' home, paid in cash to leave no trace. Outside the station, the two paraphiliacs met for the first time.

Back at the mansion the pair settled in, drinking coffee whilst naked. Small talk over, the pair adjourned upstairs to the Slaughter Room for the main event. While Armin set up a video camera to record for posterity the awful occasion, Brandes washed down a score of sleeping pills with a bottle of schnapps. It was at this point their mutual fantasies became one single, horrible reality.

In an opening act of unparalleled immorality a drowsy yet compliant Brandes allowed Armin to take out a knife and promptly slice off his penis. Following the acquiesced amputation the couple turned cannibal tasting the raw dismembered organ. When they found it too tough to swallow, the host disappeared downstairs to fry the offending article, but – in his overriding excitement – accidentally burned the meat, rendering it inedible.

Meanwhile, upstairs, Brandes had climbed into the bath, where he began to bleed to death. His host waited over three hours for his guest to die, passing the time by reading a *Star Trek* novel. Keen to partake of more human flesh, an impatient Armin then stabbed Brandes in the throat, before beginning the inglorious process of dividing up the body.

Two days later, after he had packed the juicy cuts of Brandes into freezer containers and buried the skin, guts and skull in the vast garden, Armin Meiwes sat down to tuck into his first proper meal: steak and potatoes covered in a pepper sauce, accompanied by a South African red wine. Over the next ten months he feasted on the defrosted flesh consuming as much as 20kg; with each morsel believing he grew closer to his willing victim. He would also revisit the footage of the slaughter itself many times over, masturbating to the video nasty.

STILL HUNGRY

Five months had gone by since the misdeed, his protein levels through the roof as he worked through the stock of Bernd meat. And now Armin was hungry again. Alone once more he yearned to consume another body and soon Franky was back in the chatrooms searching for a new soul mate. His desire to recreate the twisted affair would be his downfall.

In a bid to bring about quicker results and feed his appetite, Meiwes began to divulge details of what he had done, even posting up photos. When a student from Innsbruck, Austria saw these explicit images he immediately alerted the police.

Early in the morning of 10th December 2002 seven police officers came knocking on the door of the Wustefeld manor house. Seizing disks and hard drives filled with cannibal pornography and other obscene material, the authorities charged Armin with the glorification of violence. They also located 10kg of unidentified meat in the freezer, unearthed human remains from the garden and, later, found the video tape of the despicable dinner date.

COURT DILEMMA

A year went by before Armin Meiwes eventually came to trial, affording psychiatrists ample time to analyse this strange individual. In interviews he freely admitted to absorbing Brandes' masculinity and even his ability to learn English, relating the eating experience to something like taking communion.

The trial took place in nearby Kassel in December 2003. While the prosecution sought a verdict of murder for sexual satisfaction (cannibalism not being a legal term under German law), his defence focused on the fact Brandes had given his full consent to the crime – a dilemma for the jury. Following more than forty witnesses called over fourteen sessions, the court came to a decision on 30 January 2004, agreeing with the defence that the killing had not been sexually motivated and Brandes had consented to his own annihilation. He was given eight-and-a-half years for manslaughter.

In April 2005 a German court ordered a retrial following an appeal from the prosecution. After psychiatrists believed he would re-offend, Armin Meiwes was found guilty of murder and sentenced to life imprisonment.

DANIEL AND MANUELA RUDA

In a true-life tale of devilry and vampirism a freaky German couple flip from plain and pasty-faced Goths to blood-drinking death-bringers and puppets of Satan in a creepy endeavour to move closer to their dark Lord and Master.

MESSENGER OF DEATH

Life in the strange lane started early for Daniel Ruda. Shying away from ordinary human contact as a young boy, he began to lust after the metallic taste of blood from the age of twelve and by the time he was a teenager was soon to be found among the neo-Nazi movement prevalent in Germany.

From the politics of the Far Right he quickly crossed into the Gothic scene, performing in a black metal band; the portentously-named Bloodsucking Freaks. By this time Daniel was already convinced he was on speaking terms with Satan himself, who – he believed – had bestowed upon him the honour of being his personal Messenger of Death.

Yet despite this special relationship with the fallen one Daniel needed companionship and it soon became time for him to seek out a soulmate; someone with whom to share the dark times. Placing a personal ad in the classified section of *Metal Hammer*, a black metal music magazine, twenty-three-year-old Daniel called out for his queen. It read:

> *Black-haired vampire seeks Princess of Darkness who hates everyone and everything and has bidden farewell to life.*

One would be forgiven for thinking such an advert would be dismissed as mere black humour by those that read it. However, there was one girl who spotted the perverse paragraph that summer. And it spoke straight to her heart.

THE PRINCESS OF DARKNESS

Manuela Bartel was an only child raised in the small university town of Witten in North Rhine-Westphalia, far from the dark side of life that would eventually consume her. In fact, little Manuela was just an ordinary young girl who loved animals and worked hard at school until, that is, she became a teenager and the monster began to take shape. It started with radical hair styles and clothes; daring to be different, preferring to shock rather than conform. Distancing herself from friends she became an angry adolescent with a desire to rebel, attending political demonstrations. However, these protests failed to slake her thirst for disorder and at the age of sixteen Manuela ran away from her small-town life to the then European Mecca for Goths: London.

It was here in the English capital where Manuela could satisfy her cannibalistic curiosities, attending bite parties where willing donors would offer their warm blood to wannabe vampires. She would consort with others like her, frequenting graveyards where she persuaded her new friends to bury her alive.

The eerie gloom of the Scottish Highlands was her next port of call, where she befriended the infamous Leopard Man of Skye; an odd cave-dwelling hermit who had chosen to cover his entire body in leopard-print tattoos and had even altered his teeth to look more feline. These were the types of people with whom she felt she belonged.

Returning to Germany in the late nineties with a developed obsession with death and the devil, Manuela came upon Daniel Ruda's classified ad. She was the perfect candidate for his Princess of Darkness.

A MARRIAGE MADE IN HELL

When the pair met it was love at first bite; their shared mind-set allowing for a mutual descent into the dark depths of Satanism. Moving in together back in Manuela's home town of Witten, they filled their home with unique creature comforts: fake human skulls, cemetery lights and, taking pride of place, an altar in the living room.

Their obsession knew no bounds, it seemed. No doubt taking her cue from her friend, The Leopard Man, Manuela had her incisors removed and animal fangs implanted to appear more like her beloved vampires. Then in a strange Halloween ceremony the once well-adjusted girl formally dedicated her soul to Satan. It was only a matter of time before their peculiar predilection was to have an impact on others.

In March 2001, Daniel had one of his regular visions in which he would be visited by the Devil himself. The chosen messenger of Death was given four numbers: 6,6,6,7 and from this it was deduced they should marry on 6 June (6/6) and then on the 6 July (6/7) a suitable victim should be sacrificed to Satan. This was the call they had both been waiting for; an opportunity to prove their worth to the Antichrist.

And so, as planned, Daniel and Manuela married on 6 June 2001 in a wedding ceremony befitting their oddball outlook: the groom dressed all in black and his bride in a PVC bondage corset, piercings and hair dyed pink with her temples shaved to reveal tattoos of an inverted crucifix and target. A marriage made in Hell.

COME TOGETHER

Now joined together in unholy matrimony, Daniel and Manuela Ruda could now progress to phase two of their devilish plan: the human sacrifice. They had already agreed on who would be afforded the honour: thirty-three-year-old Frank Hackert, a colleague of Daniel's at the car parts centre where he worked. Hacki – as they called him – was the complete opposite to the gruesome twosome. He was warm, funny and loved the music of The Beatles. Once they said Hello, Goodbye to the Fab Four fan, they believed he would make the perfect court jester for the Prince of Darkness.

And so on 6th July 2001 the unsuspecting Frank Hackert attended a drinks party at the Rudas' home. His surprise at being the only guest rivalled only by the shock at the demonic décor, he grew more troubled with every wicked glance the newly-weds shared. While Frank squirmed on the sofa Daniel left the room only to return brandishing a hammer. As if possessed by an evil spirit he struck his work mate twice savagely about the head. The fated Herr Hackert managed to stand and walk a few paces, but would not leave the room alive.

Having watched her husband honour Lucifer with his unprovoked attack, Manuela felt it was time to demonstrate her devotion. Acting on a voice in her head, she snatched up a nearby knife and plunged it into her guest's chest again and again. Sixty-six times in total. They swore they saw the living room light flicker as Frank Hackert's own light faded.

PILGRIMAGE TO PERDITION

Following the brutal and wanton murder of poor Frank Hackert, the killer couple bathed in the euphoria of knowing they would now be welcomed with open arms into Hell. Collecting the endless outpouring of blood in a bowl they drank to their achievement at the living room altar then adjourned to the bedroom to have sex atop an oak coffin; their final act on this mortal plane before they took their own lives.

However, with each passing minute, their frustration grew at the lack of contact from Satan, as did their doubt that suicide was the way to go. In a deviation from the plan the couple fled their home, leaving the body of Frank Hackert to fester.

In a bid to garner the attention of the Antichrist, his faithful servants chose to visit the towns of Sonderhausen, Apold and Jena – all places with strong links to the world of Satanism. Yet still the call did not come.

While they drifted aimlessly around Germany, the police had been alerted to their crime. Earlier on the day of the murder the couple had sent suicide letters to their closest relatives. When Manuela's mother received hers she contacted the police and on the 9 July the authorities converged on the Rudas' apartment.

What they discovered inside made even the strongest of stomachs turn. Frank Hackert's now-decomposing body had been mutilated with various sharp instruments and a pentagram had been carved into his chest with a scalpel, which still jutted coldly from his torso. Nearby police also found a handwritten death list of fifteen names of possible future targets.

SATANIC ORDER

The Satan-smitten duo from Witten were finally arrested on 12 July 2001, thanks to a police roadblock outside of Jena. Six months later a highly-publicised trial in Bochum gave the Rudas an unprecedented platform on which to perform.

Adopting a devil-may-care attitude, Daniel and Manuela flicked devil's horn signs with their fingers and licked their lips at Hackert's parents during the entire trial. It was yet another chance to bask provocatively in the limelight.

Their defence stated they were mere puppets, instruments of the Devil's will, and were just obeying orders. As fan mail poured in from like-minded deviants, the verdicts were handed down to Daniel and Manuela: fifteen and thirteen years respectively to be served in a secure psychiatric hospital; their diminished mental capacity the reason for such light sentences. As they exited the courtroom the twisted Teutons gave one final goodbye kiss for the benefit of the cameras.

DENNIS NILSEN

Known as the Kindly Killer, Britain's worst serial killer at that time prowled the gay bars of Soho for willing playmates only to strangle and drown them before they could leave him to his loneliness.

THE WAKE OF DEATH

Dennis Andrew Nilsen was born on 23 November 1945 in Fraserburgh, Aberdeenshire, a bleak fishing town on the northeast coast of Scotland. His childhood soon mirrored the region's desolation following his parents' divorce. Forced to live under the strict Presbyterian rule of his maternal grandparents, Dennis was relentlessly lectured on the impurities of the flesh, the evils of alcohol and popular entertainment, seen as the work of the Devil.

Unsurprisingly, Dennis withdrew into a dark place, which grew even darker following the passing of his grandfather in October 1951. Forced to view the body resting on the dining room table during the wake, the six-year-old boy got his first glimpse of death. Many have suggested this became the catalyst to his future career as a killer.

School was a confusing place for the admonished adolescent as he dealt with his burgeoning attraction for other boys. With a basic education under his belt, he joined the army and travelled the world with the Catering Corps. Between 1967 and 1970 he was stationed in Germany, the Persian Gulf, Cyprus and Northern Ireland. This final port of call saw him become disillusioned with army life, and he promptly left the military. His ten year stint in the Corps had allowed him to develop a taste for alcohol, explore his homosexuality, and perfect his butchering skills that would later be used to make his male companions disappear.

Following a brief spell with the Metropolitan Police, with whom he got the chance to visit morgues, Dennis moved on again taking a job with the department of employment. Here he gradually rose within the ranks, gaining promotion to executive officer at the Kentish Town office. Both staff and clientele found the bespectacled man a kind and attentive employee. They had no idea what existed behind those myopic eyes; what transpired behind closed doors at home.

LOSING HIS TWINKLE

In private, this physically unremarkable man was

indulging in disturbingly unusual practices. His developing fascination with death found him whitening his skin and painting his lips blue to mimic a corpse, whereupon he would stare at his reflection for hours on end, often masturbating at his grim pallor. He would also walk his dog in Highgate Cemetery and let his imagination run wild as he gazed upon the graves of the dead. Teetering on the brink of evil, Dennis needed just the right emotional trigger to push him over the edge and into oblivion.

Around four years later that moment came. Dennis had been living with David Gallichan, nicknamed 'Twinkle', at 195 Melrose Avenue, Cricklewood in North London. Then, after two years of co-habiting, his friend moved on, leaving Dennis lonely and depressed. To counter feelings of rejection, he began to trawl the Soho district for company, but when each lover departed the next morning, his despair grew more acute and he reacted to his isolation in the most violent of ways.

On 30 December 1978, Nilsen met a young Irish teen named Stephen Holmes and brought him back to his bachelor pad for sex. When thoughts turned to the inevitable departure, Dennis took out a tie and strangled the boy then drowned him in a bucket of water. He now had his very own corpse, something he had fantasised about for years and he revelled in its pliability, finding beauty in its limpness. After admiring the lifeless body for some time, he placed it under the floorboards, where it remained for seven months, festering beneath his feet.

THE BAD SAMARITAN

A year went by without Nilsen resorting to murder. Then in October 1979, he picked up Andrew Ho in a pub in St Martin's Lane. Agreeing to be tied up, the Chinese student soon found his new lover's hands about his neck. He broke free and escaped, heading straight for the police, but when Dennis counter-claimed Andrew had been trying to steal from him the matter was dropped.

Two months later he met Ken Ockendon, a twenty-three-year-old Canadian student, at the Princess Louise pub in High Holborn. After showing him the sights of the capital, the pair retired to the flat, where Nilsen was overcome by urges to create another corpse. While Ockendon listened to music on a pair of headphones, his host wrapped the flex around his neck and choked him to death, making doubly sure by drowning the body in the bath. Once Nilsen had had his fun, the dead student joined Stephen Holmes under the floorboards.

Over the next twenty months, Dennis repeated his double-kill procedure of strangulation and drowning, killing ten more young men. He did not care who he picked up, and often failed to remember or even ask their names. All that was important was to find company and then never let them leave. He would spend days with a corpse until the smell became too strong, and then they disappeared beneath the carpet.

His final murder at Melrose Avenue came on 18 September 1981. The previous day Dennis had found epileptic Malcolm Barlow coping with the aftermath of a fit outside his home. The killer kindly called for an ambulance and went with him to hospital. When Malcolm returned to the house to thank him, he was invited inside for a meal. Kindness failed to strike twice and Nilsen promptly strangled his guest while he was asleep. With no room under the floor, he then squashed him underneath the kitchen sink.

TO PASTURES NEW

The body situation at the Cricklewood address had become a serious problem by the time his murders entered double figures. He had to spray the flat twice a day to keep the flies away and was forced to make midnight sorties into the large garden to dump bags filled with entrails by the fence. These would be feasted upon by scavenging wildlife. Nilsen also lit bonfires to eliminate evidence, burning a car tyre along with the human remains to mask the stench.

Knowing he needed to curb his murderous acts, Nilsen moved house in October 1981. He chose an attic flat at 23 Cranley Gardens in Muswell Hill as the residence had no garden nor easy access to the floorboards. But this attempt to break the deadly cycle, soon faltered. Within a month he was back cruising the bars of Soho, bringing Paul Nobbs back to the new pad. Luckily, he lived to see morning and when he visited the hospital to have some strange bruising examined, the doctor informed him he had been the victim of strangulation.

His first kill in Muswell Hill came in March 1982 after picking up John Howlett from The Salisbury pub. The pair struggled as Nilsen succumbed to his urges once again, but he managed to finish off his quarry by drowning him in the bath. With no easy way to dispose of the corpse, he leant on his butchering skills and dismembered the body, boiling the head, ribs and other sections in a pot on the stove, and hiding bags of bones about the flat.

Two more murders followed over the next year. He killed Graham Allen while he ate an omelette, but had no recollection of the attack. The desire to bring death had seemingly overpowered him to such an extent that now he was unaware of his evil actions. Finally, he murdered Stephen Sinclair, sleeping contently with the body for days after, using mirrors to watch himself perform with the corpse. By the time Sinclair's body had been carved up and flushed down the toilet, the end of Nilsen's savage journey was in sight.

FLUSHING OUT THE KILLER

On 3 February 1983 Nilsen's fellow residents at 23 Cranley Gardens discovered their toilets had become blocked. Dyno-Rod were called out five days later and when the engineer opened the manhole in the street, he found lumps of rotting meat. On his return the next day, he was surprised to find the strange sludge had vanished. It was then the police were called.

When neighbours informed officers they had heard Nilsen moving around that night, DCI Peter Jay paid the top-floor flat a visit, waiting for the Job Centre official to arrive home. Hit by the overpowering stench on entering the apartment, the detective knew they had the culprit and immediately asked where the rest of the body was hidden. In two plastic bags in the wardrobe came the swift reply.

After confirming the shocking truth, the police arrested Nilsen, but another surprise followed in the car journey to the station. Dennis admitted it was not just one or two bodies but fifteen or sixteen. A thorough search of both addresses took place to ascertain the true extent of this man's evil.

By the time he came to trial, only seven victims had been identified. He was subsequently found guilty on six counts of murder and two attempted murder, failing to persuade the jury of his diminished responsibility. Recommended to serve no less than twenty-five years in jail, Dennis Nilsen still resides at Her Majesty's pleasure and in 2008 was informed he would breathe his last breath behind bars.

ELADIO BAULE

In a tranquil town on a Philippine island paradise a minor infraction during a local wedding turns the worst kind of ugly, when one of the guests is forced to cater for the event.

TROUBLE IN PARADISE

As police chief superintendent, Perla Bacuel rarely had to deal with violent crime in her town. Parking tickets and bar brawls were as heavy as it usually got in Narra. Situated on the south-western island of Palawan, this peaceful municipality was in fact planning to promote itself as an ecotourism destination to foreigners wishing to experience the idyllic splendour of the Philippines. The focus was to be on the golden beaches, the luxuriant waterfalls, the trekking up in the mountains and the hot springs. Instead the town has become known for the bizarre murder of one of their own.

PROUD DAY

For many of the locals of this small town Saturday 17 July 2004 was a day of celebration; two of the residents were to be married. Looking forward to the big day was Eladio Baule. The forty-seven-year-old father would later walk his daughter down the aisle; a proud moment for the farm labourer, indeed for all there present to cherish for the rest of their lives. However, the day would be remembered for rather different reasons.

The facts are sketchy even several years down the line, adding an air of mystery to the tale. It appears during the wedding reception an incident took place. Deep in the hinterland, away from the main town, guests danced to music, drinks flowed, spirits were high. The day had gone by without a hitch. The moment came when Benjie Ganay, cousin to the happy father, stumbled and tripped on the dance floor accidentally touching the bottom of the bride-to-be. Eladio witnessed the faux-pas and, rather than taking the blunder as an honest mistake among merrymakers, flew into a rage.

WHO DOES YOUR CATERING?

The affronted father swiftly assembled a select few and conspired to teach Ganay a lesson. Eladio's young son, Gerald, along with Sabtuary Peque and Jhunnie Buyot confronted the clumsy guest and took him by motorised tricycle away from the reception and into the nearby woods. Deep amidst the tall trees things got out of hand. In a disproportionate display of violence, they set upon their prisoner, stabbing him to death. Then Eladio's murderous posse set fire to Ganay's body using coconut leaves and kerosene. Still they were not done with their victim. Taking their knives to the body once more, the fiendish four carved off pieces and ate the freshly-roasted meat. When Buyot began to choke, Eladio turned to his accomplice and held him at knife point until he swallowed.

The killer cannibals then returned to the wedding party, allegedly bringing chunks of barbecued Benjie back for the drunken guests to sample. Those who dared to snack from the buffet were completely unaware they were tucking into a friend and relative.

THE SECRET IS OUT

In the days that passed the evil secret remained hidden until it all got too much for Jhunnie Buyot. Stricken with guilt and remorse, he admitted everything to a local village elder, who forced him to confess to the police.

Agreeing to act as a prosecution witness, Buyot told Perla Bacuel and her officers the whole grisly truth, adding they had dumped the bones in a nearby creek in the hope the rains would wash them away.

The subsequent police search took two whole days to find the blackened bones of Benjie Ganay, along with strands of hair and charred pieces of clothing. With physical evidence of the heinous crime in the hands of the authorities, Sabtuary Peque quickly surrendered to police officers and Eladio and Gerard Baule were apprehended soon after.

It had now become impossible to keep this shocking tale of overreaction from the world's media. Newspaper reporters and TV stations descended on the once idyllic island. Meanwhile, in a desperate attempt to limit the inevitable damage to the area's tourism, Mayor Lucena Demaala insisted the incident was not indicative of the native population.

A number of reports focused on the indigenous tribes of many southern Philippine islands, whose histories include documented practices of canni-balism and head-hunting. This predictably fuelled speculation that such traditions are still in existence today, planting a seed of doubt in the mind of any prospective traveller planning to visit the area.

GARY HEIDNIK

With a misshapen head and a warped view on
fatherhood, this sick ex-soldier held a harem of sex
slaves in his basement, dishing out beatings and
serving up meals made up of human flesh.

FOOTBALL HEAD

Born on 22 November 1943, Gary Heidnik's subsequent childhood mirrored many a killer's troubled upbringing. When he was just two years old, his parents divorced and he spent the next four years in the care of his alcoholic mother. He then moved in with his father who had remarried. The new woman in his life created a hostile environment for him at home, and life for little Gary went from bad to worse.

Not only did he have to contend with his wicked stepmother, but he also suffered the shame of being a serial bed-wetter. Adding insult to injury, his cruel father would humiliate him by hanging the urine-soaked sheets out of his bedroom window for all the neighbours to see. Such emotional abuse soon became second nature.

Further problems came when young Gary fell out of a tree, banging his head so severely his skull became deformed. He was subsequently teased at school, where the children would call him 'Football Head'. Yet in the face of such ridicule he excelled in class, and at the age of fourteen enrolled at the Staunton Military Academy in Virginia. However, despite good grades he was forced to leave; mental problems cited as the reason. A monster was surfacing and would soon wreak havoc on those around him.

THE MONSTER TAKES OVER

After leaving the academy he joined the army and proved a model soldier, training as a medic and serving as an orderly with the 46th Army Surgical Hospital in Landstuhl, West Germany. However, in August 1962 Gary visited sick bay complaining of severe headaches, blurred vision and vomiting. He was diagnosed with gastroenteritis, but doctors also identified the more worrying symptoms of a degenerative mental illness. Three months later, Gary Heidnik was honourably discharged with a full disability pension and transferred to a military hospital in Philadelphia.

His army career over, Heidnik focused on nursing. He also indulged his considerable intellect, studying a variety of subjects at the University of Pennsylvania. Sadly, yet another blow would push him closer to the edge of darkness. On 30 May 1970, his cancer-riddled mother committed suicide, poisoning herself with Mercuric Chloride.

Following in her footsteps, Gary began a series of unsuccessful suicide attempts: overdose, eating glass, hanging and even a head-on collision with a truck. The resultant hospital visits saw him become increasingly uncommunicative, his behaviour even stranger. Nurses spoke of how he would not allow anyone to remove his favourite leather jacket, which remained welded to him like a second skin.

Over the next fifteen years or so, Heidnik's mental state slowly degraded, manifesting itself in a series of violent and heinous acts. By 1978 he had attacked his brother with a block of wood, shot at the face of a lodger and signed out his lover's mentally-handicapped sister, keeping her prisoner in his home where he raped and sodomised her. Gary Heidnik was now certainly a menace to society.

HEIDNIK'S HAREM

Past the point of no return, the mentally ill ex-soldier snapped. On Wednesday 26 November 1986 he picked up part-time prostitute Josefina

Rivera in his silver Cadillac, taking her back to his two-storey house in the heart of the Philadelphia slums. Following the sexual transaction, Heidnik handcuffed the twenty-five-year-old and dragged her downstairs into the cold, dark basement. Chaining the girl to a large pipe running along the ceiling, he then placed his head in her lap and fell asleep.

The next morning, still reeling from her sudden imprisonment, Josefina watched her captor dig a hole in the centre of the room. As he shovelled out earth from this makeshift pit, Heidnik confessed his master plan. She was merely the first of ten women he would abduct over the coming months, vowing to make them all pregnant in a warped attempt to create a large family. To prove his intent, Heidnik then raped his prisoner.

After a failed attempt to escape, Miss Rivera was joined by Sandra Lindsay, a mentally-handicapped black woman Heidnik had known for several years. Then came nineteen-year-old Lisa Thomas and Deborah Dudley either side of Christmas. On 18 January 1987 Jacqueline Askins was incarcerated below. Five girls now occupied the dank cellar. Heidnik now had half his harem.

His treatment of the cellar-dwelling sex slaves grew worse with every passing week. Forced to survive on a diet of stale sandwiches and even dog food, the girls were subjected to regular bouts of torture. One day in February, Heidnik caught Sandra Lindsay attempting to move the plywood sheet that covered the pit. She was promptly handcuffed to the ceiling and left to hang there by one wrist for two whole days.

This persecution caused her to fall seriously ill. After force-feeding her morsels of bread, Heidnik kicked her into the shallow pit, telling the others she was faking. When he lifted her out, Sandra Lindsay was dead. The others watched him drag the body upstairs. Then came the ominous sounds of a power saw as he dismembered his dead slave. The sickening stench filled every corner of the house and clung to Heidnik's clothes. Even the neighbours noticed and called the police, but when an officer paid him a visit, he simply explained it was the result of an overcooked roast dinner.

The truth was altogether more horrific. The smell exuded from the human rack of ribs in the oven and Sandra's boiling head in a pot on the stove. Heidnik had even resorted to mixing the dog food with the meat picked from her bones in an industrial food processor. This mush would then be served to the captives below. It is believed Heidnik also consumed the flesh of his poor victim.

PARTNERS IN CRIME

In the wake of Sandra's death and dismemberment, Heidnik's behaviour plummeted to new lows. Paranoid that his slaves were plotting against him, he strung three of them to the ceiling and pushed a screwdriver deep into their ears to deafen them. The one to escape such punishment was Josefina.

The first of his collection had, over the months since her capture, become Heidnik's favourite and this privileged position afforded special perks. She was permitted to accompany him on trips into town and given the dubious honour of sharing his bed. However, on 18th March 1987, she was called upon to assist her captor with a new level of torture.

Believing the three slaves in the basement deserved another more terrifying ordeal, Heidnik had Josefina fill the pit with water, while he drilled air holes in the plywood cover. The tormented trio were then shoved into the makeshift well, whereupon a bare wire connected to the mains was pushed through one of the air holes. The live feed connected with the metal of Deborah Dudley's shackles electrocuting her to death.

Forced to sign a piece of paper attesting she had assisted in Deborah's death, Josefina accompanied Heidnik to Pine Barrens, a desolate area outside

Philadelphia, where he dumped the corpse in the woods. Down one slave, Heidnik now enlisted the help of his number one girl to acquire a replacement. On 23 March Josefina persuaded Agnes Adams, a friend from her strip club days, to come back to the house. With his sixth abduction, it now appeared Heidnik had a willing accomplice to bring his master plan to fruition.

THE GREAT ESCAPE

Josefina had been biding her time. She knew the best way to survive was to stay on the right side of her keeper. Now, after weeks of playing the role of obedient girlfriend, she put her own plan into effect. On the day after the kidnapping of Agnes Adams, Josefina begged to see her family. Promising to bring him another slave, she got her wish.

With a midnight rendezvous arranged at a near-by petrol station, Heidnik dropped her off. As soon as he was out of sight, Josefina sprinted to her apartment. When her boyfriend opened the door, she finally knew she was safe. At midnight, instead of his pliant partner, Heidnik met a team of armed officers, their guns raised and ready to fire.

Less than five hours later, police turned up at 3520 North Marshall Street, Heidnik's house of horrors.

Down in the basement they found Lisa Thomas and Jacqueline Askins asleep on a mattress with the newly-abducted Agnes inside the pit.

A visit to the kitchen revealed blackened ribs in the oven, plastic-wrapped limbs in the freezer and Sandra's decapitated head still simmering gently on top of the stove.

Unsurprisingly, the defence counsel at trial pleaded insanity. As Heidnik's lawyer succinctly put it: 'Any person who puts dog food and human remains in a food processor and calls it a gourmet meal and feeds it to others is out to lunch.'

However, the testimonies from the surviving captives proved damning, and on 30 June 1988 the jury found Heidnik guilty of eighteen separate charges, including the murders of Sandra Lindsay and Deborah Dudley. Following a number of suicide attempts while on Death Row, the end came by lethal injection at the hands of the state executioner.

GEORG KARL GROSSMANN

Considered one of the most notorious killers of the
Weimar period, this sadistic butcher of Berlin lured
an untold number of prostitutes and poverty-stricken
women back to his apartment for sex. What they
endured was beyond barbaric with many of these
luckless ladies leaving in a far worse state, returning to
the streets in an altogether different form.

GROSS MAN

Georg Karl Friedrich Wilhelm Grossmann was
born on 13 December 1863. One of seven children,
he grew up with his ragman father in the small
Prussian town of Neuruppin on the western shore of
Ruppiner See in north-east Germany. While little is
known of his childhood, we do know he left school
aged fourteen before leaving his home-town two
years later. The young teen was drawn to Berlin,
hoping to find steady work in the capital and it was
here where he apprenticed at a butcher's – a trade
he would later bring into disrepute.

Released from compulsory military service due to
a hernia in 1882, Grossmann travelled around the

rural areas of Pomerania and Mecklenburg picking up small labouring jobs on farms. It was during this time that he started falling foul of the law. In 1883 he spent three days in jail for begging, theft and various indecent acts. Petty crimes compared to what lay in his future. This was merely the beginning of an escalating commitment to evil.

In 1896 Georg was found guilty of molesting a sheep in Mannheim and in the following year was convicted of sexually assaulting a twelve-year-old girl in Nuremberg. Being caught for these lewd and wicked crimes seemed not to curb their existence for in 1899 he found himself in prison yet again; this time given fifteen years hard labour for sexually abusing two young girls, one of whom suffered serious physical injury.

DANGEROUS LIAISONS

On his release in 1913 he returned to the capital. Grossmann was now fifty; too old to learn new, more moral tricks. With sexual deviance, violence and crime prevalent in many areas of Berlin, Grossman was able to blend into the background and continue with his evil ways. After living at various squalid addresses in the eastern part of the city, he took an apartment on Lange Strasse 88/89 in the centre of the Friedrichschain district – a notorious den of iniquity.

It was here in his fourth floor studio where he would begin to bring back women from the area, mainly prostitutes and single ladies down on their luck. Grossmann would lure them to his abode with promises of food, shelter and clothing, In return their benefactor demanded sex, a simple and common exchange during these hard times, but as his gluttonous lust for debauchery grew so the liaisons became all the more dangerous.

Pretty soon Karl – as he now called himself – had become somewhat of a personality around town. He was often to be found peddling his sausages outside the Silesian train station and picking up women around the fountain at Alexanderplatz, just one block north of his home. His neighbours also could not miss the steady stream of female companions as they noisily traipsed up the stairs to his top floor flat. What they failed to spot was that many of the women never left the apartment alive.

SIMPLY THE WURST

With domestic violence commonplace during the Weimar era, it is still surprising the fellow residents at Lange Strasse 88/89 turned a deaf ear to the violent screams coming from behind Grossmann's door. Even when concerns were raised at the malodorous stench emanating from within, he was able to satisfy them with fictitious tales of chicken meat gone bad.

The truth was far more sinister. The Berliner butcher would lace his victims' drinks with a sedative then pleasure himself with their bound and unconscious bodies. Once his sadistic fun was over he would bash in their brains and begin the process of dividing up the corpse into small parts, removing the women piecemeal from the studio in small paper packages to dump in the nearby river.

One might think it could not get much worse than this, however there exists a rumour some believe true. It is said that many of his victims did not end up thrown into water but rather placed into his sausages and sold outside the Silesian train station, turning the unwitting German public into cannibals.

NEIGHBOURHOOD WATCH

As Grossmann hacked his way through the female population of Berlin, unsurprisingly human remains began showing up in the numerous waterways. It was not long before the police realised they had a serial killer on the rampage. A total of twenty-three bodies between 1918 and 1921 had been discovered.

When police posted public notices around the capital in early August 1921, Grossmann's neighbours finally began to suspect there might be more to the man on the top floor. Now regarding their neighbour with extreme suspicion they kept a watchful eye on the lothario's movements, especially when bringing lovers back to the flat. At one point Helene and Mannheim Itzig, a couple living down the corridor from Grossmann, went as far as to drill a hole through his door in order to catch sight of his evil actions.

Consequently, when residents heard the usual violent screams followed by an eerie silence on Sunday 21 August, they decided it was time to call the authorities. The police rushed straight over and broke down the door to a scene of pure horror.

Inside the dingy room thick with the foul stench of blood and viscera, they found the body of a woman in a semi-state of dismemberment. Over her stood Grossmann covered in her blood. Further examination of the apartment found that at least three others had been butchered in recent weeks.

The identity of the victim was found to be thirty-five-year-old Marie Nitsche, a down-at-heel ex-con who had only just been released from a month-long stay at Moabit prison. She had met Grossman on the street from where they frequented various drinking dens. Straight out of jail without a place to stay or money in her pocket, she must have felt as if she had landed on her feet when her newly-acquired friend invited her back to his apartment. Little did she know her friend was the devil incarnate.

ONE LAST KILL

Caught red-handed, Georg Karl Grossmann was arrested and initially charged with the murder of Marie Nitsche. His defence would have a tough time finding him innocent of this crime. Police, however, had to try and connect this evil man to the mutilated bodies washed up around Engelbecken and now lying at the city morgue. This would be more difficult.

The authorities worked tirelessly to develop a series of witnesses prepared to testify against Grossmann. Many Berliner women came forward, their interviews shedding light on the perversions of this sexual sadist. Yet despite this damning evidence provided by these testimonies Grossmann was charged with just three murders in the first degree. As the judge passed a sentence of death it is said the mad butcher laughed out loud.

On the 5 July 1922, while awaiting his execution, Grossmann committed suicide, hanging himself inside his cell. In all his time in prison he never gave a full confession, for that reason the actual number of victims he murdered and mutilated is not known. Some suggest as many as fifty young women found their way from the streets of Berlin into Grossmann's apartment. How many of these filled the frankfurters served from his stall no-one dares contemplate.

ISSEI SAGAWA

*Unable to resist his lustful urges for human flesh,
this pint-sized celebrity cannibal succumbed to an
unnatural appetite, inviting a friend over for dinner.*

DISTURBING DREAMS

With Japan still reeling from the double atomic hits
upon Nagasaki and Hiroshima, Issei Sagawa entered
early into this world on 11 June 1949. As well as
being born premature, no bigger than the palm of
his wealthy father's hand, he was also diagnosed
with anoxia; a condition characterised by a severe,
lack of oxygen often causing brain damage. Such
an affliction might go some way to explaining his
future actions.

Sagawa began to have dark thoughts at a very early
age. He recalled a game he played with his father
and uncle in which they would chase him around
the house pretending to be man-eating monsters.
This idea remained with him even in sleep, often
dreaming of being roasted in a cannibal's cauldron.

Such visions of the subconscious slowly began to seep into his everyday thoughts, and he was soon fantasising about consuming a human body.

AN ABORTIVE ATTEMPT

At just five feet short with tiny hands and feet, an oversized head and a high-pitched feminine voice, Issei was never going to be a girl magnet. However, he was blessed with brains and performed well at school and soon he was enrolling at the Wako University in Tokyo. It was here, whilst studying for an English Literature degree, that he became fixated on tall, Nordic women; their white skin beguiling him into the bizarre belief that if he could consume them it would be the ultimate expression of love.

One summer day Issei chose to act upon this impulse and climbed in through the apartment window of a German woman he had seen in the street. He found her semi-clothed and fast asleep, but before he could act out his fantasy, the woman woke, screamed and he fled the scene. If there was to be a next time, he knew he would have to plan more carefully.

Following this attack, the diminutive student visited a psychiatrist to confess his depraved desires, who wasted no time deeming him highly dangerous.

Unfortunately, his rich industrialist father stepped in to cover up this evaluation and Sagawa was swiftly removed from the area. This would not be the last time Issei would need his father's help.

INDECENT PROPOSAL

Escaping further punishment in Tokyo, Sagawa finished his bachelor's degree and attained a master's at the University of Osaka. The thirty-two-year-old then went further afield to gain his PhD at the famous Sorbonne in Paris. The social side of academic life rather left him behind, ignored by his fellow students – no doubt due to his odd appearance – allowing Issei to disappear into a fantasy world.

He would daydream about killing any of the large number of fair-skinned European women he would see in the French capital, and devouring their flesh in a bid to get close to them. He began to invite prostitutes back to his 16th Arrondissement apartment, but was ultimately too frightened to deliver the final blow.

Then he saw her. A twenty-five-year-old Dutch beauty called Renee Hartevelt, a highly intelligent student, fluent in three languages and a bright future ahead of her. Knowing he would not be able to get close by any normal means, Sagawa approached her with a proposition: would she be open to teaching him German for a generous fee. The stunning blonde accepted, unaware she would be the one to pay the ultimate price.

SORBONNE APPETIT

Teacher and student began to meet regularly to improve Issei's German. They would also exchange views on European literature, art and architecture and Renee soon began to enjoy the little man's company, bonding with another intellectual mind. Sagawa, on the other hand, was dreaming of an altogether different bond. He had become infatuated with his tutor, licking the place where she had sat after she had returned home. He now made up his mind to eat her.

On 11 June 1981 Sagawa waited for the arrival of Renee Hartevelt. He had purchased a cassette recorder on which he wanted to record her reading one of his favourite German Expressionist poems. Behind the chest of drawers he had hidden a .22 calibre rifle. Today was the day he would make his dreams a reality.

Sharing pleasantries and some herbal tea, Issei cut to the chase, openly declaring his love for her. Renee revealed her feelings towards him were purely platonic. She found him engaging but sadly not sexually attractive. To avoid an awkward silence, Sagawa retrieved the poetry book from which Renee had agreed to read and turned on the tape recorder.

With her back to him as she recited, Sagawa moved for the rifle, aimed at the back of her head and pulled the trigger. By all accounts he fainted and on waking saw the lifeless body silently sprawled on the floor, blood pouring from the gunshot wound. Phase one of his despicable deed was complete.

MEAT FEAST

Having rendered her altogether more receptive to his desires, Issei undressed the object of his warped affection, her beautiful white body beckoning him onward. He tried to bite into her naked buttock, but could only leave teeth marks, so he jabbed a knife into the flesh, a corn-coloured sallow fat oozing from the punctured skin. Beneath he found the red meat he yearned for, discovering it was soft and odourless like raw tuna. He looked into her eyes and told her she was delicious.

Now he had taken his first step into cannibalism, Sagawa began sampling various parts of Renee's dead body. Serving up dish after distasteful dish with salt and mustard, he sat at the dinner table and feasted on her remains using her underwear as a napkin. Once he had eaten enough he took what was left of Renee Hartevelt to the bedroom and had sex with her corpse before falling into a deep sleep.

The next day he awoke next to the mutilated body, surprised to discover it did not smell. So Sagawa continued with the evil tasting menu indulging in the less desirable parts: genitalia, eyeballs, armpit and even anus. It was only after he had decapitated his victim, holding the head up by the hair before him, did he realise he was now a cannibal.

PARK AND HIDE

Four days passed before Issei Sagawa, lost in a world of lust-filled debauchery, realised it was time for his guest to leave the house. Her putrefying corpse had now developed a noticeable odour and had begun to attract a host of flies. Using an electric knife and hatchet, he hacked away at the limbs, cramming body parts into two wheeled suitcases, pausing only to masturbate … with her severed hand!

He then called for a taxi to take him and his shameful luggage to the Bois de Boulogne, a nearby park, where he planned to dump the dismembered Dutch girl into the lake. But a short Oriental man with a limp lugging two oversized suitcases through the grounds was anything but inconspicuous. Soon spotted, Issei panicked, dropped everything and bolted from the park.

It did not take long for the police to get the call to examine the abandoned cases. Stomachs turned as they opened them up, taking in their shocking contents, and they were swiftly traced back to Sagawa. When gendarmes searched his Parisian apartment they found all the evidence they required; Hartevelt's lips, left breast and both buttocks sitting in the refrigerator. He did not resist arrest.

EXTRADITION OF EVIL

The French court, on advice from three separate psychiatrists, declared Issei Sagawa legally insane and unfit to stand trial, and he was ordered to be held indefinitely in a mental institution. However, his father, now president of Kurita Water Industries, was to intervene once again, pulling some strings to get his son extradited back to his native Japan.

In May 1984 the thirty-four-year-old disgraced student arrived in Tokyo to a media frenzy. He was swiftly escorted to Matsuzawa Asylum, where psychiatrist Tsuguo Kanego adjudged him to be sane but recommended he remain behind bars.

Only there was a problem. Japanese authorities discovered they had no legal right to hold him. With the relevant legal paperwork back in France and the French courts refusing to send the necessary documents to build a case against him, Sagawa was able to walk out of the hospital on 12 August 1986. Unbelievably, he was now a free man.

HE'S A CELEBRITY . . . GET ME OUT OF HERE!

Sagawa became a minor celebrity in his homeland, revelling in his past atrocities, taking pride in his notoriety. Dubbed 'The Godfather of Cannibalism', he was invited on numerous talk shows, cameoed in soft core porn films and wrote a number of books, including *In The Fog*, a fictionalised account of the infamous murder, selling over 200,000 copies.

Nearly thirty years on, Sagawa lives under an assumed name in the city of Chiba thirty miles east of Tokyo. No longer able to make a living from his past crimes, he works as a freelance artist, his paintings dominated by white fleshy buttocks. Only time will tell if he will kill and eat again.

JEFFREY DAHMER

*Between 1987 and 1991 this unassuming, sandy-haired
serial killer cruised the gay bars of Wisconsin for victims
to take home. Refusing to let them leave, he strangled
them before subjecting their corpses to the most terrible
injustices, securing his place as the poster boy
of sexual perversion.*

ANIMAL LOVER

The initial years following the birth of Lionel and
Joyce Dahmer's first son on 21 May 1960 were a joy
to behold. Baby Jeffrey was a happy child who loved
life and helped bring some much-needed harmony to
the Wisconsin couple's troubled marriage. However,
events in his infancy would conspire to change their
sunny child into a monster in the making.

At the age of six Jeffrey suffered a double hernia.
The simple operation that followed appeared to
have an enduring effect on his behaviour. From this
moment on the smiling, ebullient toddler gradually
began to turn into a shy, forlorn child; his smile
replaced with a blank stare.

Uncommunicative with the outside world, Jeffrey withdrew into a dark place, preferring the company of dead animals to his fellow man. He would often roam around on his bike searching for roadkill to take back to his hideaway for examination. By the age of ten he was bleaching the bones and collecting insects in pickle jars filled with formaldehyde.

His teenage years fared little better with the discovery of alcohol and sex. Frequently drunk during lessons, his studies began to slip, acting the class clown rather than applying himself. By now Jeffrey was spiralling out of control, masturbating three times a day to pornographic images of muscular men.

DAHMER'S DEBUT

His burgeoning libido combined with his developing fascination with dead fauna soon had the now seventeen-year-old Dahmer desiring human contact. He had seen an attractive man jogging past the house and resolved to meet him. Knowing he lacked the necessary social skills to win him over, he lay in wait with a baseball bat. Luckily for the runner he never came.

His first victim would come a year later, following his parents' divorce. In June 1978, the day after he graduated from high school, Jeffrey picked up young hitch-hiker Steven Hicks. They returned to his father's house and had sex, but when his new friend decided it was time to leave, Dahmer bashed in his head with a barbell. He then slit open the body to study the innards before bagging up the remains and burying them in the nearby wood.

Carrying this secret, Jeffrey enrolled at Ohio University, sent by his father who hoped higher education would alter his behaviour. Just two semesters in, he quit. Next, Dahmer Senior issued his son an ultimatum: get a job or join the army and so in January 1978 he enlisted. Stationed in Germany, the new recruit drank himself stupid on cheap liquor and was promptly discharged for alcoholism in March 1981.

SEARCH FOR A SOUL MATE

On his arrival back home, Dahmer the serial drop-out was packed off to his grandmother's in West Allis, Wisconsin. Under Catherine Dahmer's roof, he appeared to clean up his act. He read the Bible, attended church regularly and curbed his self-abuse to just once a week. He even found work at Milwaukee's Ambrosia Chocolate Factory.

Life on the straight and narrow was fleeting,

however, and Dahmer soon returned to his wicked ways, searching for a means to satisfy his carnal desires. Once magazines failed to gratify, he stole a shop mannequin for use as a substitute partner. He then hunted the local obituaries for a fresh corpse buried at the local cemetery. Sadly, the night he crept in to exhume a suitable body the ground was frozen.

The bathhouses of Milwaukee were next on Dahmer's deplorable quest for sexual thrills. Struggling to perform while his partners were awake, he started to spike their drinks with sleeping pills. As they lay comatose, Jeffrey would masturbate and listen to their hearts beating through their chests.

STEVEN TUOMI

Like an addiction, Dahmer needed more to achieve his sexual highs. On 15 September 1987, while on probation, he killed for the second time. Outside the 219 Club he met twenty-six-year-old Steven Tuomi and invited him back to the Ambassador Hotel, where he doped his drink. The next morning Dahmer awoke on top of Tuomi's mutilated corpse with no clue as to what had happened.

Packing the body in a large suitcase, he took it to his grandmother's house, storing it in the basement cellar. Here Jeffrey dissected the cadaver, boiling the skull which he kept wrapped in a blanket on his top shelf. Two more kills in the next twelve months saw his body count double and now the putrid smell from the basement was beginning to cause his grandmother some concern.

Pushed to find somewhere else to live, Dahmer moved in to a one bedroom apartment on North 24th Street in Milwaukee. The following day on 26 September 1988, he was arrested for drugging and fondling a thirteen-year-old Laotian boy called Somsack Sinthasomphone. Pleading guilty, Jeffrey escaped a prison sentence receiving five years probation on a work release programme.

THE NIGHTS OF THE LIVING DEAD

Free to continue his labours of lust, Dahmer moved to a low-rise building on 924 North 25th Street in Milwaukee's crime-infested west-side. While his modus operandi of pick-up, spiked drink then strangulation stayed the same, his post-mortem activities became more twisted.

After cutting them open, he would caress the viscera of his victims, masturbating over the mutilated dead, before serving up the flesh seasoned with salt, pepper and occasionally steak sauce. Believing they would live on within him he started to freeze body parts for future consumption.

Over the next two years Dahmer murdered another eight men, increasing his collection of bones, organs and muscles, bleaching their skulls and painting them grey to fool any visitors into thinking they were plastic. His home now resembled an abattoir with maggot-ridden carcasses in his bed and even in the bathtub where he showered.

The problem for Jeffrey was that his rotting playmates were an impermanent source of pleasure. Craving something more he began to inject hydrochloric acid into the frontal lobes of his victims, creating zombies that would stagger about his vile apartment. It was all about control. With this home-made lobotomy he could prevent them from leaving.

LOVERS QUARREL

Despite this new development, one of his puppets managed to escape. On 27 May 1991, fourteen-year-old Konerak Sinthasomphone was found wandering the streets naked, bleeding from the rectum. Jeffrey was able to convince the police that he was his nineteen-year-old boyfriend who had ran off after an argument. Believing the calm and coherent

Dahmer, the police escorted the boy back to the apartment. That night Konerak went the same way as the others, murdered and dismembered, his skull joining Dahmer's macabre collection.

Over the summer his hunt for suitable victims intensified, averaging one prize a week. Matt Turner, Jeremiah Weinberger, Oliver Lacy and Joseph Bradehoft all succumbed to Dahmer's evil. Neglecting his job at the factory he was promptly sacked for absenteeism.

Two days later he chose what would become his final victim.

PRIVATE SLAUGHTERHOUSE
On the evening of 22 July 1991 police officers Robert Rauth and Rolf Mueller were patrolling the hot and humid streets of down-town Milwaukee. Half an hour from completing their shift, they spotted a short black male, handcuffs dangling from one wrist. Believing he was an escaped convict they pulled him over only to hear a stranger tale: Tracy Edwards had escaped from a man trying to kill him.

Knocking on the door of Apartment 213, police met Jeffrey Dahmer, his cool, calm persona conflicting with the reports of a knife-wielding maniac. However, when he offered to retrieve the key to the handcuffs, the officers soon discovered a house of horrors. Polaroid images of mutilated bodies, two severed heads in the freezer and one in the fridge, a 57-gallon vat of acid eating away at three torsos and a collection of chemicals to rival any laboratory.

THOROUGHLY EVIL

In custody Dahmer freely confessed to a long list of evil deeds and in January 1992 stood trial for fifteen murders in the first degree. The jury took five hours to find him culpable on all counts and he was sentenced to 957 years in jail. After the verdict Dahmer read out a four-page statement expressing remorse for his actions, believing himself to be 'thoroughly evil.'

Incarcerated in Columbia Correctional Institute, Wisconsin, Dahmer became a born-again Christian and was soon allowed to mix with the prison population. On 28 November 1994 during work detail in the gym fellow convict Christopher Scarver, a dangerous schizophrenic, struck him with an iron bar from a weight machine. Ironically, Dahmer died from severe head trauma. It was the same way he had despatched his first victim, Steven Hicks sixteen years earlier.

KARL DENKE

This peaceful citizen of Muensterberg feared God, abstained from alcohol and resisted carnal pleasures yet his cannibal acts over a four year period would see him become probably the worst serial killer in Poland's history.

PROBLEM CHILD

Before the border changes following the end of World War II, the modern-day Silesian town of Ziebice in south-west Poland belonged to Germany and was known as Muensterberg. It was in this small town where Karl Denke would perpetrate such crimes, the likes of which had never been seen before in this part of the world.

Born in nearby Ober Kunzendorf on 12 August 1870, this son of a wealthy farmer was a problem child from the very beginning. Far from being an academic, he left school with a basic education and ran away from home at the age of twelve, finding work as a gardener's apprentice. Little is known of his life until the death of his father, when Karl was a young man of twenty-five.

While the running of the Denke farm passed to his older brother, Karl used his inheritance to buy himself a plot of land on which to plant his own crops, but farming was not in his blood and his business failed. He sold the land and bought himself a two-storey house on Stawowa Street in Muensterberg.

PAPA DENKE

Settling in this small town, Karl would reside in the same building for the rest of his days. Even when he lost his savings to the extortionate inflation of the post-war period and had to sell the house, he remained in a little apartment on the ground floor.

Karl soon became a pleasant fixture of Muensterberg life, well-respected among the eight thousand residents. With a smile Karl would sell his leather suspenders, belts and shoelaces from a shop opposite his home, and would wave to the townspeople as he made the trek north to peddle his pickled boneless pork at the Wroclaw market.

His benevolence knew no bounds. He found time to play the organ at the local church, carried the cross at funerals and was known to help beggars and people in need, allowing them to stay the night in his one-bedroom apartment. For these reasons

Karl quickly became known as Vatter Denke – Papa Denke – by the locals. A caring soul of the community with not a bad bone in his body – or so it seemed.

AXE ATTACK

At the wintry end of 1924 the people of Muensterberg would be forced to change their view of Karl Denke. On Sunday 21 December, a coachman passing down Stawowa Street heard screams coming from the home of the much-loved figure. Rushing in to help, he found a vagrant called Vincenz Olivicr staggering along the corridor, blood streaming from a nasty head wound. Moments from collapse, the injured man muttered that Denke had attacked him with an axe.

When the police were informed of the attack they were in disbelief that Papa Denke could have done such a thing. Yet when questioned back at the station, the fifty-four-year-old friend to all admitted he had struck Olivier with an axe for attempting to rob him. This admittance of guilt saw him placed behind bars in the police jail.

That evening, shortly before midnight, Sergeant Palke was on his rounds checking on the inmates. When he looked in on Karl Denke he found him swinging from the ceiling of his cell. Somehow he had managed to fashion a noose from his handkerchief and hanged himself. Curious as to why the benign peddler had reacted so excessively to a charge of assault, the police chose to pay his apartment a visit.

LEDGER OF DEATH

On Christmas Eve policemen began the search of the ground floor flat on Stawowa Street. Inside the cramped living space they discovered an array of suspicious items. The identification papers for many of the poor unfortunates whom Denke had sheltered lay on the windowsill, and inside a closet a number of blood-stained clothes.

In the kitchen area, they uncovered two large tubs packed with meat pickled in brine and an assortment of bones and pots of fat. When lab tests found these to be of human origin, the true horror of Papa Denke's crimes became clear. The good Samaritan of Muensterberg had been murdering his visitors and pickling their remains, carting them off to the Wroclaw market to be sold as pork.

A ledger, dating back to 1921, found in the flat shed yet more light on the dark evil deeds of Karl Denke. In the ledger he had listed the names of some thirty victims along with the dates of their demise and respective weights. Police ascertained the man had been devouring human flesh and peddling it to others for around four years.

The police were unable to identify the names of all of his victims, but it is believed he pickled the remains of at least forty beggars, tramps and travellers who it seemed would not be missed.

This cannibal has a small exhibit in a museum in his home town, but who knows it could grow into an even bigger one – not all towns can boast their own cannibal!

STANLEY DEAN BAKER

Hitch-hiking through seventies America, a nomadic hippie on a hell trip succumbs to the voices in his head to murder, mutilate and make a meal of his companion.

CATCH OF THE DAY

Saturday 11 July 1970 was a balmy summer's day in the Treasure State of Montana. On the banks of the Yellowstone River a fisherman enjoying the weekend weather sat hoping to land some trout abundant in these waters. What he managed to catch that afternoon was rather larger and quite rare in these parts – caught in the river's reeds was a dead body.

One 911 call later and the authorities descended upon the tranquil spot. The body was quickly brought ashore where Sheriff Guitoni and his men examined the deceased. One look told them this was no case of drowning. The corpse looked barely human, its arms and legs having been crudely hacked off along with the head. Stranger still, the mutilated torso had a huge gaping hole where the heart should have been.

Back at the morgue at nearby Livingston, the coroner performed an autopsy. Studying the limbless stiff on the slab, he discovered the male victim had been dead for approximately twenty-four hours and had been subjected to twenty-seven separate stab wounds. The cause of death was clear but without the usual means of identification, the Montana authorities required some help in determining who this poor man was.

HIT AND RUN

A positive lead came early on the Monday morning. A twenty-two-year-old social worker had failed to turn up for work and had been reported missing two hundred miles to the north-east in the town of Roundup. His name was James Michael Schlosser and his description matched that of the corpse in the Livingston morgue. Also missing was the man's gold yellow 1969 Opel Kadett. An APB was put out for its whereabouts. They did not have to wait long.

Earlier that morning the same car with its distinctive black racing stripes was travelling along a dirt road over a thousand miles away in Monterey County, California. Speeding on the wrong side of the road it collided head on with a pick-up truck. While the truck suffered only superficial damage, the Opel was a write-off. Unhurt, the owner of the pick-up, a businessman from Detroit, approached the wreck to find two Californian hippies inside.

Wearing the customary uniform of fatigue jackets and bell-bottom trousers, the pair of bearded beatniks seemed friendly enough, although neither was able to present a driver's licence. The man from Michigan State noted the car's registration details and offered to take them to the nearest telephone to inform the police and organise a tow.

The dented truck pulled into a service station in the town of Lucia, but while the driver made the call the free-spirited duo swiftly bolted for the nearby woods. The businessman relayed the incident to police including the car's licence plate details. The missing car had been found. California Highway Patrol were immediately told to keep a look out for the absconding hippies.

I'M A CANNIBAL

At the time the call came over the police radio, Officer Randy Newton was cruising the Pacific Coastal Highway. He soon spotted the offenders walking along the side of the road just two miles out of Lucia, attempting to hitch a lift. Sirens on, the patrolman detained the suspects, who freely admitted their wrongdoing. They also gave their names: Stanley Dean Baker and Harry Allen Stroup.

When they were searched, Baker was found to be carrying a Satanic Bible and a typed recipe for LSD. Also in his pockets police discovered a handful of small bones. It was then things got surreal. When asked what they were, he replied, 'They ain't chicken bones. They're human fingers.' Then matter-of-factly he declared, 'I have a problem. I'm a cannibal.'

The twosome were taken to the nearby police station in Monterey. Here Detective Dempsey Biley was tasked with interrogating the pair, to ascertain their involvement with the mutilated corpse in Montana. In Stanley Dean Baker he found a willing interviewee, eager to tell all.

MIDNIGHT FEAST

Inside the interview room, the effusive Baker opened up. Asked to elaborate on his odd comment, the beatnik confessed he had developed a compulsion for human flesh ever since receiving electric shock therapy for a nervous disorder when he was seventeen. He then began to divulge details of his actions leading up to the weekend, actions that would shed light on the dead body in Montana.

Baker and Stroup were both from Sheridan,

Wyoming and had been travelling since 5 June 1970, hitching lifts and working odd jobs as they journeyed south. According to the loose-lipped hippie, the two separated on Friday 10 June after reaching the town of Big Timber, Montana, as Baker had managed to get a ride.

His ride was none other than James Schlosser in his Opel Kadett. He was on his way to Yellowstone National Park for the weekend, and offered Stanley the chance to tag along. On reaching the reservation they found it too crowded so chose to set up camp for the night a few miles north on the banks of the Yellowstone River.

Admitting he had taken sixty-five tabs of LSD earlier that day, Baker explained how, in the dead of night, he was overcome with an undeniable urge to kill. He crawled over to the sleeping social worker, took out his .22 pistol and shot Schlosser twice in the head. Next he proceeded to stab the body over two dozen times, before cutting up the corpse into six pieces.

After hacking off the head and limbs of his companion, Baker ended this wanton demonstration of cruelty by gouging out the man's heart, eating the organ raw. To fend off future hunger pangs, he cut off the fingers to have something to snack on, then dumped the remains in the river along with the firearm. Stanley then drove away in the dead man's car, rejoining his friend, Stroup.

SATANIC STANLEY

This unbelievable tale seemed like fiction, but when Baker escorted the police to the murder site, they found clear evidence of a homicide. Blood-spattered earth, a hunting knife along with human bone fragments and even a severed ear was sufficient proof to corroborate Stanley Dean Baker's confession.

But what of Harry Allen Stroup? The way Baker told it, he had nothing to do with Schlosser's motiveless murder. The twenty-year-old hippie had remained silent throughout his interrogation, not wishing to deviate from his friend's statement. The police had two problems with the story; they doubted the dismemberment could have been achieved by one person; the park attendant had also witnessed seeing three people in the car, not two.

The drifting duo were flown back to Montana on 20 July and arraigned before a district judge seven days later. During the trial Baker insisted he possessed magical powers and had been involved in other satanic ritual killings. On 4 August Judge Shamstrom authorised a request to send Baker to Warm Springs State Hospital for psychiatric evaluation. He was eventually sentenced to life in prison, while Stroup received a ten-year term for manslaughter.

Even in jail the one time boy scout and altar boy continued to wreak havoc. Baker persistently pressed his fellow inmates to join his own satanic cult within the prison walls. He would be known to howl like a wolf when the moon was full and often threatened the guards with a series of makeshift weapons fashioned in his cell. This beatnik cannibal was paroled to his native Wyoming in 1985, his present whereabouts are unknown.

TED BUNDY

*Looks can be deceiving and between 1974 and 1978
this dashing fiend certainly proved the rule. Prowling
campuses for coeds from the Pacific Northwest to the
Sunshine State, the handsome prince among serial killers
relied on social compliance to lure at least
twenty women to their doom.*

BECOMING BUNDY

Throughout his life, Ted Bundy went by many names.
Born on 24 November 1946 in Burlington, Vermont
to an unwed mother, this serial-killing Sagittarius
began life as Theodore Robert Cowell. His surname
would then change twice before his sixth birthday.
Young Theodore never knew his father and grew up
believing his mother was actually his older sister – a
charade to avoid social disgrace – and the pair lived
under the roof of his grandparents in Philadelphia.

At four years old, the boy and his mother moved
to Tacoma, Washington in the Pacific Northwest
and soon 'sister' Eleanor met Johnny Culpepper
Bundy whom she married in May 1951. The new
man in their lives played father figure to young Ted

who then took his name. As Ted Bundy he now had the title that, in later life, would be synonymous with extreme evil.

Despite all his stepfather's efforts, he grew up a distant child, deeply introverted and unable to fully interact with other schoolchildren. Instead the social misfit would prefer to hunt for violent and sexually explicit literature in the local libraries. At high school he started to thieve to fund his love of skiing; petty crimes that would prove the teen was on a slippery slope to more acute malevolence.

After switching institutions in his first year of higher education, Ted proved a likeable psychology student at the University of Washington. Then in the spring of 1967 he fell head over heels in love with his dream girl. Stephanie Brooks was an attractive, sophisticated student from a wealthy family and shared his passion for the pistes. The pair dated but once she graduated, Stephanie chose to end their relationship, citing immaturity and a lack of direction. This broke Bundy's heart and he fell into a depressed state, dropping out of college.

Throwing in the towel on his education, he then uncovered the truth about his parentage. This double shock to the system forced a change within Ted Bundy. The reticent, reclusive greenhorn mutated into a more confident, socially-adept young man with a new-found bravado. Yet under the surface a more sinister transformation was taking shape.

FIRST LOVE, FIRST KILL

Over the next few years, this bombastic new demeanour seemed to be a positive addition to Bundy's character. He entered the world of politics, working hard on a Republican presidential campaign and became the assistant to the state party chairman. Even when he was appointed to the Seattle Crime Prevention Advisory Committee, he still found time to complete his psychology degree. Bundy was also dating again, a divorcee named Elizabeth Kloepfer. However, despite being back on the track and showing such promise, his mind was elsewhere.

Stephanie Brooks, his first love, still plagued his thoughts and in the summer of 1973, whilst on a business trip to California, he got back in touch. She reacted well to his new attitude and political standing and agreed to give Bundy a second chance. However, following her acceptance of his marriage proposal, he broke off all contact. She then discovered this renaissance romance was Bundy's wicked plan to avenge the pain she had caused him. He had wanted revenge.

A few weeks later young women started to vanish from the Pacific Northwest area. It appeared Ted Bundy's wicked plan did not end with revenge on his former lover. On 4 January 1974 he broke into the basement bedroom of Joni Lenz, an eighteen-year-old Washington student. Her room-mates found her the next morning brutally beaten and sexually abused with a metal rod from her bed.

His first identifiable murder came a month later when he abducted Lynda Ann Healy from her student home. This twenty-one-year-old radio announcer became the first of a long line of young women who would suffer and die at the hands of Ted Bundy. Pretty, slender and with centre-parted long blonde hair, these college girls bore a startling resemblance to Stephanie Brooks. Many have suggested Bundy was still trying to even the score, seeing his ex-fiancée in the women he snatched from college campuses.

SNATCHED AT LAKE SAMMAMISH

By the summer, Bundy had perfected his usual routine. Playing an injured man in need of assistance, often sporting a sling or a cast for added effect, he would exploit the good natures of the girls who would help with a pile of books to his Volkswagen

Beetle. A blow to the head from a concealed crowbar was their only reward.

On 14 July 1974, his compulsion to kill escalating, Bundy descended on the crowded beach at Lake Sammamish. In broad daylight, he asked a number of attractive females for help with a boat he needed to unload. Many declined, some even got as far as the car before having second thoughts, yet two girls – Janice Ott and Denise Naslund – were both led unwittingly to their deaths.

King County detectives canvassing those present at the lake, several of whom had witnessed the two victims being escorted away, managed to build a solid description of both suspect and car. Fliers depicting a sketch of the killer flooded the Seattle area. Lost among the hundreds of tips the police received were calls from both his girlfriend and psychology professor.

Missing these accurate leads allowed Bundy to continue his murder spree, moving to Utah where he sodomised then strangled Melissa Smith and Laura Aime in a two-week period. The following month he altered his modus operandi, pretending to be a police officer to lure Carol DaRonch to his Beetle. She managed to fight her way out of the car and gain her freedom from the fake Officer

Roseland. Undeterred by such setbacks, Bundy persevered killing another six women over the next eight months, five in Colorado – the fourth state to be blackened by his evil.

HALF HOUR OF HELL

The authorities finally caught up with the elusive coed killer on 16 August 1975 when his VW Beetle ran a red light in Granger, Salt Lake City. A search of the car revealed a ski mask, crowbar, rope and handcuffs identical to those used during the attempted abduction of DaRonch. Singled out from a seven-man identity parade, Bundy was promptly charged with kidnapping and ultimately convicted on 1 March 1976, receiving a fifteen-year sentence in Utah State Prison.

His court appearances did not end there. Wanting him for the murder of Caryn Campbell, the neighbouring state of Colorado requested his extradition. During a court recess, Bundy – acting as his own defence – was allowed to visit the court library. From here he jumped through a second-storey window and escaped via the snowy trails of Aspen Mountain.

Evading bloodhounds and trackers for six days, he was eventually recaptured only to escape a second time six months later through a ceiling crawlspace above his jail cell. Travelling via Chicago, Bundy arrived in Tallahassee, Florida, renting a room under the name Chris Hagen, growing a moustache to alter his appearance. Within days the chameleon-like killer struck again with unparalleled force.

In the first few hours of Sunday 15 January 1978, Ted Bundy crept into Florida State's Chi Omega sorority house and strangled Margaret Bowman and Lisa Levy, who he also viciously raped. Next, he attacked two more girls with a log before being interrupted by a sister returning from a party. The whole encounter took less than half an hour.

His compulsion to kill returned a month later, grabbing Kimberly Leach from a playground, raping and murdering her, before dumping her body in Suwannee State Park. She was just twelve years old. Such boundless evil had to be stopped and three days later he was pulled over in a stolen Beetle in Pensacola. Following a scuffle with the officer, Bundy was was finally subdued and transported back to Tallahassee to face charges.

THE TRIALS OF TED BUNDY

Unable to escape justice for a third time, Bundy now faced a series of trials beginning with the

Chi Omega murder case in Florida. In front of television cameras, he played the starring role, cross-examining witnesses as he defended himself once again. However, using eyewitness testimony and matching the bite marks on Lisa Levy's buttock to his teeth via a mold, the prosecution made an irrefutable case for conviction.

Sentenced to death for both murders, Bundy attended his second trial in Orlando for his crimes against Kimberly Leach, using the court to legally marry Carole Boone. As a fitting wedding present, the judge and jury gave the groom the death penalty. After endless appeals in an attempt to forestall his state-ordered demise, his execution was set for 24 January 1989.

The penultimate night of his life Bundy granted an interview to psychologist Dr James Dobson in which he declared pornography helped to make him the killer he became. Whether a predilection for adult material can be blamed for his actions, which included the decapitation of heads and sex with decomposing corpses, is highly debatable. What is certain is that Ted Bundy will kill no more executed, as he was, at around 7am in the electric chair.

PART TWO

SERIAL
KILLERS

ANDREI CHIKATILO

As the death rattle of a dying Soviet Union sounded across the globe, one of its Communist faithful was fulfilling his necro-sadistic desires, mutilating and murdering over fifty citizens to become Russia's premier serial killer.

NOT LIKE OTHER CHILDREN

On 16 October 1936, in the rural Ukrainian village of Yablochnoye, Andrei Romanovich Chikatilo was born into crippling poverty. Stalinist rule had ensured his family – along with millions of Russian citizens – suffered under the cruel agricultural policy of collectivism which saw all crops handed over to the state. Starvation swept across large stretches of the Soviet Union and the Chikatilos grew up on a diet of leaves and grass to keep death from their door.

While his father fought in the war with the Red Army, his mother kept their son in a state of fear, telling him scare stories of an older brother devoured by neighbours to sate their hunger. With traumatising tales of famine-induced cannibalism and the regular sight of corpses littering the poverty-stricken streets it was no wonder little Andrei developed into an abnormal human being. He would wet his bed until the age of twelve.

In 1949 his father returned from the war. Having languished inside a Nazi concentration camp, he suffered the indignity of being branded a traitor by his own people. This deeply affected Andrei who was similarly vilified at school, mocked by his fellow pupils. Despite this sorrow he devoted his teens to the Communist ideal, joining the Youth League.

Here he soon realised he was not like others his own age. Preferring the company of younger children, he brought further ridicule on himself when he groped a young girl, ejaculating during the molestation. Rumour quickly spread of his impotence which would become a driving force behind his later crimes.

NO APPLE FOR THE TEACHER

Finishing school, Andrei desperately wanted away from his home country and focused on attaining a law degree at Moscow State University. Sadly, he failed the entrance exam and, following a spell of national service, moved to Rodionovo-Nesvetayevksy near Rostov in 1960 to work as a telephone engineer.

The sixties seemed to bring balance to Chikatilo's life. He married Feodosya Semyovna, a friend of his sister's who was three years his junior and, despite his impotence, they managed to conceive two children. Still unable to sustain an erection he reportedly had to push his seed into his wife by hand.

As the seventies rolled in Chikatilo acquired a degree in literature and philology at Rostov University and became a teacher. He hoped this role would bring him the respect he had missed out on in his youth, but within a short space of time history began to repeat itself. The students mocked his appearance, belittling him to such an extent he resorted to carrying a knife for protection.

His fear quickly turned to thoughts of revenge and he responded to their taunts by secretly molesting the students. In April 1973 he held a schoolgirl in detention and beat her with a ruler causing him to ejaculate. Further deviant acts resulted in his dismissal early the following year and after similar allegations at other schools in the area, he was forced to relocate to Shakhty, a small coal-mining town to the north-east of Rostov-on-Don.

SECRET SHACK
Shortly after moving the family home, the disgraced

teacher started to build a secret life away from his wife and children. Andrei wanted to allow himself the freedom to act on his perverted impulses. He bought a hideaway house, little more than a shack on Mezhevoy Lane, the perfect lair for a sexual deviant. His mind was focused on planning his first venture into a world of sin and suffering in a bid to relieve his sexual frustration.

On 22 December 1978 he plucked nine-year-old Lena Zakotnova from a bus stop, luring her to his shack with a promise of candy. A vicious attempt to rape the young child brought further dismay as he was yet again unable to perform. In a fit of rage he withdrew a knife and stabbed her three times in the stomach; the work of this substitute phallus arousing the vexed and violent Andrei.

The body was found two days later in Grushovka River but despite finding blood near Chikatilo's lair, police dismissed him in favour of a known rapist, Aleksandr Kravchenko. The wrong man was convicted and received the death penalty. The case was closed and Andrei was free to plot a repeat performance. While this close call initially scared him into restraining his urges, the fledgling killer had discovered a means to achieve a long-yearned-for release that was impossible to ignore.

IT'S ALL IN THE EYES

Laying low for the next two years, Chikatilo changed his job allowing him to travel widely on the Soviet rail system. Over the next three years he struck all across the Rostov area, murdering almost twenty victims, beginning with seventeen-year-old Larisa Tkachenko. A boarding school truant, she made the fatal mistake of laughing at her attacker when he failed to become erect. Angry frustration rose up once again and he stabbed her repeatedly with a stick. His rage was so great he even bit off her nipple before filling her mouth with dirt and leaves.

By 1984 a special task force had been created to handle the series of grisly murders. Led by Major Mikhail Fetisov, they marvelled at the uniquely violent MO of the killer. Not only did he inflict multiple stab wounds, but more significantly he attacked the eyes. This Chikatilo trademark came from a popular Russian belief that the eyes of the dead held a snapshot of what they last saw before passing.

Despite these tell-tale signs and the frequency of the murders over a comparatively small area of the Soviet Union, the police were far from catching Chikatilo. They mistook the attacks for the work of a known sex offender or someone registered insane. Even when he was caught accosting women in Rostov on 13 September 1984 and found his briefcase contained a veritable kill kit, they promptly released him. The man had no criminal record and as well as being a family man, he was a Communist party member. Surely nobody with such credentials could have committed such heinous crimes. This oversight allowed the butcher of Rostov to continue carving up the innocent with impunity.

KILLER X

In December 1984 Chikatilo took an enforced break from murder after being found guilty of theft. Stealing some linoleum from work brought a hefty year's prison term from the People's Court and during this hiatus Fetisov and his team endeavoured to obtain a better understanding of the killer. The Major brought psychiatrist Aleksandr Bukhanovksy on board to develop a workable profile.

After examining the crime scene reports, he deduced the man they dubbed Killer X was between forty-five and fifty years of age and an unsociable though not psychotic personality. His necro-sadism was the reason for his relentless stabbings; they were a way to enter his victims sexually. Even possessing this unerringly accurate description it would take another six years before the authorities would get their man.

By the late eighties Chikatilo's attacks had advanced to an even higher level of violence. On 11 January 1989, after stabbing Tatyana Ryzhova in the mouth for mocking his impotence, he cut off her head and legs and scattered them in the nearby woods. He also started to remove the tongues and genitals of those he butchered and began executing these kills in more public areas. Unsurprisingly, after more than forty murders over a ten year period he was beginning to feel unstoppable.

CAGED KILLER

With no clear leads in the case Fetisov stepped up the investigation, seconding hundreds of undercover officers to patrol the various train stations around the Rostov area. On 6 November 1990, a detective spotted a man exiting the woods near Donleskhoz station. Sporting blood on his cheek and mud on his coat, his details were taken before being allowed to continue his journey. This was Andrei Chikatilo and he had just murdered Sveta Korostik.

When her body was discovered the next day the task force checked patrol reports from around Donleskhoz bringing up Chikatilo's information.

Following nearly two weeks of surveillance, the detectives arrested the suspect on 20 November as he attempted to lure away another potential victim. In custody Andrei refused to admit to the crimes. Yet on the penultimate day before he was due to be released, Bukhanovsky, the profiling psychiatrist, was permitted to try.

The subtler approach worked and within hours Andrei was admitting to over fifty murders. He took police on tours of his murder sites revealing seventeen more victims not previously associated with the killer. He even gave a macabre workshop, showing detectives on mannequins how he slaughtered his prey.

The trial began on 14 April 1992. Held in an iron cage for his own protection, a shaven-headed Chikatilo rolled his eyes, heckled and even exposed himself during proceedings, playing crazy in an attempt to avoid the death penalty.

It was all in vain and that autumn he was found guilty on fifty-two counts of murder. Applause followed his sentence and in February 1994 Andrei was led to a Rostov prison cell and shot in the back of the head.

ARTHUR SHAWCROSS

Between 1988 and 1990 the man known to all as the Genesee River Killer targeted the streetwalkers of Monroe County, strangling them to death before dumping their mutilated corpses around the region.

MATURING TO MURDER

Born two months premature in a US Naval Hospital in Kittery, Maine, Arthur John Shawcross spent his childhood in Watertown, New York surrounded by relatives in an area affectionately known as Shawcross Corners. Yet, according to the killer, this was a far cry from The Waltons family life it resembled. His mother Bessie became a violent matriarch, one time inserting a broom handle into the boy's anus by way of punishment. He also claimed he was forced to perform oral sex on his aunt, leading to an early obsession with all things carnal. With such an unpleasant upbringing, young Arthur reacted, quickly displaying the tell-tale signs of serial killer behaviour.

From bed-wetting to bestiality, he slipped into a private fantasy world, while also falling behind at school. By the eighth grade he was some three years older than his classmates. A total outcast, he dropped out of school the following year aged nineteen.

Two years later, Arthur was drafted into the army and sent to Vietnam with the 4th Supply and Transport Company of 4th Infantry Division. Here he later attested to a series of heinous acts including the decapitation of a Viet-Cong woman, suggesting he also consumed a portion of her thigh he had roasted over a fire.

Whatever occurred in the Victnamese jungle, Arthur returned home in September 1968 and was assigned to Fort Sill, Oklahoma where he lived with his second wife, Linda. She soon witnessed first-hand Arthur's fiery temper, not only taking regular beatings herself but on one occasion watching him kill their six-month-old puppy in a fit of rage.

Following his honourable discharge from the army, the ex-soldier turned to arson, becoming sexually aroused by the flames that gutted a local paper mill and, later, a cheese factory. Serving a total of twenty-two months for these two attacks, he was released in October 1971, returning to Watertown. In less than a year Arthur Shawcross would mature from arson to murder.

THE EARLY KILLS

Early in the summer of 1972 ten-year-old Jack Owen
Blake disappeared whilst playing in a suburban area
of New York city. His mother raised the hue and
cry but a search for her son turned up nothing. The
neighbourhood had no idea he had become Arthur
Shawcross's first kill. Luring him into the woods, he
had stripped the boy naked then, forcing him to run,
hunted the child down before sexually assaulting
and murdering him. He would later maintain he also
removed and then devoured the heart and genitals.

Four months later, his appetite for murder awoken,
Shawcross snatched eight-year-old Karen Ann Hill
from under her mother's nose. Her decomposed
body was found beneath a bridge crossing the Black
River. An autopsy revealed she had been raped
then asphyxiated and had the local mud and leaves
rammed down her throat. Knowing Arthur often
fished under this bridge, police brought him in as a
suspect. He soon confessed to both murders.

Serving less than fifteen of a twenty-five year term,
he was released in April 1987, deemed fit to re-enter
society. After three communities in New York State
refused to take him, Shawcross finally relocated in
the city of Rochester, in Monroe County. Now free
to start life anew, he managed to curb his dangerous

urges for the best part of a year, until the beast within would stay silent no longer.

RED LIGHT FOR MURDER

In March 1988, his burning desire to kill pre-empted the thaw of winter, Arthur began to familiarize himself with the streetwalkers of Lyell Avenue. Picking up Dotsie Blackburn and agreeing a price for mutual oral sex, he drove to a deserted car park where, he later maintained, she bit his penis. Blood everywhere, he grabbed her throat and choked her to death, though not before biting her back. Six days later, hunters in Salmon Creek discovered the body. It had been badly beaten and had suffered distinct vaginal trauma.

As the case began to grow cold, Shawcross struck again, murdering twenty-eight-year-old Anna Steffen, another prostitute from Rochester's red light district. Two months went by before her badly decomposed corpse surfaced, found snagged on the river's detritus. The lack of physical evidence saw her death follow that of her predecessor, and as time ticked by police grew less confident of solving either case.

The following summer, Shawcross took his third life since his release from prison, shifting his murderous gaze to Dorothy Keller, a sixty year-old homeless woman working at a diner he frequented. Inviting her to accompany him fishing, he ended up beating her to death with a small log. When three fishermen found the body three months later, it lacked a head. Shawcross had been back to the spot and removed it. As the police descended on the dump site, they were unaware the killer was watching.

RISING BODY COUNT

Pretty soon more dead women started to show up, turning the once scenic Genesee River Gorge into a high-profile stage for murder. The press stirred up fear as the body count rose, charting the work of the Rochester Strangler. Police and prostitutes worked together to flush out the killer, creating a heightened sense of vigilance, yet still working girls were going missing.

On 23 November 1989, while the country tucked into their Thanksgiving turkeys, the body of June Stotts was discovered face-down in a clearing near the industrial piers. Not only had she been strangled and anally penetrated post-mortem, but when police turned her over, they realized she had been sliced open; an incision running from chest to groin. On closer inspection, it came to light her killer had also removed her labia. June Stotts had been a friend to the Shawcrosses, now she lay gutted like an animal in the autumn cold.

With a new body surfacing every week, it was time to make the call to the FBI. Agents from the Behavioural Science Unit at Quantico poured over the evidence and deduced the man dubbed the Genesee River Killer was white, about thirty years of age, working alone, and would be considered quite ordinary by the citizens of Rochester. Aside from the age the profile was spot on, but would they be able to catch this faceless loner before he killed again?

A BRIDGE TOO FAR

Three more streetwalkers disappeared in December intensifying the search in the harsh winter conditions. Police officers were pushed back by the icy winds blowing in from Lake Ontario and forced to abort as the year turned. On 2 January 1990 the authorities were back out en masse in the bitter conditions to locate the missing women of the night, but it was beginning to seem as if nothing would be found until the frozen rivers and creeks had thawed.

Then the following day, as the hunt for bodies by land and air continued, a helicopter search team decided to make one final pass along Highway 31 towards the city. Sweeping low over Salmon Creek, they spotted a human figure beneath the ice. It was the seventeen-day-old corpse of June Cicero.

She had made the fatal mistake of choosing Shawcross as her last trick of the night; it would be the last trick of her life. Squeezing her neck until dead, her final punter then savagely sawed off her genitalia before dumping her into the river. He would later claim he ate what he took away.

As the helicopter hovered over June's frozen body, the team noticed another figure upon the nearby bridge: an overweight man who appeared to be urinating. When they moved closer to him, he got into a Chevy Celebrity and drove away. It was none other than Arthur Shawcross. The killer had come to eat lunch and admire his handiwork.

Shawcross made for the town of Spencerport, disappearing inside Wedgewood Nursing Home. When State Policeman John Standing caught up with him and ran a check on his identification, he discovered he had been convicted of manslaughter. This, he believed, could be their man.

NOT MAD, JUST BAD

Not wanting to spook their best suspect, the detectives attempted to build a rapport with

Shawcross. They discussed where he liked to fish. Each spot seemed to mimic the dump sites. Slowly but surely they had him confessing to murder after murder, pointing on a map to where yet another corpse could be found.

His seventy-nine-page-long confession proved to be the focus for the trial held later that year at Rochester County Court. Shawcross was advised to plead not guilty by reason of insanity, but despite numerous tall tales of evil, many psychiatrists testified that the defendant was sane. The jury concurred and he was found guilty on ten counts of second-degree murder and sentenced to twenty-five years for each crime.

Incarcerated at Sullivan Correctional Facility in Fallsburg, New York, Arthur Shawcross would not serve even one term to completion. On 10 November 2008, he complained of pains in his right leg and was taken to Albany Medical Centre, where he had a heart attack and died at 9.50pm.

EARLE LEONARD NELSON

During the middle of the roaring twenties, a simian-looking strangler armed with a Bible and big hands relentlessly preyed on luckless landladies right across America, leaving a trail of elderly corpses behind him in memory of an overbearing grandmother.

A STREETCAR NAMED DEMENTIA

One of the recurring traits found in the backgrounds of many serial killers is the presence of a dominant maternal figure during childhood. For Earle Leonard Nelson, born 12 May 1897, this was no different. When his parents died of syphilis while he was still in nappies, he went to live with his maternal grandmother in San Francisco.

Raised by this devout Pentecostal woman, Earle became obsessed with the Bible. He would often declare his unusually large hands that would one day bring havoc to so many US States were made to hold the good book. Yet despite such a religious upbringing, young Earle soon developed into a problem child. He lacked manners, slurping his food which he soaked in olive oil, and also hygiene, refusing to bathe for long periods.

At the age of seven he was expelled from Agassiz Primary School for his continual bad behaviour. Highly temperamental, he was prone to fits of violence, becoming increasingly withdrawn. Then around the age of ten a serious bike accident involving a streetcar left him unconscious for six days. The head injury he suffered only aggravated his volatile nature and soon, plagued by severe headaches, he began a slow descent into madness.

When his puritanical grandmother passed away in 1908, Earle moved in with his Aunt Lillian. It was while under her roof that he became a chronic masturbator, a raging alcoholic, and began frequenting the red light district in Fisherman's Wharf to satisfy a burgeoning sexual appetite.

Not that he was always home. Earle would often disappear for days on end, wandering the hinterland of northern California, committing petty crimes on his travels. When he broke into a cabin he believed abandoned, he was arrested, convicted of burglary, and sent to San Quentin Prison.

The two years' incarceration gave Earle time to ponder, but unfortunately did nothing to improve his state of mind.

HOUDINI OF NAPA HOSPITAL

With the outbreak of the Great War, Earle then chose to enlist in the army, hoping to join the conflict abroad. However, he soon realized the regimented life did not suit him and he went AWOL. Two further stints as a Navy cook and an army medic ended in two further desertions before he was committed to Napa State Mental Institute aged just eighteen. His superiors had grown concerned at his refusal to work and his endless apocalyptic sermons to the other men, not to mention his increasing capriciousness.

Once in the hospital's care, Nelson tested positive for both gonorrhoea and syphilis and proved highly restless. During his thirteen month stay, he escaped three times earning the nickname Houdini from the staff. After his third flight in 1919, hospital personnel gave up the chase and simply discharged him from military service, signing off his notes that he was improved and considered non-violent.

Less than two years later he would prove his doctors wrong. On 19 May 1921, pretending to be a plumber sent to fix a leak, Earle Nelson entered the home of Charles Summers. Finding twelve-year-old Mary Summers playing in the basement, he snapped, launching himself at her, his enormous hands circling her tiny neck. Putting up a fight, the little girl screamed, alerting her older brother who fought with his sister's assailant. He was eventually apprehended and returned to his second home, Napa State Mental Institute.

ROOM FOR MURDER

Following a longer stay at the hospital with only one escape attempt reported, Earle Nelson was officially released in 1925. A year later the wild-eyed, olive-skinned ex-patient grabbed his Bible and began his reign of terror. IIis first victim was sixty-two year old Clara Newmann, who owned several boarding houses in the San Francisco area.

When a suited stranger responded to her 'Room To Rent' sign in the window, she was more than happy to show him up to the third floor of her Pierce Street home. However, once inside, his mild-mannered exterior gave way to something more sinister, his huge hands choking the life from her.

As he sexually assaulted her corpse the killer had no idea there was someone else in the house. Clara's nephew, Merton Newmann, was busy with his book-keeping in his second floor apartment. Feeling cold, he ventured downstairs to check on the furnace but as he passed the kitchen and the sound of sausages cooking on the stove, he spotted a strange man. His coat turned up at the collar and sporting a hat, the man was halfway out the door.

Before exiting, the hulking stranger turned to Merton and asked him to inform the landlady he would return to rent the bedroom. Thinking him just a prospective lodger, Clara's nephew then returned to his accounts. It would be several hours before the landlady would be reported missing. Her severely-abused corpse was eventually discovered following a search of the house by the boarders.

CROSS COUNTRY KILLING

Soon the landladies across the west coast had reason to fear this stranger. Two weeks after Clara's demise, Nelson struck again; this time in San Jose. The body of Laura Beal, another boarding house owner, was found naked from the waist down in one of her vacant apartments, strangled by the silk belt from her dressing gown. She had been raped post-mortem. It was clear to both the police and the papers that these two murders were connected and that landladies were being targeted. Telegrams were despatched across the west coast warning women not to show rooms unaccompanied.

This attempt at protecting these vulnerable ladies

out west was sadly in vain as the spectral-like killer continued to attack, strangle and sexually abuse more elderly women. Sixty-three-year-old Lillian St Mary became Nelson's third victim, her defiled body found by one of her boarders. Next he headed south to Santa Barbara and took the life of Ollie Russell, and then in mid-August, Stephen Nisbet discovered his wife's dead body crammed into a toilet area, her head violently slammed against the bathroom tiles before her death.

Three more murders of landladies followed in Oregon throughout October 1926. Nelson was now venturing further afield, crossing state lines. Over the next sixteen months the now-dubbed Gorilla Killer swept across the country, killing at will and leaving no clues. Florence Monks of Seattle, Bonnie Pace in Kansas City, and Mary McConnell of Philadelphia fell to the dark strangler as he reached the other side of the country by the following spring. After throttling Mary Sietsema in Chicago on 3 June he then chose to head north and cross the border into Canada, leaving a trail of dead American landladies stretching from one side of the country to the other.

A MURDERER MIGRATES
On 8 June 1927 Nelson crossed into Canada from

Minnesota. Hitch-hiking to Winnipeg, he traded his clothes for workman's overalls. He then took a room at Catherine Hill's boarding house on Smith Street, registering as Mister Woodcoats. Mrs Hill would be one of the lucky landladies not chosen as a victim. During his short time here would take two lives. First to fall was fourteen-year-old Lola Cowan.

Nelson met the teenager on the street selling paper flowers to make money for her family. On 8 June 1927 he charmed her into coming back to his rented room. There he wrapped a cloth around her neck and squeezed till she stopped moving. He then slept with her corpse which he kept under his bed for three nights, slowly decomposing beneath him.

The morning after murdering Lola, he came upon another house offering a room to rent. Enquiring inside, his trusted bible in his over-sized hands, he informed the owners he had no money but could fix their screen door instead. At around 11am Nelson killed Emily Patterson, his fifth victim in ten days. Her husband came home to find his wife missing. That night, after a search came up empty, he knelt by his bed praying for his wife's return. When he stood up, his eyes were drawn to beneath the bed. His prayers had been answered; his wife lay there cold, dead and abused thanks to the infamous Gorilla Killer.

The town was reeling from the attack and a search of all lodging houses eventually revealed the foul-smelling corpse of Lola Cowan beneath Nelson's rented bed. The Winnipeg police issued a manhunt. They now had full descriptions of the killer from the locals and it became just a matter of time before they caught up with the Bible-toting strangler. He managed to escape from the jail cell following his first arrest, but was eventually apprehended by one William Renton of nearby Crystal City Police Department.

Indicted for murders from San Francisco to Buffalo, Nelson first had to stand trial in Canada. Following an open and shut case at Manitoba Law Courts bringing an unsurprising death sentence, Nelson would never face the charges waiting for him in his homeland. On 13 January 1928, Nelson hanged at Vaughan Street Jail, Winnipeg at 7.30am. Reportedly, he choked for eleven minutes before dying the same way as his twenty-two victims.

H. H. HOLMES

A grisly tale of murder and deception worthy of his sleuthing namesake, H. H. Holmes surrounded himself in a surfeit of lies, luring young females to his Chicagoan castle of death going down in history as America's first documented serial killer.

FROM HERMAN TO HOLMES

The enigmatically-named H. H. Holmes began life as Herman Webster Mudgett. Born 16 May 1861 in the wealthy New Hampshire town of Gilmanton, he received a privileged upbringing although did fall foul of his strict Methodist parents on more than one occasion. Often sent hungry to the attic for long periods when he misbehaved, little Herman soon became detached from the outside world and found it difficult to make friends.

When not suffering the austere punishments of home, he would be tormented by school bullies. On one occasion they forced him to enter a doctor's office and touch a human skeleton. Rather than being consumed by fear, Mudgett was mesmerized by the articulated collection of bones. It may have been this act of cruelty that awoke in him the morbid fascination with the human body.

In spite of these early setbacks, he developed into a handsome, charming young man and, in the summer of 1878, married Clara Lovering; the daughter of a well-heeled family from nearby Alton. His new bride financed his education at Vermont then put him through medical school at the University of Michigan.

It was here in Ann Arbor where his criminal ingenuity took shape. Stealing corpses from the university laboratory, Mudgett would disfigure them then leave his handiwork around the area, but not before taking out life insurance policies on each one. When their bodies were discovered, Mudgett would appear, make the necessary identification and collect as sole beneficiary. Such devilish deception spelled the end for humble Herman Mudgett. Following his graduation in 1884, Dr H. H. Holmes was born.

NO PLACE LIKE HOLMES'

Holmes now took his ill-gotten gains to Chicago to pursue a career in pharmaceuticals and in the summer of 1886 took a job at Dr E. S. Holton's drugstore in Englewood. Shortly after, the owner succumbed to cancer, and Holmes charmed his widow into selling him the store. When he stalled on the payment, Mrs Holton filed a lawsuit. It was then she mysteriously disappeared. The new owner informed customers she had moved to be near relatives in California. In fact, Holmes had committed his first murder.

This first kill opened the floodgates and he set about orchestrating a plan of unbelievable evil. Purchasing a lot opposite the drugstore, he built an imposing three-storey edifice stretching an entire block. It was to be a hotel for the expected influx of tourists that would descend upon Chicago for the World's Fair in 1893. In fact, this was just a cover, yet another deceit in the life of H. H. Holmes.

Dubbed 'Holmes' Castle' by the neighbourhood, its construction was shrouded in secrecy. He used a number of builders to ensure only he knew the whole truth behind its devilish design. While the ground floor housed the relocated drugstore, the upper levels were a maze of over a hundred windowless rooms. Staircases led nowhere, doors opened to brick walls and secret passageways behind false partitions created a hidden world away from the unsuspecting public on the street.

CHUTE TO KILL

As if taken from the pages of a Gothic horror novel,

the evil doctor lured a series of unwitting victims to his labyrinthine lair. Pretty blonde women caught his eye. Stenographers straight out of secretarial college whom he employed at his legitimate copying company, along with those visiting the Fair, came to stay at Holmes' hotel. Many would never return home. Lost within the honeycombed house of horrors, his doomed prey were held prisoner inside asbestos-lined chambers and slowly gassed. Others were strangled or beaten to death once they had surrendered details and whereabouts of any cash and capital. At the centre of the castle ran a greased chute taking the dead down into the basement. Here in the bottom of the building the evil continued.

A medieval torture cellar equipped with large pits, some filled with acid others with quicklime, and an enormous crematorium allowed the proprietor to make his guests magically disappear. Dissecting and dismembering the corpses on an operating table, Holmes would clean up the bones and sell their skeletons for profit. No doubt memories of that night in the doctor's office bringing a smile to the mass murderer's face.

MISSING MISTRESSES
Murder was not his only crime. By the time he was

hacking up hotel guests the doctor was already a bigamist, having now married one Myrta Belknap in Minneapolis. Unaware of his first wife or indeed his predilection for preying on the city's women, she raised his family in the up-scale suburb of Wilmette, while Holmes began a series of affairs with a number of other ladies.

Employed as his secretary at the drugstore, the doctor soon took a shine to Mrs Julia Conner. Falling for his considerable charm, she left her husband and moved into the hotel with her eight-year-old child. However, when Holmes became smitten with fresh-faced southern belle, Minnie Williams, he swiftly bumped off Conner and her young daughter and installed Minnie as mistress of the castle.

In June 1893, with no notion of what horrors lay hidden inside her home, Minnie invited her younger sister Anna to join them. By July she was never seen nor heard of again. Six months later H. H. Holmes married a third time, bringing to a close his relationship with Minnie. By the spring she went the way of her sister, undoubtedly murdered by the far-from-good doctor.

HOLMES' HOODWINK
After the World's Fair, Holmes' past crimes began to

catch up with him. The creditors he had persistently failed to pay were in pursuit, forcing him to flee the Windy City. Heading south to Fort Worth, Texas, he engaged in further criminal practices, winding up in in a St Louis jail for horse theft. While behind bars he spoke of a new plan, an insurance scam that would net him $10,000 if successful. Promising his cell-mate, Marion Hedgepeth, $500 in exchange for the name of a disreputable lawyer he could trust, the convict suggested Colonel Jeptha Howe.

Also in on the scam was Benjamin Pitzel. He had agreed to fake his own death so his wife Carrie might collect on the insurance policy. While Holmes searched for a suitable cadaver to play him, Pitzel set up shop as inventor B. F. Perry at 1316 Callowhill Street, Philadelphia and waited to hear from his partner in crime.

Unfortunately for Pitzel, he failed to see the double-cross. Holmes had no intention of finding a body. Instead he killed Pitzel at the address, binding his hands and feet and burning him alive in a pool of Benzine. Following the discovery of the frazzled corpse on 4 September 1894, the police declared the death an accident, and two weeks later Holmes – accompanied by Jeptha Howe – identified the body and collected the $10,000 on behalf of Mrs Pitzel.

THE TELLTALE TWIST

Returning to St Louis with the money, it appeared Holmes' swindle had succeeded. After telling Carrie her husband was lying low in South America (while in reality he was lying six feet under), Holmes set off across the country with three of the widow's five children in tow. At every town and city he passed through he left a web of lies and deceit in his wake, cheating the innocent out of their fortunes.

That autumn, Holmes' pathological desire to hustle all those around him, would bring about his downfall. Still languishing in a St Louis jail, Marion Hedgepeth had not been paid his $500 finder's fee. Now his former cell-mate turned informant, telling police of Holmes' insurance swindle. Soon the Pinkerton Detective Agency was on the case, assigned to track him down. They caught up with him in Boston on 17 November 1894.

Struggling through an endless series of lies, investigators slowly discovered the man in custody was guilty of more than just insurance fraud. Later the bodies of the three Pitzel children were discovered. Nellie and Alice had been stuffed inside a large trunk and gassed, their bodies buried side by side in a shallow grave in Toronto. Howard Pitzel's charred bones were found in a stove at a house in Indianapolis.

Next came the shocking truth behind the castle in Chicago. Numerous skulls and other gruesome remains were seized from the cellar inciting Holmes to confess to killing twenty-seven people.

Despite this disturbing revelation, Holmes was charged with the Pitzel murders only. Found guilty, he was sentenced to death and on 7 May 1896 was hanged at Moyamensing Prison. According to his instructions, Holmes was buried in concrete at the Holy Cross Cemetery, citing fears that his body would be exhumed and dissected like so many of his victims.

JAVED IQBAL

Pakistan's most prolific serial killer shocked a nation when he openly confessed to the sexual abuse, murder and mutilation of one-hundred children in a disturbing act of vengeance.

A KILLER'S CONFESSION

Lying along the river Ravi, Lahore is home to over eight million Pakistanis. The country's second largest city, and one of the most densely populated urban areas in the world, this ancient metropolis harbours nearly five thousand children living rough on its streets. Many of them runaways escaping abusive parents, they are forced to turn to crime to survive, risking further violence to themselves. At the tail end of the last century these street children would become the easy prey to a most brutal killer.

On 2 December 1999, a letter arrived at Lahore's main police station. Signed by its author Javed Iqbal, it disclosed the sexual abuse and murder of one-hundred young boys between the ages of six and sixteen. In some detail Iqbal admitted to asphyxiating the century of victims with cyanide, dismembering their corpses and dissolving their remains in vats of hydrochloric acid. An identical letter had also been sent to a local Lahore newspaper and so in a flash police officers and journalists alike flocked to the home of this self-confessed killer.

DISPLAY OF DEATH

As the press waited for news, police inside undertook the search of the three-storey house located deep in the heart of the city's slum area. What they found corroborated the killer's claims. Blood-spattered walls and a blood-soaked floor led the investigators to a collection of photographs showing the dead wrapped in plastic. Further in they discovered two blue vats of acid with the liquefied remains of three bodies. All items had been left out in the open with neatly-written notes attached. It was clear this man wanted his handiwork confirmed.

Among this deliberate display of death, authorities found a diary giving even more information on the murders committed within. A ledger listing names, ages and dates of their demise revealed the killings had occurred over a five month period between 20 June and 13 November 1999. Iqbal had even calculated the cost of exterminating each child: 120 rupees.

MANHUNT

Included in the confession Javed Iqbal had stated he planned to commit suicide after the murders by drowning himself in the Ravi River. Police now descended upon its banks to the north of the city, dragging the waters for the corpse of a killer. The nets caught nothing of relevance. This led to what is believed to be the largest manhunt in Pakistan's history. In a bid to locate the whereabouts of Iqbal, police offered a reward of one million rupees for any information leading to his arrest. On 6 December, four days after the letter's arrival, detectives arrested two teenagers in Sohawa, some two hundred kilometres north of Lahore. In custody fifteen-year-old Muhammad Sabir confessed to assisting Iqbal in the rape and murder of some twenty-five children.

At the city's Crime Investigation Agency, a number of people were held under suspicion of involvement in the brutal slaughter of these street urchins. Among these was Ishaq Billa, accused of selling Javed Iqbal the vats of acid used to turn the dismembered remains into mush. On 7th December, the day after his arrest, he fell to his death from the agency's second storey window. It was deemed a suicide.

Meanwhile, as the hunt for Javed Iqbal continued, the parents of the missing children poured over the collection of ragged clothes and grisly photographs seized by police. By the end of the first week the identities of sixty-nine victims had been confirmed. Sadly, being in such an advanced state of deterioration, none of the bodies could be returned to the distraught families.

With each passing day that Javed Iqbal remained free, the people of Lahore became more frustrated. Protesters took to the streets, clashing with police, demanding they locate this abominable child killer in their midst. On 30 December, almost a month after his letter dropped into the laps of the police, the most wanted man in Pakistan came out of hiding.

Walking into the Lahore offices of Urdu newspaper *The Daily Jang*, Javed Iqbal surrendered, fearing for his life, believing the police were out for blood and wanted to kill him. He was subsequently arrested and gave a full and frank confession to all one-hundred murders. He also clarified his motives for this most heinous series of crimes.

MOTIVE FOR MURDER

The forty-three-year-old chemical engineer was well-known to police. He had been held on charges of child molestation and sodomy on three separate occasions in the past ten years. Each time he avoided a conviction. However, according to Iqbal, events during his time in police custody proved to be the catalyst for killing these children.

Claiming he suffered severe beatings at the hands of the police, breaking his back, crushing his head and leaving him impotent, Iqbal felt victimized. And when Pakistani authorities later dismissed allegations he had been assaulted by two servant boys, the complainant vowed revenge. He would murder exactly one-hundred children as punishment for his misery and pain. Thanks to his successful steel recasting business, Javed had the funds to put his evil plan of retribution into effect. Acquiring the necessary supplies to cut up and eliminate the corpses, he paid his accomplices to lure the street children to his apartment. Promises of a decent meal and a place to sleep was enough to bring a steady stream of the homeless and the hungry to his lair.

Javed Iqbal and three accomplices appeared in court in January 2000 for their pre-trial indictment. Once again he made clear his guilt, confessing to all one-hundred murders, proclaiming he was 'the nation's culprit' and deserved to be punished. However, the following month, Iqbal changed his tune, pleading not guilty to all charges.

Declaring it a mere publicity stunt, Iqbal claimed

none of the children had been slain; he had just wanted to bring the plight of the runaway and orphaned children of Lahore to the public's attention. Unfazed by such an appalling about-face, on 17 February 2000 the court formally indicted all four Pakistanis on charges of kidnap, sodomy and murder.

AN EYE FOR AN EYE

The next day, the trial of Javed Iqbal began in earnest. Parents of the missing children in attendance listened to his professions of innocence. His statements to the police had been made under duress, he said. Yet with a glut of physical evidence, ranging from the detailed diary to the acid-filled vats containing human carcasses, and over one-hundred witnesses testifying against him, Iqbal was eventually found guilty of every single murder.

On 16 March, Judge Allah Baksh Ranjha handed down the sentences. Accomplices Muhammad Sabir and a thirteen-year-old named Nadeem were given 63 and 253 years in jail respectively. The third accessory Shahzad Sajid was not so lucky. He, along with Javed Iqbal, received the death penalty.

Focusing on the serial killer with one-hundred souls to his name, the Judge declared he would swing by the neck before the parents whose children he murdered. He then wished for his corpse to suffer the same fate as his victims; to be cut up into one-hundred pieces and dissolved in acid. The press erroneously reported this call for an equal repayment for the crimes as his actual sentence, which had Islamic ideologists up in arms. A week later, amid the religious furore, Iqbal appealed his verdict.

CONSPIRACY?

After seven months incarceration within Lahore's Kot Lakhpat jail, the next chapter in the saga began. On the morning of 25 October 2001, Javed Iqbal was found dead in his cell. Conflicting reports as to cause of death varied from poisoning to hanging; either way police called it suicide. Faisal Najib Chaudhry, Iqbal's lawyer, believed otherwise. The timing of the death was a little suspicious. The apparent suicide had come just four days after the High Court had agreed to hear his appeal against the death penalty. An autopsy soon discovered he had been brutally beaten prior to his death leading many, including Chaudhry, to believe Javed Iqbal was murdered.

Following his death, it came to light that twenty-six of the supposed century of victims were in fact alive and well and living in Lahore. At the time of writing, the case has yet to be re-opened.

JOACHIM KROLL

Prowling the Ruhr region of North-West Germany for over twenty years, the Duisburg man-eater developed a taste for human flesh, luring little girls into secluded areas before carving out a take-away meal from their strangled corpses.

SEXUAL SLAUGHTER

Joachim Georg Kroll was born amidst a rising evil. The construction of Dachau, the Reichstag fire and the birth of the Gestapo, all part of the Nazi's quest for absolute power in Germany, were taking place when this infamous cannibal killer entered the world on 17 April 1933. Raised by a large mining family in Hindenburg, Upper Silesia, little Jocky was a fragile child. Along with his constitution his bladder was also weak, often wetting the bed throughout his youth.

Very little else is known about his upbringing. Far from a bright child, he only managed five years of primary school (psychiatrists at his trial would score his IQ at just seventy-six) and, with his father away fighting, he was soon put to work on the local farms to bring money to the table. It was during these times the boy would realize he had an abnormal sexual predilection, becoming sexually aroused by the slaughter of pigs.

Come the end of the war, as Joachim was approaching his teens, his family headed west, settling in North Rhine-Westphalia. Over the next ten years, with his father languishing in a Russian Gulag, he lived with his mother and six sisters in a cramped two-room apartment.

KROLL'S FIRST KILL

The start of Joachim Kroll's killing began following the death of his mother on 21 January 1955. Whether it was an angry reaction to the loss of a loved one or simple relief at being free to act on the thoughts in his head, this short, moon-faced German began a series of some fourteen murders over a twenty-year period.

His first victim was runaway nineteen-year-old Irmgard Strehl. On 8 February 1955, less than three weeks after losing his mother, Kroll approached the blonde in the green coat, inviting her to walk with him in the woods outside the old town of Luedinghausen. When his attempts to kiss her met with disapproval, he dragged the teenager into an outhouse, raped then stabbed her to death, disembowelling her body with a long-bladed knife.

Five days later police discovered Irmgard's body in the barn where he had left her. A thorough investigation followed but without a single witness nor piece of useful evidence, the case remained unsolved. Joachim Kroll had completed his first kill and better still had succeeded in evading detection.

TURNING SERIAL KILLER

Following his slaying of Miss Strehl, Kroll quickly sought another victim in the North Rhine-Westphalia area. The second to fall into his evil clutches was twelve-year-old Erika Schuleter, whom he raped then throttled to death in the town of Kirchhellen. Yet again the authorities were unable to point the finger and Joachim was free to plan his next attack.

Three years passed before he took his third life, securing the title of serial killer. In 1957 he moved to a small town near Duisburg, a heavy industrial city ravaged by nearly three hundred bombing raids during the war, taking a three-room apartment on Friesenstrasse. Over the years his neighbours saw him as a kindly man with a good sense of humour, unaware he spent the evenings practising his strangle holds on inflatable sex dolls.

Once he had grown accustomed to his

surroundings, Kroll resumed his attacks. Singling out a perfect spot close to the Rheinbrucke in Rheinhausen, the killer made his move on a twenty-three-year-old young woman named Erika. His target proved too strong and he was forced to flee. Less than a month later he returned to the same place, this time with more resolve to satisfy his urges.

On 16 June 1959 Kroll turned serial killer with the murder of Klara Frieda Tesmer in a meadow near Rheinhausen. Forensics discovered the body had been raped post-mortem following strangulation. A large amount of ejaculate was also found on the victim, leading investigators to think this was the work of a gang rather than one man.

KROLL THE CANNIBAL

In the summer heat, Kroll was a helpless slave to his sadistic desires, now travelling further afield to seek out a potential victim. On 26 July, he raped and strangled Manuela Knodt in the City Park of Essen nearly fifteen miles east of home. Surrendering to even deeper desires, Joachim carved sizeable portions from her buttocks and thighs to take home. His modus operandi was evolving.

Yet again Kroll slipped through the net cast by police. By February the following year detectives believed they had Manuela's killer in custody when twenty-three-year-old Horst Otto walked into a police station to confess. The fake served eight years. Perhaps fearing he was pushing his luck, Joachim refrained from any further attack for the next three years.

In 1962 the devil within him demanded to be heard once again, whereupon he took the lives of three more young girls. First was Barbara Bruder, a twelve-year-old stolen from the town of Burscheid, some twenty miles to the south. Her body was never recovered. Next he strangled Petra Giese with her own scarf after raping her in Dinslaken-Bruckhausen.

Once more he left signs of cannibalism, removing both buttocks, her left forearm and hand. He repeated this now strict routine on 4 June killing Monika Tafel in a cornfield in Walsum. Slices of flesh had been carved from her buttocks, no doubt removed for him to consume on his return home.

As in the death of Manuela Knodt, the latter two murders were pinned on the wrong man leaving Joachim free to kill again. Vinzenz Kuehn served six years for Petra's murder while the town of Walsum blamed the death of little Monika on one Walter Quicker, a known paedophile living in the area.

On 5 October, unable to take the town's constant torments, Quicker committed suicide, hanging himself in the nearby woods.

LOVER SLAIN IN LOVER'S LANE

Another three year hiatus followed until 22 August 1965 when Joachim departed from his usual routine, attacking a couple making out in a lovers' lane in Grossenbaum. Puncturing the tyre to their car, he waited until Hermann Schmitz got out of the vehicle before launching his attack. Plunging the knife several times into the young man's chest, Kroll then turned to the victim's girlfriend. It was the girl he really wanted.

Rather than freeze in fear, she reacted quickly, jumping into the driver's seat of the Volkswagen and sounding the horn. She then slammed her foot down on the accelerator almost knocking Joachim over. This near miss was enough to dissuade him from any further action and he fled unnoticed. Moments later other startled couples reached the scene only to find Hermann dying in his girlfriend's arms. He would remain Joachim's first and only male victim.

This narrow escape did little to curb his incessant hunt for prey. On 13 September 1966 he strangled Ursula Rohling in Foersterbusch Park near Marl before posing her semi-naked corpse for police to find. Just before Christmas he kidnapped five-year-old Ilona Harke, taking her by train to Wuppertal where he drowned her in a shallow ditch.

The murders continued into 1969 when Maria Hettgen received the unwanted attention of the Ruhr Hunter. In 1970 thirteen-year-old Jutta Rahn took a short-cut home from school only to become yet another victim. It was not until after a six-year break in kills that police finally caught up with Joachim Kroll.

THE BOILING POINT

On 3 July 1976, four-year-old Marion Ketter had gone missing from a playground in Kroll's neighbourhood. Police officers searched the area for the little blonde girl, enquiring door to door for any clue to her whereabouts. Nobody had seen her. She had, in fact, been lured by Joachim Kroll to his top-floor apartment to become his final victim.

The break came when Oscar Muller, a resident in the killer's apartment building, passed Kroll in the hallway to use the communal toilet. He was warned by his neighbour that it was out of order – backed up, he said, with guts. Thinking it a joke, Oscar used the facilities only to discover the bowl filled with a bright red mess. In a flash, he rushed out into the street to inform one of the canvassing officers.

Police examined the contents of the drains and were shocked to discover bloody entrails were the cause of the blockage. Following a knock on Kroll's door, he explained they belonged to a rabbit he was cooking, but when they entered his kitchen, he nonchalantly pointed to the stove. Boiling away in a pot along with carrots and potatoes was a tiny human hand!

Joachim immediately confessed to the death of Marion Kettner and over the next few days admitted to some fourteen other murders. Hoping in vain he would receive an operation to cure him of his wicked ways, he took police on a tour of his kill sites, many of which had remained unsolved over the years. With no surgical procedure to make him safe, and after a lengthy trial spanning two-and-a-half years, Joachim Kroll was convicted of eight murders and one attempted murder, receiving nine life sentences.

On 1 July 1991 Joachim Kroll died of a heart attack in Rheinbach prison.

JOHN HAIGH

No body, no murder. This was the core belief upon which one of Britain's most publicized serial killers hinged his cunning plan: to lure as many as nine victims to their deaths, dissolving their bodies in acid and thus removing the evidence of any crime.

SIGN OF SATAN

As a young child brought up in the West Yorkshire village of Outwood, John George Haigh was made fully aware of the presence of evil. Members of an evangelical movement called the Plymouth Brethren, his strict parents filled his head with a fear of society, professing the outside world which lay beyond their three-metre high fence to be wicked.

Within the confines of their secluded home, John was brought up on Bible stories and became obsessed with sacrificial fantasies, often dreaming of a forest of crucifixes weeping blood. Prevented from socializing with children his own age, he was subjected to an unending, undiluted barrage of fire and brimstone sermons, living his monastic life in fear of God's wrath.

Adding fuel to this fire, his austere father possessed a blue blemish on his forehead, which he said came from Satan as a result of his past transgressions. Terrified he would acquire a similar sign of the devil, the browbeaten boy spent much of his youth ensuring he never committed a single sin.

However as young Haigh grew older he made the inevitable discovery: each tentatively-told lie, every unavoidable indiscretion brought no mark of evil. With this sword of Damocles removed, he was free to act how he pleased. He felt invincible, and would begin a life of deception and murder, undeterred by the Lord or the law.

THE ACID TEST

Leaving school at the age of seventeen, the dauntless teenager worked a number of jobs, apprenticing at a car engineers, underwriting for an insurance company and then as a car salesman. In this latter role he made his début in crime, selling vehicles he did not actually own. Beginner's misfortune led to his capture and he received his first spell in prison for fraud.

Fifteen months later, Haigh returned to a life of endless scams to make money rather than an honest living. Moving to London he became a chauffeur for

William McSwan, a wealthy owner of an amusement arcade before moving on to trade as a phony solicitor bringing him yet more jail time. It was during this four year term, at work in the prison tin workshop, that Haigh would discover the corrosive abilities of acid. Practising on dead mice, he found it took just thirty minutes for the body to completely disappear. His cunning mind now began to forge a plan so evil it would soon make him famous.

MCSWAN SONG

In the summer of 1944 he met up with his old employer William McSwan. Becoming the best of friends, the arcade owner took Haigh to see his parents, William and Amy, who spoke openly of their recent investments in property. This caused his criminal mind to work overtime.

With summer on the wane Haigh enticed his old boss to 79 Gloucester Road, London where he rented a basement space. Once inside the cellar, Haigh clobbered McSwan over the head with a cosh. Next, after squeezing the corpse into a forty-gallon drum, Haigh proceeded to fill the container with sulphuric acid, slowly turning McSwan into nothing more than revolting dull-grey porridge. He then poured the odorous mess down the basement manhole linked to the sewer system. Informing his concerned parents that their son had simply gone away to Scotland to avoid the draft, Haigh wrote postcards to help with the deception. This worked liked a dream until the following year.

With the war coming to an end, his parents grew curious as to why he had not returned. So in July 1945 Haigh invited Mr and Mrs McSwan to the Kensington basement, disposing of their bodies in the same way.

The wilful murders of all three McSwans allowed Haigh to steal their wealth. Through forging papers and signatures, he was able to sell their five properties and amass something in the region of £6,000 – a small fortune in wartime Britain.

MEET THE HENDERSONS

By the summer of 1947 John Haigh had become an inveterate gambler. Running low on funds, he needed another mark. Answering an advert for another London property, the trickster met Archie and Rosalie Henderson. While he did not buy the house, he did become friends with the couple, sharing their passion for music, playing the piano in a bid to get them to 'sing' about their wealth.

Throughout the following winter, Haigh visited

his unsuspecting prey, taking regular trips with them to Brighton. During this time, he also moved his instruments of evil from the Gloucester Road basement to a workshop in Crawley, West Sussex. It was here that John Haigh lured Archie Henderson on the morning of 12 February 1948.

Believing he had travelled to see an invention, Mr Henderson stepped inside the storeroom only to be shot in the head with his own revolver, stolen earlier by Haigh. The killer con-artist then dumped the body in a tank of acid, returned to Brighton and delivered Mrs Henderson to the same address. She met the same gruesome fate.

Another simple forgery saw the Henderson's possessions feather their killer's nest. Anyone who questioned their disappearance was told they had chosen to emigrate to South Africa.

THE ACID REIGN CONTINUES

Haigh's ill-gotten gains allowed him to move into Room 404 of the Onslow Court Hotel in Kensington. The residence played home to a number of wealthy old widows; prime targets for this thieving murderer. Posing as a liaison officer between patent offices and would-be inventors, he soon struck up a leading conversation with Mrs Olive Durand-Deacon, a plump sixty-nine-year-old woman also living in the hotel.

Her late husband had left her around £40,000 and she was keen to invest a portion of this sum in the manufacture and sale of plastic fingernails. Inevitably, Haigh invited the heavy-set old lady to Crawley where he said he owned a factory. On 18 February 1949 he drove her down in his showy Alvis saloon to meet her doom.

Following his modus operandi, Haigh shot her dead, stripped the body of all valuables then tipped the still-warm body into the large drum. He then displayed the cold, detached behaviour possessed by many serial killers by popping out for some tea at a nearby restaurant, before returning to engulf the corpse in sulphuric acid. He made a series of trips to the factory to check on the slow dissolution of the body. Two days later, he poured the appalling gunk into the workshop yard.

The same day he disposed of Olive's inhuman remains. Haigh accompanied her friend and fellow hotel resident, Constance Lane, to Chelsea Police Station to report the rotund old widow missing. Feeling that Haigh's manner was somehow suspicious, desk sergeant Lambourne decided to run a background check on the slick-looking gentleman.

She quickly discovered his previous criminal history and Haigh became the number one suspect in Mrs Durand-Deacon's disappearance.

WEIGHTY EVIDENCE

On 26 February police paid a visit to his Crawley factory on Leopold Road. Inside this bare brick space they uncovered a host of suspicious items, including three carboys of concentrated sulphuric acid, a .38 Webley revolver and fat-stained rubber gloves. It appeared Haigh was their man.

Meanwhile, in custody, Haigh was anything but concerned. Believing the authorities were powerless to convict him of murder without a body, he freely confessed to killing Olive and rendering her body into sludge. He also admitted to killing the McSwans and Hendersons along with three unidentified others over the years. Sadly for Haigh, his knowledge of English law was somewhat lacking.

All the police needed to do was establish the fact a murder had taken place. So a forensic team set about examining the contents of the Crawley address, retrieving 475 pounds of grease in which they unearthed three gallstones, eighteen bone fragments and a set of dentures. These items had remained intact thanks to the large amount of highly-resistant fat in which they were found. The false teeth were then positively identified by Olive's dentist. Her weight may not have saved her but it helped catch her killer.

By the time the case came to trial in July 1949, John Haigh had become a celebrity. Over four thousand people flocked to Lewes Assizes to catch a glimpse of the killer before his defence – paid for by the *News Of The World* in exchange for the exclusive – made the plea for insanity. Sadly for the plaintiff, the jury rejected the tales of a maniac drinking the blood of his victims and, after just fifteen minutes deliberation, found him guilty of premeditated murder. Sentenced to death, three weeks later he was hanged at Wandsworth Prison.

John Wayne Gacy

Made Man of the Year by his local community, this fund-raising philanthropist led a double life during the 1970s. When not performing as Pogo the Clown this civic-minded saint succumbed to an insatiable lust for young men, luring his unsuspecting prey to their deaths and burying them beneath his home.

FAILING HIS FATHER

Named after the all-American film star his father idolized, John Wayne Gacy came up short in direct comparison to the famous cowboy. His father hoped his son would make him proud through manly sporting achievements but unfortunately the boy was more content helping his mother and two sisters in the kitchen and garden. This brought the overweight and often sickly child a torrent of verbal and physical abuse from his alcoholic father. Yet despite the drunken beatings, little Johnny desperately yearned for paternal affection.

It never came, even after he was struck on the forehead by a swing at the age of eleven. The numerous fainting spells throughout his teens from the resulting blood clot on the brain were deemed by his uncaring father as pure play-acting. The head trauma did little to help his failing grades and he proceeded to flunk out of four separate high schools.

By the time he was twenty years old he left the family home in Chicago for a brief stint in Las Vegas, returning three months later to enrol at North-western Business College. Following graduation, he took a job with the Nunn-Bush Shoe Company proving to be a natural salesman. What he lacked in academic prowess, he more than made up for with keen powers of persuasion. He was quickly becoming his own man; focused, determined to succeed despite his father's cold nature. The pain he had suffered during his childhood was now deeply suppressed and would later manifest itself in the most horrific manner.

A DARK CHAPTER

Transferring to Springfield, the capital of his home state, Gacy began dating shy book-keeper, Marlynn Myers, and by September 1964 the couple were married. Within two years he and his new bride had their first child, Michael, and they had moved to Waterloo, Iowa, where John had agreed to help manage his father-in-law's three franchises of Kentucky Fried Chicken.

The salesman blessed with the gift of the gab soon found being the boss suited him and his leadership skills were further enhanced after joining the Jaycees – the US Junior Chamber – along with a number of other civic organizations. His tireless volunteering work was soon acknowledged when in 1967 he made Vice President of the Jaycee's Waterloo chapter and was even named Man of the Year. A family man and leading light within the community, it seemed John Wayne Gacy's future would be an auspicious one.

However, there was a dark side to this civic-minded saint. Having been made chairman of the membership drive, Gacy appealed to the baser instincts of prospective members, arranging for pornographic film screenings and even orgies with prostitutes. Rumours were rife that he attended swinging parties and dabbled in drugs, yet the most telling tale was that this big-hearted public figure had a penchant for young boys.

A MODEL PRISONER
These whispers around the small Iowa town were true. He had already indulged in homosexual affairs with male co-workers even while his wife had been

in labour with their first child. His sexual compulsion was growing and soon this dark secret caught up with him. After luring teenager Donald Vorhees to his basement, he got him drunk and then pounced, forcing him to engage in explicit acts. When Vorhees finally told his family about the ordeal, charges of sodomy were brought against Gacy.

On 3 December 1968 he was given the maximum sentence of ten years at Anamosa State Penitentiary, where he behaved as a model prisoner. He continued to be socially active, joining numerous clubs and was even made head chef of the kitchen. To this end, Gacy walked out of jail a free man on 18 June 1970, just sixteen months after his initial incarceration.

Returning to his home town of Chicago, the now-divorced Gacy began to rebuild his life. The ex-convict moved in with his mother, worked as a short order cook and by June 1971 had saved enough money to start his own contracting business: PDM Incorporated. To reportedly keep the costs down, Gacy employed young men to perform the company's painting, decorating and maintenance work, but this money-saving act would lead John Wayne Gacy down a very dark path indeed.

By the end of the year he was well on the way to returning to a normal existence. He had bought a two-bedroom ranch-house at 8213 Summerdale in Norwood Park on the outskirts of Chicago and was now in a relationship with highschool friend Carole Hoff. Yet this reforming sodomite was unable to keep his obsession hidden. Back in February Gacy received a sexual assault charge after luring a teenage boy at a bus terminal into his car for sex. He escaped conviction when the youth failed to show at court, yet this brush with the law would not prevent his perversions from escalating.

Just two days into 1972, Gacy was back at the Greyhound bus station scouting for a suitable young man. Fifteen-year-old Tim McCoy, on his way from Michigan to Omaha, became his next sexual pick-up, bringing the teen back to his new home. The next morning, during an alleged accident with a kitchen knife, the heavy-set man stabbed the boy in the chest. Burying the body in the forty-foot crawlspace beneath his home, his sexual deviance now linked with death, this newborn killer would soon feel the need to repeat the experience.

CLOWNING AROUND

His next murder came in July 1975. By this time his second wife, Carole, had filed for divorce leaving Gacy free to bring his prey back to an empty house.

Using his natural charm, he lured many young men into his black Oldsmobile and subsequently to their deaths at 8213 Summerdale. Nineteen youths succumbed to his deadly advances over the next two years. Each one would voluntarily slip on Gacy's handcuffs, believing it was part of a magic trick. Once incapacitated, they would be subjected to sexual torture, abused by various instruments of evil and ultimately asphyxiated by the twisting of a tourniquet about their necks.

The digging of endless graves beneath the house became a chore for Gacy so he ordered his young contractors to do the hard labour for him, persuading his teenage lackeys they were trenches for pipes. With space created for more bodies he could now increase the death toll and began killing a new victim every three weeks.

While he conned his employees and bus station pick-ups back to his deadly den for sex and strangulation, he continued to pursue his philanthropic endeavours. Dressing up as Pogo the Clown, a character of his own invention, Gacy took time to brighten the days of sick children in hospital. Little did they know this jolly joker with paint on his face also had the blood of over thirty young men on his hands.

THE SEARCHES OF SUMMERDALE

His evil double existence was soon uncovered following the murder of his thirty-third victim, fifteen year-old Robert Piest. On 11 December 1978, whilst bidding on a remodelling job in Des Plaines, he lured the teenager from a pharmacy with a promise of well-paid labour. When Piest was reported missing by his mother, police found witnesses who had seen the boy with Gacy. Following a background check revealing the sodomy charge, authorities obtained a search warrant and discovered a number of possessions belonging to missing youths inside the house. Yet they failed to find a single body.

Gacy was placed under surveillance in the hope he would reveal some damning evidence. It came unexpectedly on 20 December when the two detectives staking out the home were invited in for dinner by the suspect. The policemen quickly noticed a putrid smell emanating from below stairs. Surely this was a clue worth investigating. The next day forensic teams descended on the house, the stench leading them to a number of human remains. Over the next few months Gacy's home became an excavation site as authorities unearthed over two dozen bodies under the floorboards. The community's shining light could now be arrested for murder.

SEND IN THE CLOWN

Gacy soon confessed to nearly thirty murders beginning six years back in 1972. He admitted to tricking them into the handcuffs, their unspeakable defilement and pouring quicklime on top of the bodies down in the crawlspace. The makeshift graveyard beneath his house became so full of corpses that he told police he threw the final five victims off the I-55 bridge into the Des Plaines River. These brought a total of thirty-three murders making him the worst serial killer in American history at that time.

Despite confessing in graphic detail to killings and drawing accurate diagrams of where each corpse lay buried, Gacy refused to give evidence at his trial. On 12 March 1980 the Cook County jury rejected the defence plea of insanity and found him guilty of all thirty-three murders. Judge Garripo handed down the death sentence and the roly-poly killer spent fourteen years on death row until the day of his execution.

On 10 May 1994, with a 500-strong crowd baying for blood outside the correctional facility in which he was held, Gacy received a lethal injection. Pogo the Clown would bring no more smiles to young faces and Gacy the Killer would bring no more death to the teenage population.

PART THREE

LADY KILLERS

BELLE GUNNESS

This heavyset pig farmer made an unlikely black widow, yet the nefarious Norwegian succeeded in luring as many as forty-two moneyed bachelors to her remote homestead with murder in mind.

AWAY FROM NORWAY

Belle Gunness began life as Brynhild Paulsdatter Størseth on a backwater farm in the rural community of Innbygda in central Norway. Born in November 1859 far from the Great Lakes region of America where she would later commit her crimes, the youngest of Paul and Berit's eight children was raised in relative poverty. From an early age she broke her back working on farms to bring food to the family table and soon came to realize life was a constant struggle.

Tough times came calling even when not slaving away on the land. An alleged incident in 1877 saw Brynhild, seventeen and pregnant, attacked by a man at a country dance. Kicked in the stomach, she lost the baby and suffered further indignation when her assailant escaped prosecution. Following this miscarriage of child and of justice, locals soon noticed a change in her personality.

Such adversity seemed to steel her resolve and the following year she took a job on a large, wealthy farming estate, saving all her earnings for a big move. Three years later, keen to leave Norway for a better life, she followed in the footsteps of her sister Nellie and emigrated to America. Settling in Chicago, she changed her name to Belle and began working as a servant.

In 1884, the burly Norwegian met and married store detective and fellow Scandinavian, Mads Sorenson, and two years later they decided to open a sweet shop together in downtown Chicago. The business proved unsuccessful and within a year the store burned down, apparently due to an exploding kerosene lamp. The pair collected on the insurance and with the money bought a new home in Austin.

BOUGHT THE FARM

Over the next few years, Belle gave her husband four children. However, when two of them, Caroline and Axel, died in infancy it appeared bad luck had followed Belle across the Atlantic. Acute colitis was presumed the cause of death, yet the symptoms of abdominal pain and nausea mirrored those of poisoning. Nobody suspected a thing even when the couple received another payout from the babies' life insurance policies.

As fortune begat misfortune, a pattern started to emerge. Then on 30 July 1900, Sorenson suffered heart failure and died. His death fell on the only day on which two separate policies on him overlapped. When the grieving widow wasted no time in claiming the day after the funeral, it became clear this was less a case of bad luck and more of bad Belle. An inquest was ordered following suspicions of foul play but when the body was exhumed and no trace of poison found, the matter was dropped.

The two policies paid out a combined $8,500 with which she bought a pig farm on the McClung Road in La Porte, Indiana. Shortly after her move to the Maple City area she met Peter Gunness, a fellow expatriate from Norway, who agreed to marry Belle on the 1 April 1902 – a most apposite wedding date, it would turn out.

Just one week after tying the knot, Peter's young daughter mysteriously died alone in the house with Belle. Before the year was out Peter Gunness would also be dead. In December 1902, the experienced butcher met with a tragic end when a meat grinder fell from a high shelf and split open his skull.

When Belle banked a $3,000 insurance claim, the neighbourhood cried murder. Pregnant with her son, Phillip, Belle stood before a jury and was cleared of any wrongdoing.

HEART STRINGS TO PURSE STRINGS

Emboldened by her two lucky escapes from justice, Belle began placing adverts in Scandinavian newspapers across the Midwest, searching for eligible bachelors and rich widowers to take Peter's place. Soon a steady stream of middle-aged men began to arrive at her farm ready and willing to combine fortunes. One of the first was John Moe from Elbow Lake, Minnesota, who brought over $1,000 to pay off her mortgage. He disappeared within a week.

The citizens of La Porte witnessed Belle, dressed in all her finery, bring her gentlemen callers into town one by one, making a bee-line for the bank where they would cash in their savings. Ole Budsberg, an elderly widower from Wisconsin, was last seen withdrawing funds here on 6 April 1907 before going missing. In January 1908, Andrew Helgelien followed the same routine after he had been hooked by Belle's letters declaring undying love.

Her suitors were not the only ones to disappear. Jennie Olsen, her adopted child, vanished in

December 1906 never to be seen again. When concerned locals inquired after the teenager, Belle informed them she had sent her to a Lutheran College in Los Angeles. The truth was far more sinister; she remained on the property, buried in the backyard.

SMOKING GUNNESS

While the neighbourhood smelled a rat there was one man who knew the truth. Ray Lamphere had been employed to run the farm shortly after the death of Mister Gunness. He quickly grew jealous of her endless suitors, developing an infatuation with the heavyset lady of the house. Consumed by envy, he began to cause trouble and on 3 February 1908 she fired him. Belle then paid a visit to the local courthouse and declared her former employee a menace to her and others, and even made out a will with her lawyer, M. E. Leliter, making it known she feared for her life.

In the small hours of 28 April, Joe Maxon, Lamphere's replacement, woke to the smell of smoke in his second-floor bedroom. Discovering the house on fire, he called for Belle and the children but received no reply. He escaped the blaze and went for help. When the fire department arrived the place was in ruins. Four bodies were found in the cellar, trapped under a grand piano. Three of them were quickly confirmed as Belle's three children: Myrtle, Lucy and Philip. The remaining corpse proved to be more difficult to identify as she was missing a head.

Belle's lawyer then came forward and informed authorities of his client's misgivings regarding Lamphere. When a witness admitted seeing him running from the farm moments before the flames took hold, Sheriff Smutzer arrested and charged him with murder and arson.

Members of the sheriff department, aided by a number of volunteers, began sifting through the ruins for evidence. Their attention was directed to an area surrounded by a high-wire fence containing a number of filled-in holes. In the first week of May, the diggers discovered the bodies of Jennie Olson and Andrew Helgelien. Both had been cut into pieces, wrapped in oil cloth and buried in four feet of earth. Further excavation revealed as many as forty men and children dumped in shallow graves.

NO HEADWAY

As the shock of such a find spread through the town, many locals came to look at the charred remains of the headless woman and all refused to believe it was the body of Belle Gunness. Even bearing in mind the missing head and burnt flesh it looked nothing like her. Beefy Belle was known to be at least five feet eight inches tall, weighing as much as 280 pounds, yet the corpse lying in the morgue was five inches shorter and over a hundred pounds lighter.

Doctor J. Meyers examined the internal organs of the dead woman and found evidence of strychnine. Together with some surviving bridgework found in the ashes deemed insufficiently touched by fire, it looked more and more as if Belle Gunness had faked her own death and had escaped justice for a third time. The authorities hit a dead end, unable to confirm with any degree of certainty who the headless woman was. Yet again, Ray Lamphere was able to shed light on the mystery.

DEATHBED CONFESSION

Lying on his deathbed dying of tuberculosis, the convicted arsonist finally revealed his long-held secret to Reverend Schell in January 1910: Belle was still alive. He went on to confess to helping her bury many of her victims after she had either poisoned them or bashed in their heads while sleeping. He spoke of her decapitating a Chicagoan woman who had been lured to the farm by a promise of work.

This was the mysterious headless woman found next to the three children; the three children Lamphere revealed she had murdered.

Before his death, the besotted accomplice explained how Belle had amassed great wealth through these murders. By his reckoning as many as forty-two men had met their end at the Gunness farm; their cashed-in savings filling her coffers to the tune of around $250,000, around $6 million in today's money. Later, the banks revealed Belle had indeed withdrawn all her funds the day before the fire.

Many sightings of the elusive pig farmer were reported over the years. From Chicago to New York to Los Angeles, witnesses believed they had finally found her. Then, in 1931, twenty-three years after her disappearance, a woman named Esther Carlson was arrested in Los Angeles for the murder of August Lindstrom. Following her death in prison while awaiting trial, two former La Porteans managed to view the body and swore blind they had seen the body of Belle Gunness.

BEVERLEY ALLITT

*Over an eight week period, the malevolent
ministrations of this angel of death transformed
a care-giver into a life-taker, breaking parents'
hearts when she stole their babies' lives.*

ATTENTION!

Many a child is forced to vie for attention when
growing up in a large family. It was the same for
Beverley Gail Allitt. Born on 4 October 1968, the little
girl had to compete with three siblings in order to be
heard. Yet unlike most children young Beverley would
resort to extreme acts of odd behaviour, demanding
the spotlight in increasingly disturbing ways.

It began with feigning injury to pull her parents'
gaze towards her. When this became commonplace
she took to wearing dressings and casts over
apparent wounds but would refuse to let anyone
examine the injuries. Through her teenage years her
weight ballooned and with each pound she put on,
her behaviour became more aggressive. She even
manipulated boyfriends, faking pregnancy and even
crying rape to get her own way.

At the same time her need for attention increased. She started making endless trips to the hospital for a variety of simulated illnesses. From blurred vision to gall bladder pain, from ulcers to urinary infections; Beverley would use any condition to waste healthcare resources. And she was good at it. Her display of suffering was so realistic she even managed to convince doctors to remove a perfectly healthy appendix.

Picking at the stitches to ensure the wound remained a source of attention, she continued along this dangerous path to self-harm, cutting herself with glass and using a hammer to create new physical injuries. Her incessant hospital visits soon made her a well-known face and she was forced to resort to doctor-hopping; moving from hospital to hospital in order to receive the attention so clearly craved.

PATIENT TO PRACTITIONER

With her strong connection to the medical profession, Beverley unsurprisingly chose to train as a nurse. This failed to curb her strange behaviour. During her training at a nursing home, she smeared faeces on the walls and even left excrement in the fridge. Along with these foul outbursts, Beverley notched up an inordinate number of sick days, persistently ill from a series of feigned ailments. Despite her poor attendance record and numerous failed attempts at passing the nursing exams, Beverley managed to find a job at a hospital. Grantham and Kesteven Hospital in Lincolnshire had suffered a series of budget cuts and were chronically understaffed. Having only two trained personnel on the day shift and just one for the night, they were in dire need of a nurse on their children's ward. So Beverley Allitt was thus granted a temporary six-month contract in 1991.

She joined Ward 4 and quickly settled in, proving a keen worker, always finding time to be close to the sick children that came in for care. Unaware of her troubled history, the staff were equally clueless that they were working side by side with a dangerous, unstable and twisted individual who would turn from care-giver to life-taker in a matter of weeks.

SPECIAL CARE

On 21 February 1991, seven-month-old Liam Taylor was admitted to Ward 4 with a chest infection. The new nurse on the team seemed to go that extra mile to help reassure the anxious parents who were told to go home and get some rest. On their return, Beverley broke the bad news; Liam had suffered a respiratory attack in their absence. Relieved to hear their son was showing signs of recovery, Mr and Mrs Taylor were heartened to find Nurse Allitt had volunteered to pull a double shift to keep an eye on Liam through the night.

Moments before midnight, Beverley sent her colleagues on an errand, leaving her alone with baby Liam. It was during this time that his condition took a dramatic dive. Ghostly pale and developing nasty red blotches on his skin, the child stopped breathing. Allitt reacted quickly, calling for the emergency doctors. So focused was the crash team on resuscitating poor Liam, that they overlooked the disquieting fact the alarm monitors had failed to sound.

After a long struggle, fighting to revive the infant, they were forced to put the baby on life support. All through the chaotic ordeal a detached Nurse Allitt watched silently from the sidelines. She then put on her coat and went home leaving the Taylors to make the worst of all decisions; to turn off the machine keeping their little son alive.

ARRESTS ON WARD 4

Two weeks passed before Beverley struck again. Suffering from cerebral palsy, eleven-year-old Timothy Hardwick was wheeled into Ward 4 following an epileptic fit on 5 March 1991. Left alone with the merciless nurse, the boy began to fade. The resuscitation team rushed to the scene to find young Timothy turning blue with no sign of a pulse. Despite a paediatric specialist being on hand to assist, the team were unable to revive the patient. The subsequent autopsy found no obvious reason for his death.

Three days later, Kayley Desmond went into cardiac arrest in the same bed in which Liam Taylor had died. Once again Allitt was the attending nurse. This time the doctors were able to resuscitate the one-year-old girl and she was transferred to the larger hospital in Nottingham. She had only come in with a chest infection. After her transfer, a strange puncture wound was located underneath her armpit. This clue to the crime was dismissed as being from an accidental injection. But it had been anything but an accident.

Encouraged by the lack of suspicion surrounding her, Beverley continued to tamper with alarms and aggravate the conditions of her charges. On 20 March, five-month-old Paul Crampton suffered insulin shock prior to discharge, slipping dangerously close to a coma on three occasions. Revived each time, the decision was made to transfer him to

Nottingham, but this was not the end of the ordeal for baby Paul. Accompanying him in the ambulance, Allitt ensured another insulin overdose befell him. Thankfully, the patient survived the journey with evil by his side.

The unexpected cardiac arrests and inexplicable spikes in insulin levels suffered by the children on Ward 4 caused concern among the staff but still nobody was pointing the finger at Nurse Allitt. In fact, many remarked how attentive and eagle-eyed she was to have raised the alarm on each occasion. Over the next couple of days two more innocent children came close to losing their lives; both patients transferred to Nottingham hospital before she could administer the kill shot. Twice foiled, it would not take long for Beverley to succeed in murdering for yet more attention.

OH GOD MOTHER

On 1 April 1991, baby Becky Phillips was rushed to Grantham Hospital with gastroenteritis. One of twin girls recently born prematurely, she remained stable in the children's unit under the watchful, attention-seeking eye of Beverley Allitt. Two days in, she reported the two-month-old infant cold to the touch but after an examination found nothing wrong, she was sent home with her mother. That evening, little Becky suffered convulsions and, despite a diagnosis of mere colic from an on-call doctor, sadly passed away.

The subsequent autopsy was unable to find a clear cause of death so, as a precaution, Becky's surviving twin, Katie, was admitted to Ward 4. As bad luck would have it, Allitt was working her shift that day. History repeated itself as the second Phillips twin endured a similar fate as her sister. Katie arrested twice in forty-eight hours, both times she responded positively to the resuscitation procedure. Following her transfer she was found to have broken five ribs, developed cerebral palsy, partial paralysis and sight and hearing difficulties, all owing to her oxygen deprivation. But she was alive.

Discovering Beverley was the nurse to have raised the alarm and due to her constant close attention paid to both daughters, Sue Phillips approached Allitt, asking her if she would be Katie's godmother. Revelling in this false heroism, the nurse accepted, undeserving of such an honour having inflicted such permanent damage on the child.

HARSHEST VERDICT

One more life would be taken before Allitt's

destructive forces were brought to an end. On 22 April 1991, fifteen-month-old Claire Peck was admitted after an asthma attack. Two brief moments alone with the nurse from hell brought on two arrests, the last of which took her life. Her autopsy revealed she had died of natural causes, but this did not sit right with Dr Nelson Porter, a consultant at the hospital, who initiated an enquiry. Tests revealed high levels of Lignocaine in her system; a substance never prescribed to babies. The police were called, and they discovered twenty-four suspicious episodes over the previous two months all linked by one common factor: Beverley Allitt.

Suspended from duty while sufficient evidence was collected, she was formally charged in November 1991. While she awaited trial, psychiatrists attempted to understand her motivation behind the attacks. It soon became apparent she was suffering from a rare factitious disorder named Munchausen By Proxy, characterized by the causing of physical injury upon others to gain attention for oneself.

Attending just sixteen days of her two-month trial due to apparent illness, Beverley Allitt was convicted on 23 May 1993 and given thirteen life sentences for murder and attempted murder, the harshest verdict handed down to a woman. Behind bars, she reverted back to her past, self-harming by stabbing herself with paper clips and pouring boiling water over her hand – all in the name of attention.

ELIZABETH BÁTHORY

Luring an unending line of young girls to her creepy castle, this medieval menace delighted in the torture and mutilation of her slaves to satisfy an insatiable bloodlust; an obsession that became legendary and earned her the sickening sobriquet: the Blood Countess.

PURE EVIL

During the sixteenth century the Hungarian aristocracy enjoyed enormous power in Eastern Europe. As part of a great empire ruled by Austria to the west, each of these families possessed untold riches and vast lands. To protect these huge estates bloodlines were kept pure by the intermarrying of relatives. On the 7 August 1560 two branches of one such dynasty were fused together with the birth of Elizabeth Báthory.

Counting cardinals, princes and even a future king as family, the young noblewoman spent her childhood at Ecsed Castle, growing into a highly-intelligent, raven-haired beauty. She did, however, suffer from seizures, possibly a by-product of the inbreeding, and would often fly into a rage much to the alarm of her governesses.

In addition to her studies, Elizabeth became well-versed in violence. Hungarian nobles were renowned for their mistreatment of the lower classes and at Ecsed Castle servants were severely beaten on a daily basis. On one occasion the wild youngster witnessed a gypsy thief being sewn into the belly of a horse as punishment; his head protruding from the incision, the culprit was left to die. Elizabeth grew up believing such savagery was just the way of the world.

At eleven years of age, she was betrothed to Count Ferenc Nádasdy, an accomplished warrior known among the people as The Black Hero of Hungary. Her adolescent promiscuity almost scuppered the arrangement, however, when she fell pregnant to one of the peasants on the estate. Sent away to give birth and give up the child, Elizabeth returned and married the Count the following year. She moved in with her new husband at his castle in Sárvár, where he introduced her to a new level of perversion.

STAR-KICKING AND SCREAMING
The newlyweds immersed themselves in the dark world of the occult, casting spells, chanting incantations during satanic rituals until Nádasdy was called away to war. The Ottoman Empire was

encroaching on the Christian kingdom seen as the last bulwark against the invading Muslims. Elizabeth was left to her own devices and travelled from castle to castle, visiting relatives including an aunt who opened her eyes to the pleasures of bisexuality and flagellation.

Once she had completed the tour of her estates, she settled at the thirteenth-century Cachtice Castle, a wedding gift from her husband, set in the remote Little Carpathian mountains. Here she busied herself with her many duties as a noble, assisting the poor and defending the land from Turkish attack. Yet such responsibilities were not enough to prevent Elizabeth from indulging in her favourite pastime.

The countess delighted in whipping her servants with a barbed lash or beating them with a stick. She would amuse herself by having her maidservants dragged naked into the snow to have cold water poured over them. The water would then freeze creating human ice sculptures for her perverse entertainment. A trick picked up from her husband called star-kicking also became common practice. Paper soaked in oil would be placed between the toes of a victim then lit. Elizabeth was assured the recipient saw stars due to the burning pain.

Not all her servants lived in constant fear of the

cruel countess. She had a select few who agreed to help her bring suffering to the rest. Colluding with her was Ilona Jo, her wet-nurse from childhood, Dorothea Szentes or Dorka, a heavyset woman believed to be a witch, and Johannes Ulvary also known as Ficzko, a crippled dwarf. These collaborators assisted in bringing Elizabeth's creative visions of violence to life.

BLACK WIDOW

In January 1604, Count Nádasdy died. A wound sustained in battle or, as many claim, received from a Bucharest whore whom he had refused to pay, had become infected making Elizabeth Báthory a widow. His death served only to allow her more freedom to indulge in her evil fantasies. She took a female lover called Anna Darvula, a kindred spirit who supported her reign of terror, and together they revelled in an escalating binge of brutal torments.

Handmaidens would be stripped, forced to lay on the floor and tortured so severely that buckets were needed to scoop up the blood. From burning hands to mutilating genitals, nothing was too loathsome for this evil countess. Not even illness could curb her inhumanity; asking Szentes to bring a maid to her sickbed, she leapt out like a rabid dog and sank her teeth into the girl's flesh, biting her cheek, shoulder and breast.

While the countess played rough with the young girls in her employ rumours began to circulate within the surrounding villages. The poverty-stricken peasants living in the shadow of Cachtice Castle had always aspired to work inside its walls. Thrilled by the promise of high wages, families waved their virginal daughters off with a smile, but when their loved ones failed to return a growing consternation took over. However, fearing retribution from the potentate, the townsfolk mustered no more than guarded whispers and nervous gossip.

With the locals hamstrung by terror, Countess Báthory's wickedness continued unimpeded. Bodies piled up inside the citadel causing an unimaginable stench, forcing her accomplices to dump the corpses in ditches and rivers outside. Then in 1609 a death occurred for which Elizabeth was not responsible: her lover Anna Darvula passed away. She immediately took another, a widow named Erszi Majorova, who would make a suggestion that would bring about her downfall.

FINISHING SCHOOL

As a younger woman Elizabeth's beauty had always

been beyond compare, but she was approaching fifty now and her best days were behind her. Gazing long into the mirror, as she was known to do, would now only disappoint. Then one day she struck a servant girl for accidentally pulling her hair while brushing. Blood spattered on to her hand and the countess declared it had a rejuvenating effect.

Legend tells us that she instructed her cohorts to bring young virgins to the castle. The innocent girls would have their veins slit with knives allowing Elizabeth to shower in their blood. When this failed to restore her good looks she figured it was down to the victims' breeding. It was then that Erszi Majorova, her lover, proposed a move that would finally bring this unending trail of death and disorder to an end.

Daughters of lesser noblemen from the surrounding lands were invited to attend a finishing school at the Báthory residence. These etiquette classes lured as many as twenty-five girls at a time who, once inside the castle, found social grace distinctly lacking. Those chosen would allegedly provide the countess with high-born blood in which she would bathe to bring back her former allure.

STORMING THE CASTLE
Moving on to such respectable prey was a mistake,

bringing the considerable power of their families down on Elizabeth. Soon the Lord Palatine of Hungary, Count Thurzo, was told of the vast number of missing girls. As cousin to the countess he was keen to avoid a family scandal, but soon public pressure became too great to ignore and in March 1610 he sent two officials to investigate the claims.

By the onset of winter Thurzo had sufficient evidence to warrant action. On 30 December, the count and a band of soldiers ventured to the castle under cover of night. Beyond the heavy wooden doors lay a living nightmare. In the main hall they found a girl lying dead on the stone floor. Further on, another lay close to death from severe wounds to her body. Deep inside the dungeons more victims were discovered, awaiting their turn in the torch-lit torture chambers.

Elizabeth was placed under house arrest within her own castle, escaping the ignominy of a trial thanks to her noble birth. Her accomplices were not as lucky. Found guilty on eighty counts of murder, Szentes and Ilona Jo had their fingernails torn out by red-hot pincers before being burned at the stake. Ficzko the dwarf was beheaded for his crimes and his headless body tossed into the flames.

Despite keeping a diary listing over 650 victims

of torture, and even with the Emperor Matthias II demanding her execution, Countess Báthory eluded the death penalty. The bloodthirsty noblewoman was, however, walled up in a single room in Cachtice Castle from which she did not escape. On 21 August 1614 she was found dead inside this makeshift cell and her body laid to rest in the family crypt at Ecsed. Her evil actions blackened her name throughout Hungary where any mention of Elizabeth Báthory was forbidden.

ILSE KOCH

*From humble beginnings this vicious redhead rose
to become one of the Nazi elite during World War
II, striking terror among the inhabitants of the
concentration camp her husband commanded.*

NAZI NOBILITY

Born Ilse Koehler on 22 September 1906 this
daughter of a factory supervisor showed little sign
of any sadistic tendencies during her childhood.
In fact, she was a blithe spirit while growing up in
the Saxony capital of Dresden, passing through her
school years without incident. Keen on working
with finances she attended accountancy college,
acquiring the necessary qualifications to land her a
job as a book-keeping clerk shortly after.

Throughout the 1920s, while Ilse worked in
relative obscurity, Adolf Hitler was reorganizing
the Nazi party in his quest to govern Germany. In
April 1932 she became one of its early members
and, through her new fascist friends, met Karl Otto
Koch. Nine years her senior, Koch was a veteran of
the Great War and, following the open oppression

of the Jews, had begun to earn a reputation for himself as a strict camp commandant. This perfect Nazi couple were married in 1936.

In the summer of the following year, Koch was transferred to take command of the newly-created hard labour camp at Buchenwald near Weimar. In stark contrast to the prisoners' short miserable existence, Ilse lived the high life in their luxury villa on Officers' Row. Treated like Nazi nobility, her sadistic fantasies were given the freedom to become grim reality.

HEINOUS HOUSEWIFE

As the Camp Commandant's wife, Ilse held no official rank at Buchenwald, yet over time she became a much-feared monster among the incarcerated. With her striking appearance, long red locks and tight clothes she flaunted her sexuality, teasing the inmates. Indeed, any prisoner caught looking at her ran the risk of being shot on the spot.

Wielding such power over those held captive, this simple housewife soon became known as The Commandeuse, using the compound as her own personal playground. Whipping prisoners on a whim and forcing captives to sexually abuse one another for her amusement, Ilse revelled in her unconstrained role at Buchenwald. With nobody to tell her no, her mind was given free rein, thinking up vile ways of making the most out of the inmates' wretched lives.

Many have since told tales of how she would demand a line-up, order the men to strip then proceed to march down the rows searching for tattoos she liked. As if picking out curtains, the Commandeuse would point at those designs she found appealing and their owners were escorted away to the camp hospital. If the chosen were ever seen alive again, they would be missing their inked flesh.

No one could have imagined the reason behind this tattoo selection. It soon came to light the patterned skin had been tanned then stitched to make a patchwork. With this macabre material a number of appalling artefacts were created, from lampshades to book covers to knife cases, many of which were given away as gifts to friends in the SS.

DELIVERANCE

Her crimes were not confined to the torture of prisoners. Whilst ordering the stripping of skin, Ilse and her husband were also ripping off the Reich, and it did not take long before the Gestapo came calling. In August 1943 the couple were arrested for embezzlement of SS funds totalling more than 700,000 Reichsmarks and put on trial the following winter. The special Nazi court found Karl Koch guilty and he was executed in the yard of his own camp on 5 April 1945. Ilse, on the other hand, was acquitted due to lack of evidence and, at the end of the war, endeavoured to return to normal life.

The court ordeals of the Commandeuse, however, were not complete. Following the liberation of Buchenwald by Allied troops in the spring of 1945, Ilse was tracked down and arrested by US authorities in June. Brought before an American military tribunal at Dachau, she was among thirty-one defendants charged with aiding and abetting in the murders at the death camp. Former inmates testified to the killing orders given by Ilse for tattooed skin helping those passing sentence to hand down a life term.

Later, the Bitch of Buchenwald, as she had become known, had this judgement commuted to four years. Having already served this period of time, she was freed from Landsberg prison much to the dismay of many Americans. In 1949, after pressure from the US Senate, Ilse was re-arrested and tried before a West German court.

On 15 January 1951, she was once again given a life sentence. After serving twenty years in prison,

Ilse Koch committed suicide, hanging herself with twisted bedsheets in her cell at Aichbach prison. She left a note stating death was the only deliverance.

IRMA GRESE

*Transformed by the Nazi uniform under
the conditions of war this evil, whip-cracking
woman became one of the cruellest guards in all
of the death camps, taking great delight in causing
undue suffering to her charges.*

FROM BANAL TO BRUTAL

Few would argue, were it not for the outbreak of war
and the Nazis' fixation with the Final Solution, the
life of Irma Grese would have been very different.
Born on 7 October 1923 in the rural German town
of Wrechen, this future brutal camp guard was
raised by a dairy farmer and his wife along with four
siblings in relative banality. Even when her mother
committed suicide, following marital problems in
1936, she showed no sign of deviant trauma that
might hint at the evil she would later display inside
the concentration camps.

Two years after her mother's death, Irma left school
aged fifteen. Never the scholar, she had struggled
with her studies, obtaining a basic education that
essentially made her unfit for anything other than

casual labour. Simple farm work seemed to be her future. In an attempt to better herself, Irma tried twice to become a nurse, but on both occasions her application was rejected. The closest she could get was a two-year stint as an assistant at an SS sanatorium in Hohenlychen.

Little did she know her talents lay in terror. She had already developed a fascination with Nazism, much to the disapproval of her father, joining the League of German Maidens. Following her second failure to join the healthcare community in 1942, Irma was sent by the employment exchange to Ravensbrueck Concentration Camp where she received training to become a female guard or Helferin. Here she learned the malicious methods of abuse and punishment that would form the basis of her barbarity.

EAGLE-EYED IRMA

Showing the necessary aptitude for cruelty, Irma was despatched to Birkenau camp at Auschwitz in March 1943. She quickly rose through the ranks to become Oberaufseherin or Senior Supervisor; the second highest ranking position for a woman at the facility. In charge of around 30,000 Jewish female prisoners, she revelled in the responsibility, suitably conditioned by Nazi doctrine to believe the inmates were nothing but subhuman scum.

Various reports of wanton brutality have been levelled at her. Whether it be shooting, whipping, raping or stabbing it appeared nothing was beyond the call for Irma Grese. In fact, she often broke camp rules, even crossing the line drawn by the Third Reich, in her desire to inflict pain and suffering. Her half-starved German Shepherds were let off their leash to attack bound prisoners on more than one occasion, and she often indulged her bisexual urges by raping the Jewish women.

During the selection parades in the main square, Irma often displayed her merciless streak. In September 1944 a mother, chosen for the gas chamber, escaped the line and joined her daughter in a row due to be spared that day. The eagle-eyed supervisor spotted the death dodger and ordered a guard to have her shot where she stood.

Such ruthlessness came as no surprise to the inmates of Birkenau. Earlier that summer they had witnessed Irma, nicknamed The Beautiful Beast by those she terrorized, personally assist the notorious Dr Mengele in a mass selection of between two and three thousand doomed captives. Her oppressed wards came to tremble at the very sound of her heavy boots, turning pale at the sight of her plaited whip, knowing full well anyone of them could be next to feel her cold malevolence.

In January 1945, Grese briefly returned to Ravensbrueck before ending the war in the Nazi concentration camp at Bergen-Belsen. Now she had a whole new batch of victims to brutalize. To their relief, on 15 April 1945, the British 11th Armoured Division liberated the complex. While many of the guards had fled, Irma remained behind and was promptly arrested.

Accused of murder, torture and the general mistreatment of prisoners, she stood trial at Lueneburg before a British military tribunal between 17 September and 17 November 1945. On the fifty-third day of proceedings, a remorseless Irma Grese was sentenced to hang for her crimes.

Less than a month after the verdict was announced, the Blonde Angel of Belsen was escorted out of her cell at Hamelin jail to meet Albert Pierrepoint, the famous English executioner. Remaining defiant to the end, she approached the gallows like a martyr, ordering her hangman to be quick. Pierrepoint duly obliged and, dropping through the trapdoor, Irma Grese became the youngest woman executed under British jurisdiction in the twentieth century.

JANE TOPPAN

More Sister with a Syringe than Lady of the Lamp,
this early American murderess showed no mercy
to over thirty victims, delivering injections
of death to the ill and infirm.

MADNESS IN MASSACHUSETTS

This Angel of Death began her days as Honora
Kelley, born in 1857 to Irish immigrants and raised
in the Bay State of Massachusetts. What little is
known of her childhood paints a traumatic picture;
with her mother dying of consumption and her
elder sister confined to an asylum, life was grim for
poor Honora. And it got worse. Peter Kelley, her
father, was a renowned eccentric who ran a tailoring
business in Boston. His bizarre behaviour allegedly
escalated to such an extent that, on one occasion, he
sewed his own eyelids closed. The Kelleys were, it
seemed, touched by madness.

Unable to cope with two young girls in his
unhinged state, Peter took six-year-old Honora and
her sister Delia to the Boston Female Asylum, an
orphanage for little girls. He pleaded for the officials

to take them from him and, on seeing signs of neglect and possible abuse, they agreed. Two years later, in November 1864, Honora left the asylum to become an indentured servant at the home of Mrs Ann C. Toppan of Lowell, Massachusetts. While not officially adopted, she took her keeper's surname and, leaving her past behind her, became known as Jane Toppan.

Life was much improved in Lowell. Jane worked hard for her benefactor and in turn received a stable upbringing. But living in the shadow of her elder foster sister, Elizabeth, brought out the green-eyed monster in her. The object of her envy was pretty, dainty and slim – all the things Jane was not. While Elizabeth received endless attention from suitors, she was left on the shelf, unwanted. Even when she managed to land herself a fiancé, he left the nineteen-year-old at the altar. This had a profound effect on the plump Irishwoman, adding to her already-developing neuroses, that would later reveal her own madness to the New England area.

JOLLY JANE

Jane remained at the Toppan house beyond her contract, and after her foster mother passed away, worked for Elizabeth and her new deacon husband,

Oramel Brigham. Then, in 1885, she moved out and began training as a nurse at Boston's Cambridge Hospital. She became a well-liked member of the team. Patients and personnel alike found her good company and a competent carer, and she soon acquired the nickname: Jolly Jane.

However, there was a dark side to this new trainee. Those in her care whom she liked would be prescribed unauthorized doses and have their charts falsified to ensure they stayed bedridden. Those patients she disliked she used as guinea pigs, secretly experimenting with various levels of morphine and atropine, bringing them in and out of consciousness. On several occasions these victims would die.

Her disturbing behaviour did not stop there. While she played with the lives of the sick and elderly, she found she derived a sexual thrill from watching them slip away. In their last moments she would slide into bed with the dying and snuggle up close to witness the final throes of death.

Amelia Phinney later would testify to finding the plump frame of Jolly Jane in her bed as she slipped in and out of a coma, kissing her face until she was interrupted. The delirious patient put it all down to a strange dream until hearing news reports of Toppan's actions years later.

SISTER SLAIN

Despite around a dozen patients dying on her watch, Nurse Jane managed to persuade a number of influential doctors to give her glowing references, allowing her to continue her training at the prestigious Massachusetts General Hospital. Here she continued her deception, doctoring charts and sleeping with her sick charges, until rumours of her stealing from the patients forced the authorities to dismiss her in the summer of 1890.

Next, Jane returned to Cambridge Hospital for a brief spell until she was fired for improper provision of opiates to patients. Unbowed, she forged a nursing licence and began a career as a full-time private nurse in the following year. Her talents as a care-giver became much sought after, despite enduring rumours of petty theft and fabricating stories, and over the next few years her benevolent role in the community blossomed.

However, in May 1895, she abused this respected position, poisoning her landlord, Israel Dunham. Jane then moved in with the dead man's wife who, two years later, also fell foul of this live-in nurse. Next, she turned her evil attention to someone she hated with a passion. In August 1899, she invited her envied foster sister to her holiday home in Cape

Cod. Over a period of several days the resentful wretch spiked her drinks with strychnine, allowing her to slip into a death-delivering coma.

DEATH AT THE DAVISES

Moving on, Jane rented a cabin on the property of the Davis family. Alden and Mattie had two daughters, Minnie and Genevieve, portraying a vision of familial bliss – something Jane had never enjoyed. The fact that the Davis girls were also married stuck in her craw and she secretly plotted to bring misery into their lives.

The Davises, however, took to their overweight lodger, often allowing her to fall behind on rent. When the missed payments reached $500, Mattie Davis decided to collect, paying Jane a visit at her new accommodation. Using her signature move, she spiked mineral water with poison causing her former landlady to fall violently ill. Nurse Toppan played carer during the sickness, toying with her lucidity for seven days before she died. She even attended the funeral, scattering earth upon Mattie's grave.

Such rare attentiveness caught the eye of the grieving Davis family and they asked Jane to move in and help run the house for the elderly Alden. Little did they know they were inviting death into the home. Soon after her arrival a series of mysterious fires broke out in various rooms and then, on 26 July 1901, the youngest daughter Genevieve fell ominously ill. The sickness took her life and all agreed the cause was suicide; a desperate reaction by a grief-stricken daughter to her mother's death.

Less than two weeks later, the widower Davis followed his wife and daughter, gradually poisoned by their new housekeeper. Doctors missed the truth and deemed his death the result of a massive stroke. Jane was still not finished with the family.

In mid-August she brought out the vials of venom to poison the last remaining daughter, Minnie Gibbs. After imbibing the morphine-tainted cocoa wine, the dying girl suffered the pain of having her poisoner cuddle up to her whilst she held her ten-year-old son.

By the summer's end Jane Toppan had successfully wiped out four members of an entire family. She then returned to her home town and set her sights on Oramel Brigham, her late foster sister's husband. Nobody was going to get in the way of luring the deacon into wedlock, not even his seventy-year-old sister whom she poisoned to death. Next, she fed the object of her affection a deadly cocktail to prove, quite literally, he could not live without her.

Happily, while he had ingested the poison, Oramel refused to swallow the ruse and kicked her out of the house.

PARANOID POISONER

Meanwhile, Captain Gibbs, father-in-law to the final Davis victim, had returned from sea and, on hearing the horrific tales of the Davis deaths, instantly suspected foul play. He contacted Dr Wood, an eminent Harvard professor and toxicologist, and demanded tests be made on the exhumed body of Minnie Gibbs. Following the discovery of morphine and atropine in her system, Jane Toppan was swiftly arrested in late October 1901 and held for trial at Barnstaple Jail House.

Her psychiatric evaluation revealed the disturbing sexual gratification she obtained from holding the dying as well as traces of mental ill-health in her family history. The attending doctors diagnosed an irresistible sexual impulse that caused her to kill. With such a damning judgement, it took less than twenty minutes for the jury to find her guilty of the four Davis murders, and she was sentenced to life in Taunton Insane Hospital. She took the news with a smile.

Her surprising reaction to the verdict came from the mistaken belief that due to her court-supported insanity she would be free within a few months. A post-trial confession published in the *New York Journal* revealed she wanted the jury to find her insane and went on to declare she had killed more than thirty-one people.

In fact, she would spend the rest of her life inside the asylum, accusing her carers of giving her poison, until she died of natural causes aged eighty-one.

KARLA HOMOLKA

*Portraying a damsel in distress, this Barbie
doll deviant masked her evil soul from the
world while helping her violent boyfriend
sexually abuse young girls, proving beauty
is only sin deep.*

ANIMAL LOVER

Born on 4 May 1970 into a Czech immigrant family,
Karla Leanne Homolka grew up in a lower middle
class neighbourhood on the southern shore of Lake
Ontario in Canada. Blessed with affectionate, loving
parents, who doted on Karla and her two younger
sisters, she developed into an attractive well-adjusted
young girl. She excelled at school, proving a studious
pupil, and with her blonde locks, doe eyes and Eastern
European features soon became popular with the
boys at Sir Winston Churchill High.

However, despite such a perfect start in life, the
teenage Karla began to demonstrate a disturbing
fascination with sexual violence. After dabbling
in self-mutilation, Karla experimented with early
boyfriends, allowing them to tie her up and beat her

during sex. Her masochistic tendencies awoken, she now longed for a man who could play her sexual master. She would not need to wait for too long.

Leaving school with her high school diploma, Karla found work as a veterinary assistant – the ideal role for a life-long animal lover. On 17 October 1987, she travelled to Toronto to attend a pet convention, staying at the Howard Johnson in Scarborough, a nearby suburb. That evening, in the hotel dining room, she met Paul Bernardo; a confident, fresh-faced twenty-three-year-old, who charmed her into coming up to his room. Such an instant connection sparked between them that within hours of meeting the pair were engaging in wild sex. Karla had found her soul mate.

SISTER ACT

The new man in her life appeared to be the perfect catch. He was training to be an accountant, welcomed into the Homolka family and made Karla extremely happy. But Paul harboured a sinister secret. Since May 1987 a number of young women had been sexually assaulted alighting from buses by an unknown assailant dubbed the Scarborough Rapist. Unbeknownst to Karla, the perpetrator of these attacks was none other than her Paul Bernardo.

The couple grew ever closer as the years passed. Karla's infatuation with her deviant boyfriend created a disturbing dynamic in which she would do almost anything for him. Throughout the summer of 1990 Paul made it increasingly clear to Karla that he wished to deflower her fifteen-year-old sister, Tammy. Rather than reprimand him, Karla considered the twisted request and set about planning the most sickeningly-inappropriate gift anyone could give.

On 23 December 1990, following a Christmas party at the Homolka house, Karla and Paul invited Tammy downstairs to watch a film with them in the basement den. Karla slipped her tipsy sister some sleeping pills and then smothered her face with a cloth soaked in Halothane – a general anaesthetic she had stolen from work. Handing Paul his early Christmas present, she recorded him raping the young virgin on videotape, taking time out from directing duties to perform oral sex on her own comatose sister.

Such shocking defilement and debauchery brought about one final surprise. Thanks to the concoction of drugs and alcohol in Tammy's system, she started to choke on her own vomit and soon stopped breathing. The demonic duo cleaned the poor victim and redressed her before calling 911 ensuring by the time paramedics reached the scene Tammy was long gone. The subsequent autopsy deemed her death an accident, leaving Karla and Paul free to continue their evil sexual escapades.

CONCRETE PROOF

Two months later the perverted lovers rented a wood-panelled bungalow in Port Dalhousie, and by the summer the pair were back on the prowl for prey. In the early hours of 15 June 1991, fourteen-year-old Leslie Mahaffy returned to her Burlington home after attending the wake of a friend. Finding she was locked out, she walked around to the rear of the house only to find Paul Bernardo sitting on a bench in the backyard.

His magnetic personality quickly charmed the young girl, luring her to his car with a promise of a cigarette. In a flash, Paul had Leslie at knifepoint, bundling her into his ride and spiriting her off to the house some fifty kilometres away. On their arrival, Karla awoke and joined her boyfriend in sexually abusing the teen, though not before prettying herself in front of the recording camera.

Even when left alone with Karla, Miss Mahaffy's pleas fell on deaf ears. The evil vet assistant simply plied her with more sleeping pills before the couple garotted the girl with an electrical cord. The next day a circular saw was taken to the corpse and, with the heads and limbs removed, her body parts were encased in quick-drying cement.

They then travelled out to Lake Gibson and dumped the eight blocks into the water. Two weeks later, a husband and wife canoeing on the lake came upon the odd concrete blocks. Paddling over to them, they discovered some had split, revealing human remains. On the very same day, sixteen miles away at Niagara-on-the-Lake, Karla and Paul were exchanging their wedding vows before a packed church of friends and relatives. Off on their Hawaiian honeymoon, the couple were now bound together in holy matrimony as well as by murder.

THE WINTER OF DISCONTENT

The infernal newlyweds' next victim disappeared into their sick and twisted world of sadomasochism on 16 April 1992. Fifteen-year-old Kristen French was spotted by the couple in a church parking lot and this time it was Karla's turn to lure in the victim. Pretending to need directions, the siren-like beauty baited Kristen towards the car whereupon she was snatched by Bernardo.

Back at their bungalow, Karla and Paul abused, tortured and raped Kristen for three days running. Due at the Homolkas for an Easter dinner and feeling unable to leave her alive, they murdered the teenager on 19 April, returning after their meal to discard the body. The naked corpse was found eleven days later in a Burlington ditch.

The following month the Green Ribbon Task Force was set up to handle the murders of Leslie Mahaffy and Kristen French, but was hampered from the start thanks to erroneous witness testimonies. The couple were sufficiently spooked to file for a change of surname from Bernardo to Teale. This move would not come in time to help them.

By the winter of 1992 the killer couple's volcanic relationship had reached eruption point. Following a savage beating with a torch, Karla left her husband and moved in with relatives in Brampton. By the end of January, the investigation into the Scarborough Rapist case finally matched Paul Bernardo's blood sample, given after an earlier interview, to the physical evidence at the crime scenes. On 17 February the violent sexual deviant was taken into custody. By the time of the arrest Karla had already taken steps to distance herself from her accomplice.

HOMOLKA HOODWINKS

A week before Bernardo's arrest, Karla had confessed her involvement in the murders to her aunt and uncle. She then went to Metropolitan Police Station where she told detectives she was frightened for her life, explaining she had been coerced into performing sinister acts by her dominating husband.

Playing the victim became Karla's focus to ensure blame for the deaths fell on her husband. The authorities, keen on building an airtight case against Bernardo, offered the blonde Jezebel a plea bargain. Agreeing to turn state's evidence, Karla received the guarantee of a reduced sentence and total immunity from prosecution in the murder of her sister. This pact would later be dubbed the worst deal in Canadian history.

With the deal set in stone, Karla stood trial, pleading guilty to manslaughter. On 6 July, she received her commuted prison sentence of twelve years. Nearly two years later, Paul Bernardo's trial began and the evidence shown in court caused a public outcry, thanks to some hidden videotapes held back by the defence counsel. These clearly revealed that Karla was by no means a victim. The footage showed her smiling at the camera, licking her lips and actively engaging in the sexual abuse of their victims. Having already been tried and sentenced for her involvement in the crimes, this conniving Canadian had successfully avoided the full force of the law.

Amid protests across the nation, Karla Homolka moved from Kingston's Prison for Women to the medium security Joliette Institution, nicknamed Club Fed for its leniency. She engaged in a lesbian affair with a fellow convict and even acquired a degree in Psychology while inside. Examined by numerous psychiatrists prior to her incarceration the pretty blonde was diagnosed an hybristophiliac – someone sexually aroused by a partner's violent sexual behaviour.

On the 4 July 2005 she received her independence. Two years later, following a string of death threats, she gave birth to a baby boy and left Canada for the Antilles in the West Indies. Ontarians locked up their daughters in December 2009 when news reports suggested killer Karla was back in the area studying law and living with a new man.

KATHERINE KNIGHT

*This landmark case in Australia's court history
covered the evil acts of a demonic butcheress
whose fits of overreaction and treatment of
her partners have become the stuff of legend.*

BUTCHERY IN HER BLOOD

Born the youngest of twin girls on 24 October
1955, Katherine May Knight did not receive an
ideal upbringing. Her father, an alcoholic abattoir
worker, used to violently rape her mother as much
as ten times a day, and even she suffered a similar
fate at the hands of other members of her family
until she was eleven years old.

These episodes remained hidden from public
view within the small valley town of Tenterfield,
New South Wales and at school she came over as
a normal if slightly introverted young girl. One or
two incidents of bullying were recorded as puberty
struck but nothing to indicate the evil she would
perpetrate in later life.

However, there were cracks beginning to show
in her personality. In 1969, her beloved uncle Oscar

committed suicide leaving a distraught Katherine believing his ghost would regularly come to visit her. On leaving Muswellbrook High School at fifteen, she eventually followed in her father's footsteps and joined him at the local abattoir. Cutting up offal and boning carcasses seemed to be her idea of heaven. She would even hang her own set of butchering knives above her bed, gazing at them before she went to sleep, to dream of death and dissection.

OFF THE RAILS

In 1973 the tall, wiry slaughterhouse worker met truck driver David Kellett and within a year they agreed to be married. On the day of the wedding Katherine's own mother allegedly took the groom-to-be aside and warned him about her daughter. 'She'll kill you!', she said.

That night he would experience first-hand her fierce temper. Having fallen asleep, exhausted after three long sessions of sex, he was awoken by his bride's hands around his throat, attempting to squeeze the life out of him.

The violence did not stop there and it soon developed into a regular occurrence. In May 1976, following the birth of their first child Melissa Ann, Kellett chose to leave his wife for another woman, moving to Queensland. Depressed and angry at this affront, Katherine placed their two-month-old child on the tracks of the nearby railway line. Thankfully, a local old man out foraging in the woods heard the little girl crying and rescued her from certain death.

Having abandoned her own baby, the deranged twenty-one-year-old now headed into town, wielding an axe and threatening to kill random members of the public. Arrested before she could do any damage Katherine was taken to St Elmo's Hospital in Tamworth where she was diagnosed with post-natal depression.

It took only days following her release before Katherine embarked on another wild and crazy mission. Slashing the face of a woman with one of her trusted knives, she forced her to drive to Queensland where she planned to kill both David and his mother. When her driver managed to escape at a petrol station, Katherine then took a small boy hostage, causing a stand-off with local police. Finally officers managed to disarm her using a number of brooms and, once again, she was admitted into psychiatric care.

Deemed no longer a public threat, Katherine left Morisset Psychiatric Hospital and moved to Woodridge near Brisbane. Her husband had decided to return and care for his unhinged wife. He remained by her side, with the pair conceiving another child, until abruptly in 1984 Kellett arrived home to find Katherine had left him. Two years later this she-devil had found herself a new victim.

GREEN-EYED MONSTER

Following a back injury sustained while working at the abattoir, Katherine drew a disability pension and ended up in government housing in Aberdeen. It was here in 1986 where she met thirty-six-year-old David Saunders and in no time at all the pair were living together. Everything seemed perfect to begin with but it was not long before her violent nature reared its ugly head.

She grew extremely jealous, fearing he was seeing other women, and would often give in to fits of excessive violence. In May 1987 she slit the throat of his two-month-old puppy right in front of him purely as a warning never to cheat on her. Katherine then struck Saunders over the head with a frying pan, knocking him unconscious.

Despite this, Saunders stuck by his green-eyed girlfriend and in June 1988 the couple extended their family with the birth of daughter, Sarah. Needing more space they purchased a two-bedroomed home on MacQueen Street which quickly became Katherine's pet project, decorating it in her own inimitable style. Rather than evoking a family feel, she opted for homicidal hunter chic, covering the walls with animal skins, rusty traps, pitchforks and skulls.

Allowing Katherine to create her design master-piece failed to put a stop to the violence that had undeniably crept back into their relationship. Her partner took an iron in the face and was even stabbed in the stomach with a pair of scissors. This particular incident proved the final straw for poor David and he moved back to his old apartment in Scone.

VIDEO NASTY

With Saunders scared away into hiding, Katherine next shacked up with forty-three-year-old John Chillingworth, a former co-worker at the slaughter-house. The couple had a child together but after just three years the romance was over; the crazy Knight had found another with whom she had been having an affair for some time. This new inamorato would prove to be the unluckiest of all her companions.

His name was John Price and known to his many

friends as Pricey. Well-liked, honest and true, the divorced father of three was well aware of Katherine's reputation. Au fait with her fiery temper he allowed her to move into his three-bedroom bungalow, simultaneously moving himself inexorably closer to his dark destiny.

Their relationship followed a similar path to all the others. Over-the-top outbursts from Katherine would result in some form of suffering for her partner. In 1998, following his refusal to marry her, she made a videotape of some out-dated medical kits he had taken from a skip at work. She then sent the evidence to his boss who promptly fired him from a job he loved and had held for seventeen years.

Living in constant fear of her extreme actions, John Price visited Scone Magistrate's Court on 29 February 2000 and took out a restraining order. That afternoon at work he told his colleagues that if he failed to show up the following day it would be because she had killed him. When he arrived home he found the house empty; his children were at a sleep-over and Katherine – to his relief – was not there.

Sometime after eleven his dangerous darling returned, climbing into bed with him where they had sex. Price soon fell asleep, sealing his fate. The next morning his neighbour spotted his vehicle still in the driveway. His employers were also concerned he had not turned up for work and quickly the hue and cry was raised. The police arrived around eight in the morning and resolved to break in via the back door. Nothing could have prepared them for the horrific sight that lay within.

NEVER TO BE RELEASED

Once officers entered 84 St Andrews Street their eyes focused on an odd piece of drapery that seemed out of place. On closer inspection they realized what it was: hanging by a meat hook from the door arch an entire human hide complete with nose, ears, and genitals. Further inside, the skinned body of John Price lay on its back, legs crossed; he had been decapitated.

The missing head was discovered in a cooking pot stewing with assorted vegetables, and on the side dinner had been prepared for the children: slices of their father's buttocks served with baked potato, pumpkin, zucchini and gravy. A handwritten note accompanied the meal falsely accusing the victim of sexually abusing the youngsters.

Finally, after following a trail of bloody hand-prints to a double bed at the back of the house, they came upon an unconscious Katherine Knight.

Charged with the murder of John Price on 6 March 2000, it took well over a year for this hyperbolic butcheress to stand trial. Refusing to accept responsibility for her actions, she became hysterical when the gruesome details were mentioned in court and required sedation.

On 8 November 2001, after being found guilty by the jury, Justice O'Keefe handed down a landmark sentence of life behind bars with no possibility for parole; a first in Australian legal history. A failed appeal in June 2006 ensures Kathcrine Knight still remains a prisoner at Silverwater Women's Correctional Centre.

ROSEMARY WEST

Not your average Wild West story, this evil murderess along with her husband engaged in a series of violent and incestuous crimes that ultimately led to murder inside their basement torture chamber.

A THORNY ROSE

When Daisy Letts gave birth to a baby girl on 29 November 1953 the chances of her developing into a stable, well-adjusted child were slim. Her gene pool far from blessed, Rosemary Pauline was the product of a schizophrenic father and a mother who suffered from chronic depression. To make matters worse Daisy underwent electric shock therapy for her condition while pregnant, an aggressive treatment that ran the risk of causing significant prenatal injury.

Life failed to get much better outside the womb for Rosemary. Her father ran their Barnstaple home like a borstal and regularly beat his children for minor indiscretions. For hours on end the youngster would sit alone, rocking her head back and forth as if in some trance-like state, possibly in reaction to her tyrant father's late-night visits to her bedroom.

At school it was equally tough. She was a pretty girl but not bright and languished in the lower classes. Weight problems provoked teasing and she responded by lashing out, getting a reputation as a bad-tempered loner. Finding it hard to make friends at school, she focused her attentions on older men and quickly began sleeping around, having under-age sex with truck drivers. Her keen sexual precocity had developed at an early age, having been known to climb into bed with her younger brother and touch him inappropriately.

By 1969 Rosemary's parents had separated and, after a brief spell living with her mother, she made the somewhat surprising decision to move in with her sexually-abusive father. At the same time she met Fred West, a simian-looking, convicted child molester with a thick West Country accent. William Letts disapproved of the man twelve years older than his daughter and made numerous attempts to break the couple up. But Rose and Fred were inseparable, and together would share a life so deviant it would shock the nation.

BOUND BY BLOODSHED

The following year Rose fell pregnant with Fred's child. Not yet seventeen, the young mother was forced to care for two additional children from her boyfriend's previous marriage in their tiny house on Midland Road. Fuelled by resentment, she became violent, hurling abuse at her charges. Then, in June 1971, while Fred was doing time for theft, Rose snapped and murdered Charmaine West, the eight-year-old daughter of Fred's former wife.

Informing Charmaine's stepsister, Anne-Marie, that her mother had come to take her away, she hid the body until Fred's release. He then dismembered his own daughter and buried her in the garden. When Rena Costello, the murdered girl's mother, came asking questions she met a similar fate, ending up below ground.

Enchained by a bond of bloodshed, the pair next joined in unholy matrimony, marrying at Gloucester registry office in January 1972. Rose then gave birth to another daughter six months later. The growing family moved into 25 Cromwell Street, a three-storey end-of-terrace house in the centre of town.

The new home came equipped with a large basement which the pair swiftly transformed into a soundproofed torture chamber. The first reluctant guest was Fred's eight-year-old daughter, Anne-Marie. Bound and gagged, the helpless child was held down by Rosemary and viciously raped by her

own father. Regular trips down into the cellar were
backed up with threats if she ever told a soul.

CONSENTING TO CRUELTY

The apparent freedom to inflict such suffering on
those closest to them allowed the Wests to indulge
a burgeoning lust for the sadistic. Rose turned to
prostitution, allowing her voyeur husband to watch
as she engaged in bondage and violent sex acts with
her equally-deviant clients. Yet those that came to
25 Cromwell Street were not always consenting
adults. In late 1972 Caroline Owens came to the
house to serve as the couple's nanny.

In next to no time, the husband and wife team
had the seventeen-year-old in the basement against
her will with Rosemary taking the lead in a series of
sexually-abusive acts. The malicious mother of two
would then laugh as her husband beat the captive
teenager, threatening to bury her under the paving
slabs of Gloucester if she ever revealed their dirty
secret.

Despite the blackmail attempts, Caroline spoke
out, informing the police of the suffering she had
endured. Charges of assault were brought against
the couple in January 1973 but a pregnant Rose and
a persuasive Fred somehow convinced the court

magistrate that Caroline was a willing participant in their S&M games. Escaping with a mere fine, they moved on undeterred.

UNLUCKY HEATHER

Over the next five years Rose and her husband murdered at least another eight young girls between the ages of fifteen and twenty-one. All were enticed to the house with promises of work, a bed or board; all ended up dismembered, decapitated and buried on the property. Stuffed into vertical holes in the earth, the victims had endured their last days being subjected to increasing levels of carnal cruelty.

For every dead girl buried below, it seemed Rose produced another baby above ground, conceiving six more children over ten years. The perverted parents succeeded in maintaining strict control over the brood, allowing their debauchery to go unnoticed by the local community. However, when Anne-Marie moved out and daughter Heather became the focus of their obscene desires, Rose and Fred came close to having their evil world revealed to all.

By the time Heather reached her mid-teens she had become feisty and headstrong. After countless trips into the cellar to suffer at the hands of her parents, she made the mistake of telling a friend about life at home. When her mother and father found out, they reacted with unconstrained violence, ending in her death. They then made their thirteen-year-old son, Stephen, help with digging her shallow grave.

SAVAGE SEARCH

Heather's burial, the ninth to be interred on the property, highlighted the fact that the Wests were running out of room. But these partners in crime refused to curb their immoral self-indulgence, inviting more playmates to the house. Soon reports began to filter through to the authorities regarding the activities in a house filled with young children and, on 6 August 1992, police produced a search warrant to the loathsome owners.

Inside investigators found hardcore pornography littered about the home along with evidence of Rose's prostitution. The children were interviewed, revealing disturbing accounts of rape and torture. However, when the case came to court in July 1993, proceedings collapsed when their abused daughter refused to testify.

Leading the investigation had been DC Hazel Savage who refused to quit following this disappointment. While the Wests had seemingly got away scot free, the case had brought to light the mysterious disappearance of Heather West and the the dogged detective continued to search for the truth. She repeatedly questioned the West children, now out of harm's way in the care of foster parents, and amassed sufficient circumstantial evidence to get a second search warrant.

On 24 February 1994, police entered 25 Cromwell Street with a view to probe the fifteen by sixty foot garden. Initial excavation unearthed the remains of two headless and hacked-up females and, after Fred claimed sole responsibility, he directed detectives to the cellar. Here nine more dismembered bodies were found, leading to his immediate arrest. Rose, on the other hand, denied all knowledge of the murders. It was time for some desperate self-preservation tactics for the West woman.

ROSEMARY AND TIME

With her husband taking the blame for the bodies underneath their 'House of Horrors', Rose decided to distance herself from her partner in crime and allow him to take the fall on his own. She told police he made her sick and avoided his touch in public in her bid to convince those watching she was the victim and not the perpetrator. Rejected and alone, Fred West stood trial for twelve murders, confessing to as many as twenty before committing suicide in his Winson Green Prison cell on the first day of 1995.

Failing her own suicide attempt, Rosemary was unable to avoid her own trial which took place on 3 October 1995 amid a media frenzy. Both Anne-Marie and Caroline Owens testified against the dowdy defendant in large glasses, giving evidence that she was, at the very least, an equal member of the sadistic couple. Their revelations of the depravity that existed inside the Gloucester home shocked those present in court with many requiring counselling.

Rose's lawyers then made the mistake of allowing her to take the stand and give testimony. During her cross-examination, the jury witnessed her violent temper and dishonest nature, helping them to unanimously find her guilty of ten murders at the end of the seven-week trial. Judge Mantell sentenced her to life imprisonment, which was later revised by the Home Secretary to a whole life tariff. She now resides at HMP Low Newton, an all-female prison in Durham, and has had two appeals rejected.

PART FOUR
CULT KILLERS

Adolfo de Jesus Constanzo and Sara Maria Aldrete Villareal

The son of a teenage Cuban immigrant to Miami,
Adolofo Constanzo was introduced to black magic by
his mother at an early and impressionable age and used
his perceived powers to gruesome effect.

THE GODFATHER OF MATAMOROS

By the time he achieved notoriety as a cult leader, drug dealer and serial killer in the late 1980s, his own depraved and horrific brand of torture resembled that of the apparently far-fetched cruelty depicted in the 'video nasties' that were synonymous with the same era.

As part of his ritual torture and of his victims, Constanzo, who also became known as El Padrino de Matamoros – The Godfather of Matamoros – would rip out their brains and hearts for his *nganga*

– a cauldron. This, he believed, would guarantee him success in his career of choice dealing drugs. Sara Aldrete, a promising Mexican student, joined Constanzo's cult in 1987, becoming its High Priestess the following year.

Constanzo was born in Miami in 1962 and spent the early years of his childhood there until his widowed mother moved him to Puerto Rico where she remarried. There, he was baptized a Roman Catholic and was an altar boy in his local church.

When he was only nine years old, Constanzo's mother introduced him to the Santeria religion and even took him on trips to Haiti to learn more about the dark art of Voodoo. Around a year later, his family returned to Miami and his stepfather died soon afterwards, leaving the young Constanzo and his mother financially secure. This didn't stop them from staying out of trouble with the law, with his mother arrested over thirty times for petty crimes and Adolfo himself twice arrested for shoplifting among other minor offences.

In 1976, Constanzo became the apprentice to a practitioner of Palo Mayombe, a form of religion that involves animal sacrifice, and was told by his mentor – who also imparted his experience of drug dealing – that non-believers should be allowed to kill themselves with drugs and that the likes of Constanzo should profit from this. It was around this time that his mother began to believe that he had psychic powers, later reporting that he had prophesied future events including the attempted assassination of President Regan in 1981.

By 1983, Constanzo had pledged his allegiance to Kadiempembe – his religion's equivalent of Satan – when he also visited Mexico City on a modelling assignment. There, he met three men who became his first disciples, Martín Quintana Rodríguez, Jorge Montes and Omar Orea Ochoa. He seduced both Quintana and Orea into a homosexual ménage a trois, calling one his 'man' and the other his 'woman'.

After a brief return to Miami, Constanzo made the permanent move to Mexico City where his reputation as a man of magic continued to gain him more followers. True to his chosen path – the worship of evil for profit – he cultivated a successful business of sorts, whereby he cast spells that involved animal sacrifice to bring his clients good fortune. Naturally, these didn't come cheap; documents found after his death showed that he had thirty-one regular customers and that he charged in the region of $4,500 per ceremony. There was even a menu detailing the costs of the various sacrificial animals available. At the low end of the scale were roosters which cost $6 each and at the other extreme, $1,100 and $3,100 would buy a zebra and lion cub respectively. These high prices were, of course, designed to attract rich criminals and corrupt police officers and Constanzo was soon using these connections to become acquainted with the city's drugs cartels.

SACRIFICING LIVE HUMAN BEINGS

As his cult following – which included a wide cross-section of Mexican society – continued to grow he turned his attention to grave robbing in order to obtain human bones to put in his nganga to increase his strength and power. This phase was not to last for long, however, as he promptly moved on to sacrificing live human beings. There is no recorded total available for how many people he slaughtered, although twenty-three cases are well documented and there were several other unsolved mutilation killing cases in the Mexico City area at the time, which many experts believe were his doing. Constanzo believed that his magic was solely responsible for the success of the narcotics cartels and demanded to be made a business partner with the Calzadas – one of the most powerful families he knew. His demand was rejected with dire consequences; no fewer than seven of the Caldaza family disappeared and were found dead with body parts missing. The absent body parts included brains, toes, ears, fingers and, in one instance, part of the spine.

Constanzo then befriended another cartel, the Hernandez brothers and, in 1987, engineered a 'chance meeting' with Sara Aldrete who was dating Gilberto Sosa, a drug-dealing affiliate of the new cartel's family. A matter of weeks afterwards, Sosa received an anonymous telephone call stating that Aldrete had been having an affair and duly ended their relationship. Aldrete turned to Constanzo for support, who told her that he had seen her break-up coming on his tarot cards. A brief sexual liaison followed, although Constanzo made no secret of his preference for men. Already hooked on the occult element of their relationship, however, Aldrete seemed to accept this rejection and became High Priestess or La Madrina – the godmother – of his cult and contributed to the torture of its victims.

RANCHO SANTA ELENA

The sadistic violence of Constanzo, Aldrete and their followers escalated after the cult moved to Rancho Santa Elena in the nearby desert. On 28 May 1988, he shot dead two victims, one of whom was a rival drug dealer. Unsatisfied with these killings – as they didn't die screaming – he ordered the execution and dismemberment of a cult member's transvestite ex-lover on 16 July and had the remains dumped on a street corner where they were found by children.

In November of the same year, he made a gory example of one of his flock – a former policeman named Jorge Valente de Fierro Gomez – for disobeying his ban on drug use.

Valentine's Day 1989 witnessed the torturous murder of rival Ezequiel Rodriguez Luna and when two other dealers, Ruben Vela Garza and Ernesto Rivas Diaz, arrived uninvited to the 'ceremony', they too were brutally murdered. More deaths followed, including the fourteen-year-old cousin of Ovidio Hernandez – who by this point had cemented Constanzo's alliance with the Hernandez family by joining the cult – and Sara Aldrete's ex, Gilberto Sosa. A fortnight prior to Sosa's death, however, the cult had unwittingly made a fatal mistake that would ultimately result in its demise.

THE BEGINNING OF THE END

On 13 March 1989, Constanzo, angered by his latest victim not screaming, despatched cult members to find a new offering for his nganga; they returned with twenty-one-year-old Texan student, Mark Kilroy. Unlike the cult's other numerous casualties, at least three of whom were never identified, the American was not someone who could disappear without trace; he came from an affluent and well-connected family who were determined to bring his killers to justice. It was the beginning of the end for Constanzo. With Kilroy's disappearance threatening to become an international incident, the Mexican police were eager to solve the case quickly and received a very welcome piece of luck that simultaneously made a mockery of Contanzo's alleged powers.

On 9 April, cult member, Serafin Hernandez, drove past a police road block under the illusion that Constanzo's black magic made him invisible to the authorities. He was pursued and arrested along with fellow disciple David Martinez and driven to Rancho Santa Elena. There, police found a huge stash of marijuana and firearms. Two other cult members, Elio Hernandez and Sergio Martinez, then arrived and were also arrested. The four men were interrogated through the night in which they were almost boastful about their barbaric acts of ritual sacrifice. Over the next couple of days, the ranch was raided. Constanzo's cauldron was found, which held a human brain, a dead black cat, scorpions, spiders and deer antlers among other items and the corpses of fifteen victims exhumed.

THE GODFATHER IS DEAD

Constanzo, along with Aldrete, Quintana and Orea as well as Hernandez family hitman, Alvaro de Leon Valdez, fled to Mexico City moving from the home of one cult member to the next.

Their eventual discovery on 6 May 1989 was by chance – in spite of a note thrown out of the window by Aldrete being dismissed as a joke and kept to himself by the passer-by who found it a few days beforehand. Police were conducting a door-to-door search for a missing child when they were spotted by the cult leader. He panicked and opened fire, only for the apartment building to be surrounded by 180 police officers. After a forty-five-minute siege, it became apparent to Constanzo that there was no escape. He ordered Alvaro de Leon to shoot both him and his lover, Quintana. Upon arrival in the apartment, police discovered the bodies of Constanzo and Quintana slumped against each other in a closet. Aldrete, Orea and de Leon were arrested immediately. In total, fourteen of

Constanzo's surviving disciples were convicted for a number of offences.

Aldrete and two of the Hernandez brothers, Elio and Serafin, were found guilty of multiple murders and sentenced to over sixty years each. Although Constanzo was dead and his accomplices imprisoned, his influence on others was not; disturbingly, a smiling and self-assured Alvaro de Leon told police: 'The godfather will not be dead for long.'

CHARLES MANSON

One of America's most infamous criminals, Charles Manson achieved notoriety in the late 1960s as the head of a hippie cult known as 'The Family'.

TURBULENT AND UNHAPPY

Manson was born an illegitimate child to sixteen-year-old Kathleen Maddox. At first, he was known as 'No Name Maddox', but within weeks he was Charles Milles Maddox. He gained the surname he is now known by, when his mother married labourer, William Manson. It is thought that his biological father was one Colonel Scott, who his mother successfully filed a bastardy suit against in 1937.

Manson's early years were turbulent and unhappy; apparently unwanted by his mother who rejected him on several occasions – indeed, she once tried to sell him for a pitcher of beer. He also spent a significant amount of his youth in correctional centres. He would later go on record as saying that his solitary happy childhood memory was being embraced by his mother after she was released from prison.

After spells inside – and escapes from – the Gibault School for Boys in Indiana and Boys Town in Nebraska, Manson was sent to the harshly disciplinarian Indiana School for Boys.

In 1951, he made his latest escape and embarked on a spree of petrol station robberies before being apprehended again. This time though, he was sent to a federal institution in Washington. It was in this latest episode of custody that Manson would commit his first violent crime, holding a razor blade to another boy's throat while raping him.

He was released in 1954 and married Rosalie Willis the following year, but trouble was never far away. Soon after their marriage, Manson was arrested twice for stealing cars and was sentenced to three years. While he was incarcerated, he missed the birth of his son, Charles Manson Junior, and Rosalie divorced him.

He was paroled in 1958 but was soon earning a living as a pimp. A year later, he received a suspended sentence of ten years for attempting to cash forged cheques. Inevitably, he broke this probation too; conning a woman out of $700 – making her pregnant in the process – before drugging and raping her roommate and was sent to the U.S Penitentiary at McNeil Island, Washington.

'THE FAMILY' WAS BORN

In prison, Manson developed a series of fanatical obsessions. At first, these were in the form of various religions including Scientology and Buddhism, but these would give way to music; specifically that of The Beatles. He learned to play the guitar and believed that he had the ability to be better and more successful than his heroes, writing between eighty and ninety songs and devoting hours on end to playing them.

In 1967, having been transferred to Terminal Island, California, Manson was released although he wanted to stay in custody. He pleaded with the guards to keep him locked away, citing his belief that prison was now his home and that he would not be able to adjust to a life of freedom in the much-changed world he was being released into. His request was ignored by the authorities, with devastating results.

He moved to San Francisco where he managed to blend into the hippie scene. Here, he learned about drugs and observed that LSD in particular could be used to control others. A mysterious man who played the guitar and came across as deep and meaningful, it didn't take Manson long to attract followers. Most of them were rebellious but impressionable young women from respectable backgrounds and it wasn't difficult for him to manipulate them with his enigmatic philosophies and drugs. In Manson, they believed that they had found their true leader and 'The Family' was born.

Although his new-found role as a guru to a throng of young women was a major preoccupation, Manson still dreamt of becoming a successful musician and thought he had received the break he craved in 1968 when he met Denis Wilson of the Beach Boys after befriending Gary Hinman, a music teacher who knew the star. The leader and his groupies would hang around Wilson's home at every opportunity. Wilson was initially receptive to Manson, paying for studio time for him, introducing him to industry contacts and even persuading his fellow Beach Boys to record one of his songs. His interest didn't last though and The Family were thrown out of his mansion when he became uneasy about their leader's manipulative presence.

The Family found a new home in a ranch owned by the elderly George Spahn. Manson persuaded Spahn to allow this in exchange for cleaning services and sexual favours from one of his followers. It was here that Manson began to cultivate the twisted philosophy that would end in a killing spree. He believed that the Beatles song *Helter Skelter* from their *White Album* contained a hidden warning about an uprising by black people. He was a racist and this attitude had been exacerbated by the fact that many of the inmates who raped him in prison had been black. His theory was that the blacks would kill the whites but not be able to retain power due to their perceived inferiority. He and The Family would hide in a bottomless pit in the desert of Death Valley until the racial holocaust was over – by which time, he estimated, there would be 144,000 members of The Family. Then they would rise up and take the power back. His beliefs also incorporated his interpretation of the *Book of Revelation* in the New Testament; he was Jesus Christ and would lead The Family into a new world. Meanwhile, he had still not given up on becoming a musician and turned to Doris Day's son, Terry Melcher, who he had met through Denis Wilson. Melcher listened to a live performance, but was not impressed and didn't grant Manson the studio time he so desperately wanted. This enraged the cult leader and acted as the catalyst for the evil acts that were soon to follow.

10050 CIELO DRIVE

Manson told The Family that they might have to

show the blacks how to start it and on 27 July 1969, The Family claimed its first victim.

Manson had sent three of his followers, namely Bobby Beausoleil, Mary Brunner and Susan Atkins, to the home of Gary Hinman two days beforehand to extort money from him. Hinman was uncooperative and was held hostage. Manson turned up with a sword and slashed his ear before instructing Beausoleil to stab him to death. One of Manson's three followers then wrote 'Political piggy' on the wall in their victim's blood and also drew a panther's paw in an attempt to pin the blame on the Black Panthers, a black separatist group. This vicious killing was merely a warm up for the atrocities that were to follow and on 8 August, Manson instructed Charles 'Tex' Watson, Susan Atkins, Linda Kasabian and Patricia Krenwinkel to visit Terry Melcher's old home on Cielo Drive.

'Now is the time for Helter Skelter,' he told them. 'Totally destroy everyone in it as gruesome as you can.'

The house was now home to film director Roman Polanski and his wife, Hollywood actress, Sharon Tate. Upon arriving at 10050 Cielo Drive in the early hours of 9 August, Watson climbed the nearest telephone pole and cut the wires to the house while the rest of the gang climbed the walls. Their first victim was eighteen-year-old Steven Parent who was driving out having visited the caretaker who lived in the property's guest house. Watson shot him four times from point blank range. He then broke in to the house with Krenwinkel and Atkins while Kasabian was sent to the gate on lookout duty. Polanski was working abroad, but Sharon Tate – who was eight months pregnant – was home and she was not alone; Polanski's friend Wojciech Frykowski and his girlfriend Abigail Folger – a coffee heiress – were also present, along with Jay Sebring, a hair stylist of international fame.

As Frykowski awoke from sleeping on the sofa, Watson stood over him, 'I'm the devil and I'm here to do the devil's business,' he said.

Atkins and Krenwinkel rounded up the other occupants before Watson tied Tate and Sebring to each other at the neck. It is thought that Sebring broke free and, protesting over the treatment of his pregnant host, was shot by Watson and then stabbed several times. Folger, meanwhile, was briefly taken back to a bedroom to get her purse, believing that they were being burgled. When she was returned to the living room Frykowski, who had been bound with a towel, attempted to take Watson's gun. He failed and was beaten around the head with its butt and shot twice. Kasabian then showed up and tried to put a stop to the brutality by claiming that somebody was coming, but her appeals fell on deaf ears. As Frykowski struggled to the door screaming for help, he was caught by Atkins and Krenwinkel who stabbed him a total of fifty-one times. Watson then stabbed Folger repeatedly as she tried to escape. The terrified Tate had watched this all and knew she was next. She pleaded for her own life and that of her child, but her assailants showed no compassion; Atkins stabbed her sixteen times.

With all four occupants dead, Atkins wrote 'PIG' on the front door in Tate's blood.

3301 WAVERLY DRIVE

Apparently displeased with elements of the Tate murders, Manson ordered the same four Family members – as well as Leslie van Houten and Steve Grogan – to carry out another set of murders the following night. This time he went with them to 'show them how to do it'. After directing them to 3301 Waverly Drive – chosen as it was next door to a house where they had been to a party the previous year – Manson and Watson broke in and tied up the occupants Leno and Rosemary LaBianca, putting pillow cases over their heads. Manson then left, sending van Houten and Krenwinkel in to kill the couple. Watson stabbed Leno in the throat with a chrome-plated bayonet and, hearing a struggle in the bedroom, went in and stabbed Rosemary several times. He then returned to Leno, carving 'WAR' on his stomach while van Houten and Krenwinkel stabbed Rosemary with a kitchen knife.

The messages 'Rise' and 'Death to Pigs' were written on the walls with the blood of the LaBiancas, while 'Healther Skelter' (sic) was scrawled on the refrigerator.

The already dead Leno was then stabbed fourteen more times and was left with a carving fork in his stomach and a steak knife in his neck.

BACK TO WHERE HE WANTED TO BE

Amazingly, despite the common denominator of blood-scrawled messages on the walls of all three murder sites, police failed to make any connections between the killings. It wasn't until Atkins was later arrested for prostitution and boasted about them to her cell mate – during which time, she also revealed plans to kill Richard Burton, Elizabeth Taylor, Frank Sinatra, Steve McQueen and Tom Jones – that the authorities made any progress. Manson and his followers were duly arrested and legal proceedings began. Kasabian was granted immunity for testifying against the Family.

On 25 January 1971, Manson, Krenwinkel and Atkins found guilty on seven counts of murder. Leslie Van Houton was found guilty on two counts. All four were sentenced to death, but these were overturned a year later and replaced with life sentences when the US Supreme Court ruled that the death penalty was unconstitutional. Manson remains in Corcoran Prison, California where he will spend the rest of his life. Given the fact that he has spent most of his life in custody and his plea to be retained in 1967, many believe that he is exactly where he wants to be.

DAVID KORESH

In an event that bears similarities to those that took place in Jonestown in 1978, cult leader David Koresh and seventy-six of his followers died in controversial circumstances, on 19 April 1993.

The horrifying news footage of the prolonged FBI siege in Waco, Texas, culminating in the burning of the Mount Carmel religious compound, is one of the enduring images of the late twentieth century.

DAVID KORESH

Born Vernon Wayne Howell, he legally changed his name in 1990 to the one that would earn him notoriety three years later. Koresh never met his father, Bobby Howell, who abandoned his fifteen-year-old mother, Bonnie Sue Clark, before the future sect leader was born. Apparently unable to cope, she handed him to her parents to bring up, although at some point she introduced him to the Seventh Day Adventist Church which the Branch Davidians, the organization he would end up leading, had descended from as a result of a schism in the 1930s.

His childhood was a difficult one; he was dyslexic and was bullied by his classmates, dropping out of school by the ninth grade. Despite his supposed illiteracy, he was fascinated by the Bible and studied it fervently, memorising large sections of it.

After a failed attempt at becoming a rock star, he joined the Branch Davidians in 1981. Its leader – or 'prophet' – at the time was seventy-six-year-old Lois Roden who had assumed control when her husband, Benjamin, died. Howell – as he was still named at this point – seduced her, later claiming that God had ordered that the two conceive a child that would be the 'Chosen One'. Any attempts there may have been failed, but two years later Howell's influence on Lois was reflected when she allowed him to preach. This caused friction with Roden's son, George, and a power struggle ensued.

When his mother died in 1986, George Roden forced Howell and his followers from Mount Carmel at gunpoint. Howell returned a year later in an attempt to rejoin the sect; the episode was both bizarre and violent. Roden had exhumed a corpse which he challenged Howell to bring back to life; seeing an opportunity to remove his opponent, Howell reported Roden to the police but was told that photographic evidence would be required.

Howell returned to Mount Carmel with seven of his disciples in tow, where Roden responded by opening fire. Amazingly, nobody was killed. Howell and his seven companions were accused of attempted murder but all eight were acquitted. Roden was soon imprisoned for another offence and was eventually transferred to a mental hospital where he spent the rest of his days.

In 1990, Howell became the leader of the Branch Davidians and changed his name to David Koresh. He apparently chose his first name as he believed himself to be an heir to King David and his second after an ancient Persian King who had allowed Jews to return to their homeland. During the infamous siege, however, he told an FBI negotiator that Koresh also meant 'death'. Once he had taken control, Koresh announced that he was the only member of the cult who could be married and annulled the marriages of his followers. Although several members left at this point, a number of them clearly accepted his reasoning, as they stayed. He perceived the women – and, allegedly, some of the girls – as his wives, while the men were seen as his guardians.

Koresh wanted to create a divine army and believed that he alone could father these children. The members who had left the cult asserted that

Koresh was a hypocrite who seemed immune to his own rules and also made allegations of child abuse against him, reporting that he would beat them until they bled; these claims were investigated but never confirmed. One former Branch Davidian claimed that Koresh had fathered at least fifteen of the children on the compound.

His teachings, meanwhile, began to focus on the concept of martyrdom for the cause. Clearly paranoid, he contended that the Apocalypse would begin when the US Army attacked the Mount Carmel compound. In anticipation of this, he had already begun preparations for a siege. A school bus was buried to act as a bunker while resources such as food and weapons were stockpiled. It was his hoarding of the latter that would arouse suspicion and ultimately result quite literally in an explosive ending for the sect.

THE SIEGE BEGAN

On 28 February 1993, agents belonging to the Bureau of Alcohol, Tobacco and Firearms (ATF) raided Mount Carmel – which Koresh had now renamed 'Ranch Apocalypse' – in an attempt to arrest and charge the leader for possessing and modifying illegal weapons. This came after rumours about the cult's weapon stash had gathered pace and, in May 1992, a delivery driver had reported that a package he delivered to the compound had become damaged, revealing grenade casings in the process. It remains unclear as to which side was first to pull the trigger, but gunfire was exchanged. Four ATF agents were killed and a further sixteen of their colleagues were wounded. Six of the Branch Davidians perished and others, including Koresh himself, were injured. Control of the escalating situation was handed to the FBI and a tense fifty-one-day siege ensued. Negotiations began and, initially, it appeared that a peaceful resolution could still be achieved as ten children were released. The FBI's next move was to surround the perimeter of the compound with armoured vehicles. This incensed Koresh and his anger would only be fuelled when it was discovered that the FBI had diverted the compound's phone lines so that the Davidians could only dial out to them. Negotiations continued, nevertheless, and Koresh promised to surrender and release his followers if the Bureau arranged for a tape of his teachings to be broadcast on national radio. The tape was duly played on the Christian Broadcasting Network, but Koresh changed his stance, telling negotiators that, during prayer, God had told him to wait.

At some point during the standoff, proceedings took a bizarre twist, as the FBI blasted the compound with a loud and eclectic range of music as well as recordings of Koresh that had been made during telephone negotiations. Koresh responded by releasing a video of members talking about why they were there of their own free will and that they would only leave when God told them to. Any rapport that there may have been between the Davidians and the FBI seemed to collapse during the next few days. Koresh refused to surrender and his only statements were threats of violence and long-winded religious proclamations. This breakdown in communications caused the FBI to become concerned that the cult would commit mass suicide rather than surrender. A letter sent by Koresh to the FBI on 9 April did nothing to change this growing fear; when experts analysed its contents they concluded that he had no intention of leaving. Like Jim Jones' chilling warning to authorities that they would die if they tried to take any of his followers from Jonestown in 1978, Koresh made a similar threat to the FBI the week before the grisly end to the standoff: they would be consumed by fire if they tried to harm him. This threat was echoed by Davidians on the penultimate day of the siege. As tanks pushed aside vehicles from the front of the compound, members held children up at windows as well as a sign that read: 'Flames Await'.

After the Davidians refused a final ultimatum, the FBI commenced a tear gas attack in the early hours of 19 April. Tanks punched holes in the building's wooden walls before pumping the gas through the holes, cult members responded with gunfire. At around noon, a fire was spotted at one end of the building and FBI snipers reported witnessing two men starting the blaze. The wooden compound was soon engulfed in flames and a large explosion indicated that its weapon store, the initial cause of the authorities' concern, had been breached.

Although a handful of cult members escaped as the fire took its grip, a devastating toll was taken as the bodies of seventy-seven cult members, including that of Koresh, were recovered. At least twenty of them, including their leader and five children, had died of bullet wounds. The FBI's heavy-handed management of the situation was roundly criticized and its intervention certainly seems to have confused the issue as to whether the tragedy was a mass suicide or a mass murder. What is clear, however, is that whether deluded or conniving, David Koresh's hypocrisy and dictatorial manipulation of others had earned him the epitaph of cult killer.

ERVIL LEBARON

Many a fanatical cult leader has claimed to have heard the voice of God telling him to carry out – or, more appropriately, execute – orders fundamentally opposed to the very doctrines he should be promoting. Ervil LeBaron, however, surely ranks amongst the most hypocritical, ruthless and deranged.

THE LEBARON FAMILY TRAIT

He remained stone deaf to accusations of expropriation of property, wealth and power through violent exploitation of family, friends and their offspring, including rape, paedophilia and murder. Conversely, ideas satisfying his lust, greed and urge to manipulate everyone around him were heavenly music to his ears. Unfortunately, nobody on record had the temerity to tell him he should stop talking to himself and try normality for a change. Easier said then done, perhaps, since madness was a definite LeBaron family trait.

Sects generally shut themselves off from the world, which they judge to be evil, heathen and dangerous. Sect leaders present as wise and caring

Police lead the handcuffed serial killer, Dennis Nilsen, into the back of a van the day after his arrest in February 1983. Nilsen kept the bodies of his mutilated homosexual lovers in this apartment in Muswell Hill, London, before disposing of them in his own garden. (Credit: Getty Images)

On the afternoon of 12 June 1981, a Japanese student by the name of Issei Sagawa, walked into the woods in Bois de Boulogne in France, carrying a pair of suitcases. Inside the suitcases were the body parts of a female classmate of his, that he had killed the day before. When the French police asked why he had killed her, Sagawa replied, 'I killed her to eat her flesh!' (Credit: AFP/Getty Images)

Three portraits of Russian Andrei Chikatilo, who has the reputation of being one of the world's worst serial killers. He preyed on young girls and boys and is believed to have murdered as many as fifty-three between the years 1982 and 1990, when he was finally captured. (Credit: Time & Life Pictures/Getty Images)

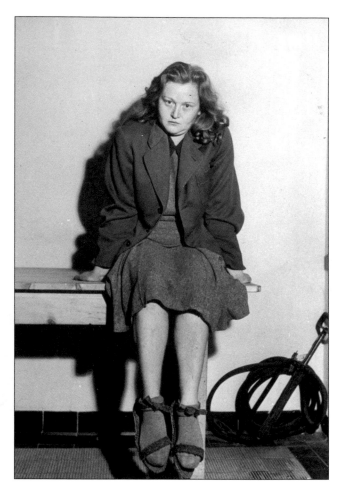

During World War II, Ilse Koch became kown as the Bitch of Buchenwald because of her cruelty and sadistic behaviour towards the inmates of the prison camp where her husband was the Kommandant. Her hobby was making lampshades, book covers and gloves from the skins of specially selected inmates that had recently been exterminated. (Credit: Time & Life Pictures/Getty Images)

Another infamous wartime female was Irma Grese who rose to the rank of Senior SS-Supervisor and was put in charge of around 30,000 women prisoners in the Bergen-Belsen concentration camp. After the war prisoners testified to her acts of sadism, beatings, shootings and the savaging of inmates by Grese's own dogs. (Credit: Getty Images)

General Idi Amin Dada seized power of Uganda after a coup in January 1971. The cruelty of his repressive regime became legendary. An ex-officer in the Ugandan Army, Tom Masaba, is stripped of his clothes and tied to a tree before his public execution at Mbale in 1973. (Credit: Getty Images)

Founder of the Branch Davidian sect, David Koresh (above) playing in a music video. Koresh and 83 of his followers were involved in a 51-day stand-off with the FBI at the sect's headquarters in Waco, which ended in a mass suicidal fire. Nine Davidians escaped but 74 died, including 21 children. Survivors of the fire (right) can be seen filing out of the federal courthouse after an initial hearing. (Credit: AFP/Getty Images)

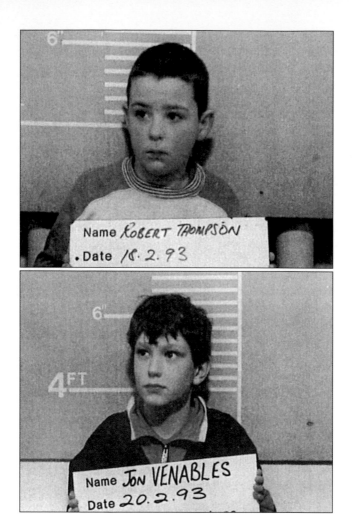

Both Jon Venables and Robert Thompson were ten years old when they abducted, tortured and killed two-year-old James Bulger in Bootle, England. Despite a public outcry to keep them under lock and key, they were both released in 2001 having been given new identifies. (Credit: Getty Images)

guides to the hordes of followers they attract – or lock in – with promises of paradise in the afterlife. Doubtless, these were precisely the guiding principles of Joseph Smith, founder of the Mormon Church, who attributed his *Book of Mormon* to his vision of an angel bearing holy tablets engraved with ancient scriptures. Clearly, his message from God told him to lead an exemplary life away from the wicked world, in his own, 'pure' community; and, since the Bible also told of patriarchs taking many wives to fulfil such projects, Smith also embraced polygamy, both literally and figuratively. Small matter that he took more than thirty wives – despite his denials when polygamy, already against the law, was condemned by the Church – his was a holy mission, his lies essential for the greater good. Towards the end of the nineteenth century, however, the pressure of the real world told and the practice of polygamy officially ceased within the Mormon Church ... prompting breakaway groups of Mormons to decamp to Mexico, safely removed from evil society, corrupting influences and, most importantly, the law.

CHURCH OF THE FIRSTBORNERS
In 1924, Alma Dayer LeBaron and his family of

two wives and eight children also found their way to Mexico, more precisely to Galeana, Chihuahua, where they set up a farm called 'Colonia LeBaron'. Colony, sect or just plain harem, it provided the ideal setting for the launch of a philandering psychopath the following year. Born 22 February, 1925, Ervil Morrell LeBaron was, nevertheless, unlucky enough to have an elder brother barring his way to leadership of the sect. Joel LeBaron became the leader on his father's death, in 1951, with Ervil second-in-command. Together they led the so-called Firstborners, from the Church of the Firstborn of the Fullness of Times.

Though lazy and openly self-indulgent, Ervil was smart enough to realize that his encyclopaedic knowledge of the *Book of Mormon* and the Bible both impressed and intimidated sect followers. Conveniently for the tall, handsome sexual predator, LeBaron claimed God had told him to spread his seed freely. No second bidding required, as he accumulated some thirteen wives and allegedly fathered more than fifty children, never baulking at molesting under-age girls, seducing the young wives of friends and even bedding grateful, older women. Satisfying his voracious sexual appetite was, nevertheless, still not enough to sate his lust for power.

Ervil's blatant siphoning off of sect funds and desperate attempts to close lucrative but decidedly shady business deals threatened to leave him exposed, not only to critical fellow members of the sect but also to opponents, especially rival sect leaders. Time for another message from God. The latest revelation saw LeBaron reinterpreting the Ten Commandments and reviving the long abandoned Mormon Church concept of Blood Atonement. Originally, Blood Atonement, clearly a means of punishing by death the crimes of Mormons, was also supposed to represent joyous, early entrance to the kingdom of God. Ervil LeBaron's version, called Civil Law, simply represented vengeance for the wrath of God, requiring the ultimate, human sacrifice: breaking any of the new commandments – in short, doing anything to oppose or upset LeBaron – would inevitably incur death, the more painful and violent the better. Now he could repress and suppress at will, armed with the ultimate sanction, granted by God's decree.

When Joel demoted the cavalier Ervil, in 1970, he could scarcely have guessed the depths of depravity his younger brother would plumb. Outraged at his humiliation, Ervil soon formed the breakaway Church of the Lamb of God, in San Diego. Then, in

1972, he had Joel eliminated by two of his assassins – Ivan, Joel's fourteen-year-old son, found his father, shot twice in the head at close range.

Instead of asking Ervil to lead them, the Firstborners of 'Los Molinos', in Baja, California, chose his younger brother, Verlan, and publicly accused Ervil of Joel's murder. Ervil promptly ordered the execution of Verlan, the first of many unsuccessful attempts to kill the second 'false prophet' of the family. Nevertheless, two of Verlan's men perished during Ervil's unsuccessful assassination raid on 'Los Molinos'. After Ervil handed himself in, in Mexico, in 1974, he was tried, convicted and sentenced to twelve years imprisonment. After just twelve months he was released. Though many suspected bribery, the verdict was officially overturned on a technicality.

PARANOIA AND WEAPONS

As if psychosis, delusions of grandeur and blood lust were not enough for one man, Ervil LeBaron now began to suffer from paranoia. His failed murder of a second brother left him feeling vulnerable to attacks from vengeful followers of Verlan. Cunningly, he harnessed the condition by passing it onto his followers. Convincing them that they, too, were potential targets, he moved the Church to Utah and armed them with new identities and, more significantly, weapons. From there it was a short step to persuading some of them to kill on his behalf, in the name of the Church.

He also tightened up on security, fearing treachery could be his undoing. A chance soon presented itself for two of his wives to permanently silence an enemy within, namely Noemi Zarate Chynoweth, one of Ervil's – albeit illegal – mothers-in-law through his marriage to her daughter, Lorna. Noemi, an undercover 'plant' at 'Los Molinos', had taken fright when Ervil's attack on Verlan's headquarters failed. She ill-advisedly let slip that she was unhappy about Ervil's cruelty and violence and was thinking of exposing him to the police. With total support from Noemi's husband, Bud, LeBaron sent wives Vonda White and Yolanda Rios to do his dirty work: Vonda drilled her friend, Noemi, full of bullet holes and Yolanda helped Vonda bury the corpse.

Next on the death roll was Robert Hunt Simons, whose business, property and, no doubt, wives, Ervil coveted. A rival, polygamous sect leader, Simons was, it seems, equally deluded about his own God-given mission, reportedly to save the souls of Native Americans by converting them to the Mormon faith. Once again, LeBaron's assassins did his bidding, leading Simons into an ambush and shooting him in the back of the head, before concealing the body. With business looking up in 1977, LeBaron finally ordered the killing of Rulon C. Allred, rival leader of another group of polygamous Mormon fundamentalists, who had long since bad-mouthed the Firstborners. LeBaron's thirteenth and last wife, Rena Chynoweth, abetted by Ramona Marston, executed Allred at LeBaron's behest, but walked free from her trial for murder – to which she confessed in her 1990 memoir, *The Blood Covenant*.

Vonda White's second victim, Dean Grover Vest, one of LeBaron's men who wanted to leave the Church, earned her a life sentence. However, not even the murder of his own, seventeen-year-old, pregnant daughter, Rebecca, who also wished to leave the Church, resulted in conviction for LeBaron. His stepson, Eddie Marston, and brother-in-law, Duane Chynoweth apparently strangled her with a rope, in April 1977.

What did for him had already happened: he was arrested in Mexico and extradited to the United States, on 1 June 1979, for ordering the murder of Allred. In 1980, he was sentenced to life imprisonment at the Utah State Penitentiary in

Draper, where he died, some say of a heart attack others claim suicide, on 16 August 1981.

The postscript to LeBaron's demise reads like a sickening catalogue of vengeance killings from beyond the grave. It started ironically with the coincidental death of his brother Verlan, in a car crash two days after Ervil's own death. The first on LeBaron's post mortem death list may not have perished at the hands of the infamous henchmen, but many more would. Following LeBaron's hit list, composed in jail and incorporated into his voluminous Book of the New Covenants, it appears that at least twenty-five opponents have so far been murdered, including wives Lorna and Yolanda and children Isaac and Arturo. In the infamous four o'clock murders, Duane Chynoweth, Eddie Marston and Mark Chynoweth, were all shot simultaneously at 4 pm on 27 June 1988. The long arm of the lifeless outlaw, Ervil LeBaron, seemingly still locks his hapless opponents in its vile embrace, choking the truth to death and prolonging the terrible myth of blood atonement.

GLENN TAYLOR HELZER

*The sudden appearance of duffel bags containing
dismembered body parts, in the Mokelumne river in
California, heralded one of the most unusual murder
trials of recent years. In a case that implicated a
Playboy centrefold model, a witch and a would-be army
of Brazilian orphan assassins, lapsed Mormon Glenn
Taylor Helzer pleaded guilty to five grisly murders he
had carried out with the intention of bringing about the
second coming of Jesus Christ.*

NICE KIDS

Born to devoutly religious parents, Glenn Helzer
– who was known to most by his middle name,
Taylor – and his younger brother, Justin, had an
ordinary childhood and were referred to as 'nice
kids' by witnesses who knew them in their early
years. Taylor was the more outgoing of the two,
whereas Justin was more introverted and looked
up to his older brother. Taylor embraced the sense
of superiority afforded him by his younger sibling
and would often tell him: 'I'm No. 1 and you're
No. 2.' The normality seemed to continue into the

time when both brothers fulfilled the Mormon requirement of two years' mission work. Justin spent this time in Texas while Taylor went to Brazil where, it seems, he conceived at least one of the many unusual facets to his elaborate plan. On his return to America, things still seemed to be unexceptional; he got a job as a stockbroker, got married and became a father to two girls. In 1996, however, the first signs of what were to come became evident as, three years after getting married, he left his wife. He cited the restrictive nature of the Mormon faith and his desire to expand his life beyond the confines of the church as his reasons. He wanted to drink, smoke and have sex with other women and started wearing black as a sign of rebellion. Eventually, he was excommunicated by the church, but not before he had met one of his future accomplices, Dawn Godman. Godman was a loner with a troubled history; she had lost one child shortly after birth and lost custody of the other to her ex-husband. Seeking some purpose, she made what would prove to be a life-changing decision as she joined the same church as the Helzer brothers.

I AM PERFECT

Around this time, Helzer started to develop his own

belief system, one of the fundamentals of which was that 'good' and 'evil' were fraudulent concepts and that society was foolish for buying into the notion that there were such things as right and wrong. A hastily scribbled, twelve-point manifesto formed the basis of his prospective cult and included maxims such as 'I am already perfect and therefore can do nothing wrong.' Ultimately, he believed that he was a prophet and that God was telling him what to do. Godman soon became acquainted with the brothers and actually ended up dating Justin, but the sibling who had made the real impression was Taylor. This didn't go unnoticed by the latter, who became her spiritual leader and convinced her that he was a prophet who planned to start a self-help group called Impact America that would destroy Satan. Taylor planned to fund the group via drugs, prostitution and blackmail. He also planned to adopt some of the orphans he had met during his mission work in Brazil and train them to be assassins, in order to eliminate the fifteen Elders of The Church of Jesus Christ of Latter-day Saints in Utah, so that he could take over. He also told her that it was his destiny to take over the Mormon church and that he would kill its leaders if he needed to. Finally, he divulged the only one of his deranged plans that would come to pass; he would extort money from a client to start his group and that he would need her to kill in God's name. She agreed and, along with Justin, became Taylor's follower and did his bidding.

Before they could carry out their plan, Helzer and his two followers needed to recruit one more unwitting accomplice to their cruel plan to launder the money. Taylor soon found the ideal candidate when he met Selina Bishop, a young woman newly arrived from a small town and looking for love. He was the tall, dark stranger she was looking for and he knew it. He told her that his name was Jordan and acted mysteriously, shunning opportunities to meet her friends and family or to divulge his surname, but she fell for him. She willingly agreed to open bank accounts to deposit Helzer's stolen money in and gave him a key to her apartment, oblivious to his true motives and the dire consequences becoming involved with him would have for her.

VICIOUS MURDERS COMMENCED

With Bishop unwittingly on board, Helzer could put his extortion plan into action. He exploited his contacts at work to draw up a list of potential victims who he thought could be manipulated – and killed, if the need arose – easily. The first victim on the list was out when Taylor and Justin called at his home; undeterred, the brothers simply moved on to the next target: Annette and Ivan Stineman, an elderly couple who had actually come to think of Taylor as a friend. After forcing the Stinemans to drink rohypnol – which he had acquired on a trip to Mexico in 1999 with his then-girlfriend and future Playboy model, Keri Mendoza – he coerced them into writing cheques to the value of $100,000 payable to Selina Bishop. The couple were then led to the bathroom where they were viciously murdered; Annette Stineman's throat was slit by Taylor while Justin smashed Ivan's head against the floor. Taylor then summoned Godman – who had witnessed the entire episode – to join him and Justin in kneeling beside the corpses to thank them for giving their lives for his cause. Ever calculating, Helzer had gone as far as getting a Rottweiler to eat the remains of his victims. This, however, didn't work, so their bodies were cut to pieces with a power saw after their teeth had been knocked out with a hammer and chisel to complicate identification.

Once the money obtained in the brutal attack on the Stinemans had been paid in to the relevant account, Helzer decided that Bishop was no longer needed. Afraid that she may suspect him, the only option as far as he was concerned was to have her killed. He offered her a massage and she accepted, lying face down on the floor. Justin crept into the room before hitting the back of her head several times with a hammer. Taylor then called Godman into the room.

'Spirit says you get to know this isn't a dream,' he told her, before lifting Bishop's head and slitting her throat.

With the key witness to his scheme eliminated, Helzer remained paranoid that he could still be caught. He had briefly met Bishop's mother, Jennifer Villarin, and quickly came to the conclusion that she should be slain too. Using the key that Bishop had given him to her apartment and knowing that her mother would be there house sitting, Helzer descended on his latest victim in the small hours. However, she wasn't alone; her partner, James Gamble, was also present. Unfazed, Helzer approached the sleeping couple, shot them at point blank range and hurriedly left the scene of his latest crime. A neighbour immediately reported the gunshots and police were soon on the scene. Similarly, it didn't take long for the first three of his victims to be missed with the Stinemans' daughter and Bishop's colleagues reporting them missing respectively. Wanting to talk to the mysterious 'Jordan', law enforcers were soon in pursuit of Helzer and his cronies and found damning evidence at the brothers' home. After a protracted chase, the Helzer brothers and Godman were all apprehended before, later the same day, the duffel bags containing the body parts of their first three victims – which had been mixed up to hinder identification – surfaced.

Once legal proceedings began, it emerged that a woman who described herself as a Wiccan witch had provided the three suspects with a phony alibi before realising the extent of their crime and confessing to police. With all the evidence against them, there was little doubt that the case would be decided quickly. Realising this, Godman struck a deal with prosecutors; in return for pleading guilty to five counts of murder and testifying against the Helzer brothers, she would avoid the death penalty and be sentenced to thirty-eight years for her part in the killings. Despite a plea of insanity, Justin Helzer was found guilty and sentenced to death for three of the slayings while Taylor was given the death penalty for all five.

JEFFREY LUNDGREN

*What is it that makes otherwise normal, decent,
caring people fall under the spell of misguided and
deranged individuals, such as Jeffrey Lundgren?
Could it be the sheer force cult leaders derive from their
delusion that they have been chosen to usher in The
Second Coming of Christ that subdues the reason and
conscience of followers, who then acquiesce in ritualistic,
brutal human sacrifice?*

EMBRACED THE ROLE OF AVENGING ANGEL

Does 'temporary' insanity absolve them from guilt
and qualify them for sympathy?

Whatever the conclusion, there can be absolutely
no doubt about the deluded ravings of Jeffrey
Lundgren, even though he, too, rediscovered some
logic once he was in custody and facing the death
penalty. Like the worst of all cult leaders before him,
having deceived, browbeaten, robbed and, in some
cases, violated his gullible followers, he joyfully
embraced the roles of judge, jury and executioner –
or, as he would have preferred it, avenging angel.

LAST PROPHET ON EARTH

With hindsight, Lundgren might appear to have
always had in mind his life's project, the return of
Christ in the Temple of Kirtland, Ohio. Lundgren's
destiny, to be God's last prophet on earth, was, he
felt, beyond question. His visions, like those of his
Mormon predecessor, Joseph Smith, concerned
the ancient, golden tablets from which the Book of
Mormon evolved. Lundgren convinced his utterly
biddable disciples that the tablets were buried close
to the Temple, established by Joseph Smith. To
counter what would be undoubtedly formidable
opposition to the Second Coming, he argued,
opponents needed to be extinguished and sinners
'spiritually cleansed'. Such a project would require,
of course, a massive arsenal of weapons to fight the
good fight. Nevertheless, the events of Lundgren's
unremarkable life give the lie to this notion of a
predestined, holy mission.

Lundgren was born on 3 May 1950, in
Independence, Missouri and grew up in the 1950s
and 1960s as a member of the Reorganized Church
of Jesus Christ of Latter Day Saints (RLDS), allied
to the Mormon Church. Some claim his father
was abusive, others merely that he was a strict
parent, though all seem to imply a less than happy

childhood for Jeffrey. However, the aloof schoolboy certainly spent a lot of time acquiring from his father the hunting, shooting and survival skills which would serve him to such devastating effect in later life. Father and son frequently went off on hunting trips, and the young Lundgren became an expert marksman.

His education appears not to have suffered unduly from the alleged poor parenting and Lundgren was clever enough to enrol on an electronics degree course at Central Missouri State University. His membership of the church also stood him in good stead, as he found accommodation in an RLDS youth house. Here he befriended Alice Keehler, who would later become one of his followers and, in 1970, his – pregnant – wife, after they had both dropped out of university. In order to support his family, Lundgren enlisted as an electronics technician in the US Navy for four years, by the end of which time Alice had given birth to two sons. By then, he seemed preoccupied with money problems and disenchanted with and abusive to his wife, who allegedly suffered a ruptured spleen as a result of his violent behaviour. No evidence as yet of a coherent series of events and actions on the part of Lundgren, to support his claim to be Christ's messenger on earth – but proof aplenty to suggest an unbridled bully and poor husband and father without a plan.

In 1984, Lundgren and his family moved into a church house, next to the Kirtland Temple in Ohio, and he secured a position as a tour guide of the Temple. As a lay preacher since 1981, he now had access to a congregation and tourists, on whom he could try out his theories and reading of the Bible. His simplistic take on interpreting scriptures, along with increasing references to violence and sexual acts, nevertheless apparently persuaded many followers. Unsurprisingly, it also attracted criticism from more traditional church members, who felt ill-at-ease with his unchristian teachings and questionable ethics.

THE SECOND COMING

Significantly, in 1987, he was evicted from the house and, accused of stealing as much as $25,000 of church funds, lost his job as tour guide. So, Lundgren's honourable, early discharge from the Navy in 1974 had now been matched by a dishonourable removal from a position of trust and an accusation of theft from the church that had nurtured him. Was this to be the key moment in Lundgren's 'life project', a mere thirty-seven years after his birth? Just like Ervil LeBaron, when he was demoted within the

Mormon Church Firstborners group, Lundgren abandoned his RLDS church group and eventually moved his family to a rented farm house, where he started his own sect. Although sect numbers remained small, the twenty or so followers were sufficient for Lundgren's needs: credulous disciples prepared to hand over some or all of their money to the cause and to subscribe to otherwise unthinkable deeds in the name of the Second Coming.

In order to exercise complete control over his followers and their assets, Lundgren insisted that they move in with him and his family. Small wonder, then, that he started to turn against Dennis and Cheryl Avery, who, after selling their home, effectively refused to be totally manipulated by Lundgren, when they found a rented house of their own and only donated part of their house sale profit to the sect.

PLAN OF ACTION

Lundgren made sure his followers accepted that his vision, directing him to Kirtland, revealed that on 3 May – coincidentally his own birthday – Christ's successful Second Coming depended entirely on Lundgren and his followers taking the Kirtland Temple by force. He proposed spiritual cleansing of the people, land and property around the Temple, implying burglary and the deaths of those resisting the group's objectives. Unfortunately for the Avery family, Lundgren soon identified softer targets, Dennis and Cheryl, as alternative major sinners and opponents and set about convincing sect members that the Averys should be put to death.

It was time for the practised hunter-killer to put together his plan of action. Thanks to his successful use of control techniques during his classes, members accepted that talking among themselves was disloyal and sinful and remained passive, as Lundgren became angry and intimidating whenever anybody, such as Dennis Avery, tried to raise objections. However, he needed reassurance that no-one would back out of the proposed murders. He invited his followers to dinner at a motel, on 17 April 1989. There, he questioned each of his co-conspirators separately; all of them swore their allegiance to the cause.

At the farm house, Lundgren and Ron Luff tricked Dennis Avery into going into a barn, on a pretext of helping them with some camping equipment. Bound and gagged, Avery was thrown into a pit dug beforehand and shot dead by Lundgren. The same fate awaited the rest of the family in succession: first, wife Cheryl, followed by fifteen-year-old daughter,

Trina, then Becky, aged thirteen and, finally, Karen, six years of age. All were bundled into the communal grave and executed without a flicker of emotion from their killer. Lundgren's accomplices finally buried the bodies with soil and lime, to speed up decomposure.

Lundgren and his cronies, with their families, fled to West Virginia and set up a military-style camp in order to repel any attacks, especially from officers of the law. Now completely dominant, having subdued both physically and psychologically all of his followers, Lundgren became even more extreme in his teachings, going so far as to demand the right to cleanse through impregnation some of the wives of his followers. By the autumn, with group funds running low, the members dispersed and Lundgren and his family went back to California. Then, nine months after the slaughter in Kirtland, the bodies of the Averys were discovered by police following a tip-off. The net soon closed on Lundgren's followers, who helped police to secure the arrest of thirteen in total, including the Lundgren family, in 1990.

So, how did the Supreme Court of Ohio react to Lundgren's tale of spiritual cleansing and revelations of the Second Coming? Despite multiple, seemingly reasoned appeals, they rejected the arguments that had crucially swayed Lundgren's followers – yet another murdering, false prophet met his maker, executed on 24 October 2006, at the Southern Ohio Correctional Facility. Alice Lundgren received five life sentences for conspiracy, complicity and kidnapping. And the rest of Lundgren's cruelly brainwashed, formerly decent, law abiding disciples? Culpable in their own right, albeit on reduced charges, they attracted swingeing sentences that will keep many of them imprisoned without hope of parole until well beyond the end of their natural lives.

JIM JONES

When the shocking news broke that US Congressman, Leo J. Ryan, and four of his party had been gunned down while attempting to board a plane in Port Kaituma, Guyana on 18 November 1978, it was merely the tip of the proverbial iceberg.

Within a few hours, an already grieving America was to learn of a horrific mass suicide orchestrated by cult leader, Jim Jones. Under his guidance, 913 members of his cult The People's Temple – the majority of them American citizens – prematurely ended their lives in what some have called a suicide pact and others a mass murder.

HOLY ROLLERS

Born in 1931 in Indiana, Jim Jones became fascinated with religion from an early age. He was later described by those who knew him in his early years as being a strange child who was morbidly obsessed with death. Some accounts refer to rumours that he regularly held funerals for small animals and that he once stabbed a cat to death. He was also an avid reader, studying the likes of Adolf Hitler and Joseph Stalin during his High School years. By the time he was sixteen years old, Jones had already become part of a local Pentecostal congregation known as the Gospel Tabernacle – whose members were scornfully referred to as 'holy rollers' by others in the community – and also believed that he had spiritual powers. He started to preach on street corners of mixed-race communities. He believed in equality regardless of race or social standing which were still perceived as radical notions at the time, but it was these values that would attract scores of people to his cult in years to come. In contradiction to his egalitarian principles, however, the young Jones quickly developed a strong belief that he was superior to others and began to think of himself as their leader. One early indication of this occurred when a friend refused to comply with his demands by leaving church early to go home; Jones took his father's gun and shot at him.

After he married Marceline Baldwin in 1949, other disturbing personality traits became noticeable. An insecure man, Jones developed a paranoid fear of being abandoned by those he loved, becoming jealous and highly emotional when his wife paid attention to anybody else. He also lost his faith, stating that the existence of poverty proved that there was no God. So vehement was hc in this belief that he threatened to kill himself should his wife pray. This view had changed by 1952 when he learned that the teachings of the Methodists – the denomination followed by Marceline – were similar to his own values. He eventually became a Methodist preacher and, within a couple of years, was attracting considerable crowds to Pentecostal meetings in other churches. In 1956, his success resulted in the foundation of his own now-notorious church, The People's Temple. The church advocated communalism and provided shelter and a soup kitchen for the needy. At around the same time, Jones and his wife adopted a black child and a Korean orphan as well as celebrating the birth of their own biological son in 1959. With the Cold War and America's fear of Communism both constant concerns, Jones had a vision of an imminent nuclear attack and set about trawling the world for a safe location for his church. Following visits to Hawaii and Brazil, Jones visited Guyana and was impressed by its government's socialist leanings. After moving his congregation from Indianapolis – where, for a while, he actually was Director of the Human Rights Commission – to

California and his hypocrisy, thirst for power and extra-marital affairs resulting in the collapse of his family and a dramatically reduced following, Jones applied for affiliation with the Disciples of Christ, an organisation with 1.5 million members, in 1968. The request was accepted and, five years later, The People's Temple's flock had swelled to over 2,500 spanning San Francisco and Los Angeles.

JONESTOWN

In 1974, Jones made another application; this time to the Guyanese government for a 300-acre plot 140 miles from Georgetown. Again, his wish was granted and a commune that he named 'Jonestown' was founded. The Temple soon attracted criticism from the local Catholic Church, whose representatives were disgusted at the fake healings and so-called miracles that took place. Jones returned to the USA where it was said that he had members' rubbish searched for information that he could incorporate into his phoney clairvoyance routines, while prospective members were carefully screened with those of a more conservative ethos rejected. Despite its supposed status as a socialist utopia, the growing cult was more like a dictatorship. Believing himself to be a reincarnation of Jesus Christ, Jones manipulated his followers into pooling their incomes and surrendering their possessions through his Christian communalism teachings. In return, they received bed, board and a weekly allowance of $2, but he was the only authority figure and his staff were not permitted to question his plans. Further contradictions were evident in his teachings about sex; he was a keen believer in sexual freedom but was a staunch advocate of marriage; he claimed to be a devout heterosexual but privately sodomized a member of his church to prove that the man was homosexual. He was even arrested for lewd conduct in a known gay meeting place, although he successfully concealed this from his followers.

The People's Temple continued to grow, but attracted increasing criticism from outside. Jones used his increasing influence – which he obtained thanks to relationships with dominant political figures as well as money taken from his followers – to attempt to prevent this criticism from being published in the press. Jones was unable to keep all of these stories from reaching the awareness of the public, however. A notable instance was the defection of member, Grace Stoen, who left in protest at the severe beating of a fellow member who had condemned Jones and his teachings.

The self-appointed Reverend responded by falsely claiming that Stoen's son was his child and entered into a custody battle. Inevitably, this led to negative publicity for the Temple and it was this, along with his paranoia, that saw Jones hasten the preparations for moving his followers to Jonestown and towards the horrifying events that would result in their deaths.

CONGRESSMAN LEO J. RYAN

His status as a megalomaniac was confirmed on arrival in Guyana by the fact that members' passports were confiscated in order to stop them from defecting from his twisted cult. Jones now had the dictatorship that he seemed to crave, although this was soon to be threatened with dreadful consequences when a delegation led by Congressman Leo J. Ryan visited the commune seeking answers about The People's Temple. Following concerns raised by relatives of those who had moved with Jones to Guyana, Ryan had been conducting investigations into the cult for several months before his fateful trip to Jonestown. These included interviews with defectors, some of whom alleged that there had been brutal beatings, rehearsals for a mass suicide and even murders. Ryan's visit clearly exasperated Jones, whose increasing paranoia resulted in a bloody denouement. One recording of Jones taken in the days approaching the congressman's visit goes as far as announcing the impending massacre. 'If by any chance you would make a mistake to try to come in and take any one of us, we will not let you, you will die, you will have to take anybody over all of our dead bodies,' he preaches with a disconcerting urgency. In another recording, he says: 'They won't leave us alone. They're now going back to tell more lies, which means more congressmen and there's no way, no way we can survive.'

Predictably, relations between the two sides were hostile and tense over the following days and things came to a head when Ryan himself was attacked by a Temple member, prompting the congressman and his group to beat a hasty retreat; fifteen defectors leaving with them. As they were boarding their plane at Port Kaituma airport at around 5pm, members of Jones' cult arrived in a tractor and opened fire killing the politician, three members of the media and one defector. At about the same time, Jones gathered his followers together and told them of his 'premonition' that Ryan would be shot and that the political forces who had been hounding the Temple would respond by killing them all. The only answer, he concluded, was the mass 'revolutionary suicide' that they had chillingly rehearsed for. An audio recording of the sickening events that followed reveals the final minutes of the Jonestown cult. A barrel of Kool-Aid, a soft drink, laced with cyanide and sedatives was given to everybody congregated and, after a few protests from those with young children who said that their offspring should be allowed to live were dismissed by Jones either persuading them to the contrary or forcing them, the horror began. Babies and children were the first victims of Jones' evil; the poison administered by syringes squirting it into their mouths. The adults followed suit.

A total of 913 bodies were recovered from Jonestown, including Jones himself who was found with a single gunshot wound to his right temple which, authorities believe was self-inflicted. Sadly, the bodies of 412 cult members were never claimed by relatives and were buried in a mass grave in Oakland, California. Jones' legacy leaves a number of questions; most notably that of whether the events of Jonestown constituted a cult suicide or a mass murder. Most share the view that, in the very least, the children were murdered at his whim while many others have concluded that the majority of the adults were manipulated by an evil and calculating man who had falsely gained their devotion. This leads to the question of how one man could exercise such control over so many people. Some theories state that Jones created and resolved 'threats' before telling his followers about how he had saved them, thus earning him a position of trust that he abused with devastating results; the like of which would tragically be seen again in other religious sects.

JOSEPH DI MAMBRO

When firefighters were called to tackle a blaze at a privately owned property in Morin Heights, Quebec, on 4 October 1994 they could be forgiven for thinking that the distressing presence of two charred bodies would be the extent of their unwelcome discovery.

ORDER OF THE SOLAR TEMPLE

The building belonged to a Joseph di Mambro and officials assumed that the deceased were the sixty-nine-year-old and his friend, Luc Jouret. When closer inspection revealed that one of the dead bodies was that of a woman and that the male victim was neither di Mambro nor Jouret, it was the start of a string of such gruesome discoveries that would ultimately unmask the landlord and his friend as co-founders of a religious sect known as the Order of the Solar Temple which was accountable for the deaths of over fifty people both in Canada and thousands of miles away in Switzerland.

Born in the inter-war years in southern France, Joseph di Mambro was a mysterious man who was attracted to esoteric religions from an early age. The first half of his life does not seem to be very well documented, although it is known that he trained as a jeweller and watchmaker. In January 1956 he joined the Ancient and Mystical Order of the Rosae Crucis (AMORC), a secret philosophical society, becoming the head of its lodge in Nimes, France by the end of the following decade. In 1970, he became a lecturer in the burgeoning New Age Movement, founding the Centre for the Preparation of the New Age three years later. He then established a commune for this organisation in his native France close to the Swiss border. It was during this time that he began to claim to be both a member of the Great White Brotherhood – a group that occultists believe to be superhumans who shape the development of the human race – and also the reincarnation of a number of notable religious figures including Moses and Osiris.

COSMIC MARRIAGE AND CHILDREN

In the early 1980s, di Mambro met Jouret, a Belgian homeopathic physician. The pair struck up an instant friendship, bonding over their shared obsession with the occult and, in 1984, the Order of the Solar Temple was founded; di Mambro was essentially the director of operations, dictating rituals from behind the scenes while the charismatic Jouret became its figurehead and, to all intents and purposes, its leader and recruiter. The cult has been described as a fusion of traditional occultism and a belief in the coming of a 'New Age'. The manipulative di Mambro used his growing reputation to convince his followers to hand over their money and possessions to him so that he could take care of their collective interests. He believed that his daughter Emmanuelle, born in 1982, was a cosmic being who was destined to lead the world into the New Age and set about arranging cosmic marriages among his followers, dictating which couples had cosmic children to assist Emmanuelle in her perceived role of messiah. Rumour has it that Jouret convinced members that, in a previous life, he had been a member of the Knights Templar, a Christian military order during the middle ages, and that he also believed himself to be the third incarnation of Jesus Christ. He preached to them about his belief that death was an illusion and that after they left their mortal bodies, they would be transported to the star Sirius. Things went well for the organisation during the remainder of the 1980s with membership reaching its hundreds and considerable wealth being accrued as a result. In the early years of the next decade, however, its fortunes changed; di Mambro's health began to fail him and people began to question his authority, some demanding their money back and leaving the sect. His family began to fall apart after Emmanuelle herself rebelled against his orders and his older child, Elie, denounced him to members of the sect. Then, in 1993, Jouret was arrested for buying illegal weapons. The reputation of the cult, along with that of di Mambro, plummeted. He concluded that the world was not ready for the New Age and that he and his followers should therefore 'leave' for a higher dimension, almost quite literally sparking the infernos that would help get them there.

MEMBERS OF THE ORDER OF THE SOLAR TEMPLE

After the initial discovery of the two bodies at the property in Quebec – both of which turned out to belong to members of the order – the building was searched in case there had been further casualties. Tragically, there were; the remains of three more people – a man, a woman and a child – were found in a cupboard. Further analysis revealed that the departed had not perished in the fire and had, in fact, been dead for a few days before the building was consumed by flames. The three corpses discovered in the cupboard belonged to Antonio

Dutoit, his wife, Nikki and their three-month-old son, Christopher-Emmanuel. The parents had been killed by multiple stab wounds to their backs, chests and throats while the child had been stabbed in the chest six times with a wooden stake. The police were understandably baffled, apparently left with more questions than answers. The truth slowly began to surface when it was ascertained that the Dutoits had previously been members of the Order of the Solar Temple cult. Various theories exist as to why they were murdered; some simply state that it was felt that the couple may have known too much, whereas others relate to their infant son. One is that he was conceived against the cult's wishes while another rumour is that di Mambro became convinced that the child was a reincarnation of the Anti Christ and ordered his shocking execution.

On the same day as the grisly discovery in Canada, a similar fire was discovered in an outbuilding at a farm all the way across the Atlantic in Cheiry, Switzerland. The victim was retired farmer, Alberto Giacobino, who had a plastic bag over his head and appeared to have been shot. As police combed the property for clues as to what exactly had happened, they found incendiary devices that had started the fire as well as what appeared to be a meeting hall full of people's abandoned possessions. Then, an astounding discovery was made. One of the walls in the hall was found to move and it concealed a lavishly decorated chamber full of mirrors. Inside this new room was a carefully arranged circle of twenty-two corpses, most of which were clad in ceremonial robes. Like the first body, the majority had plastic bags over their heads and had been shot. Some of the bodies had their hands clasped, presumably in prayer, and there were champagne bottles strewn around the room. There was a makeshift altar with a rose, a cross and a photograph of Luc Jouret on it. Further incendiary devices that had failed to go off were then discovered. Investigators believed that the macabre events had taken place the day before and were aided with the grim results heralded by yet another fire on 5 October, this time around 100 miles away in Granges-sur-Salvan, also in Switzerland. Three ski chalets had been rigged to burn in the same way as the hall in Cheiry had been. Inside two of them were some more horrifyingly similar discoveries; twenty-five badly charred corpses – including children – many of which had multiple bullet wounds to their heads had been arranged into a circle. International arrest warrants were issued for both di Mambro and Jouret, although it was eventually established that the ring leaders were among the dead. It later emerged that that the puppet master of the cult had gathered together his closest confidantes for a last supper before the carnage began and, in another development, that several suicide notes stating the cult's intention to 'leave for a higher dimension' as per di Mambro and Jouret's teachings had been left behind by its members.

Based on the post mortems of the victims in the weeks that followed, magistrates concluded that only 15 of the deaths in Switzerland were willing suicides while at least seven were presumed to be executions. The majority had taken tranquilizers before being shot. After the events in Switzerland and Canada had taken place, more dark secrets about the Order of the Solar Temple emerged. It had an extensive portfolio of property across the two countries as well as in France and had been involved in some large-scale money laundering operations. It had also been implicated in arms trafficking, stockpiling them to allegedly prepare for the end of the world. A year later, a further 16 members of the cult were found dead in France and a further five took their own lives in Quebec in 1997; di Mambro may have been dead, but his evil legacy had lived on.

SHOKO ASAHARA

It seemed to be just another unremarkable morning on the Tokyo underground on 20 March 1995 – until the heart of the city was rocked by a sudden and virulent act of terrorism. Panic ensued as sarin – a fatal nerve gas – was deployed; twelve commuters never made it out of the subway alive and thousands more were taken seriously ill in the sickening attacks masterminded by cult leader Shoko Asahara.

CHIZUO MATSUMOTO

Born Chizuo Matsumoto in 1955, his childhood was one of adversity. Not only was he born into an impoverished family, but he was also diagnosed with infantile glaucoma at birth. As a result of this condition, he was left blind in his left eye and only partially sighted in his right, and this resulted in him becoming the victim of schoolyard bullying. His parents responded by having him enrolled in a government-funded school for blind children, where his fortunes changed. As the only pupil with any sight, he turned this to his advantage by becoming a bully himself and forcing the other children to do whatever he said, only doing favours for them in exchange for money. In these, his formative years, it was already becoming evident that he was a calculating and manipulative individual motivated by financial gain and control over others.

After leaving school in 1977, the ambitious Matsumoto attempted to gain a place at university, but was rejected. Furious at not being granted a place that he felt he deserved, he was arrested for assault shortly afterwards. He decided to move to Tokyo to focus his attention on another goal: a career in Chinese medicine and acupuncture. Here he met and married his wife, Tomoko, who persuaded her family to fund a business. This venture was a success, but wasn't without its controversy. It was alleged that the remedies offered by Matsumoto were dubious and he was charged for a related offence in 1981. Despite this minor setback, his reputation was growing and he was achieving his lifelong ambition of acquiring wealth, but this was seemingly not enough for him as he suddenly sought a new direction. He turned to spiritualism and spent vast periods of time studying a diverse range of beliefs and ideologies. One account of this part of his life tells of how he claimed to have experienced a strong energy while meditating that enabled him to see the auras of evil people. His enthusiasm for spiritualism, coupled perhaps with an inherent desire to have power over others, resulted in the formation of a so-called religious group in 1984.

REINCARNATION OF SHIVA

After a pilgrimage to the Himalayas in 1987, Matsumoto changed his name to Shoko Asahara and that of his cult to Aum Shinrikyo – Aum is a sacred Hindu symbol while Shinrikyo means 'supreme truth'. The cult combined Hindu and Buddhist beliefs and the writings of the sixteenth-century French prophet Nostradamus. During his trip, he had briefly met the Dalai Lama for a photo opportunity. He would later claim that the great religious leader told him that he had the mind of a Buddha and was destined for a divine mission to bring to the Japanese the true teachings of Buddhism. Clearly believing himself to be a messiah figure, Asahara's teachings were apocalyptic; the world was soon to be consumed by evil, he said, but those who followed him would be saved. He even claimed to be a reincarnation of the Hindu god Shiva and a Christ figure. By the mid 1980s, he had grown a straggly beard and was regularly seen in white robes. In contrast to the peaceful associations of this look, though, there were disturbing activities taking place under his guidance. Followers could drink his blood – for a price, of course – while the teachings included chemical-induced survival training. Some Aum members reportedly died during some of his severe rituals while others were allegedly murdered for attempting to challenge its authority or escape its control. The majority of its 10,000 army of followers across the nation were from stable family backgrounds and had no history of violence. It has been speculated that this made them easy targets for Asahara, who exploited the naivety by duping them into believing that they were helping to improve the world by joining his organisation.

Following the alleged murders of two dissenting members in 1989, the suspicion of one missing man's family was aroused. Lawyer Tsutsumi Sakamoto became involved, offering his services and publicly criticising Aum. The cult leader's response was to distribute defamatory leaflets about the legal representative who, in turn, increased legal pressure. Asahara's answer to this was shocking and brutal. He sent a handful of his men to Sakamoto's home armed with syringes of potassium chloride. The men broke in, waking Sakamoto's baby son,

Tatsuhiko, who they immediately injected with the deadly toxin. Sakamoto himself was then struck over the head with a hammer. His wife, Satoko, was woken by this and, after a struggle, strangled. Both adults were then injected with the same substance before Sakamoto was strangled as he continued to fight for his life. The depravity of the attack wasn't over, however. The bodies were taken to three different locations and disposed of, but not before their teeth were smashed beyond recognition to obstruct their speedy identification. Asahara told his returning thugs that they had carried out holy work and, despite media and police interest, seemingly got away with murder.

CHEMICAL ATTACKS

After visiting Russia in 1992 to initiate a new branch of the cult, it was evident that Asahara's reputation was mounting overseas as well as in Japan; by now there were 30,000 Aum followers in Russia alone. His growing influence enabled him to buy arms from the Russian military, setting in motion a chain of events that would ultimately result in the attacks on the Tokyo underground three years later. His thirst for power, meanwhile, saw him run for election, but his overtures and underhand tactics failed spectacularly with the public showing little interest. Aum as a whole was beginning to be the subject of great scrutiny and it was this pressure, combined with his anger at the electorate for shunning him, that seemed to motivate the sect leader to teach the world a shocking lesson. He had his chief scientists devote their time to developing chemical weapons. As the dangerous fruit of their labours was refined and with suspicion of Asahara's doomsday cult continuing, Aum purchased property in a remote part of western Australia in 1996. There it established a sarin factory, testing the deadly product – some of the ingredients of which were allegedly smuggled into the country in sake bottles – on sheep. The results were the twisted success that the evil leader was hoping for and, the following year, he ordered sarin to be used against human subjects. After a failed attempt to trial it on the leader of a rival religious group, the deadly nerve gas was used on three judges who, it seemed, were about to deliver an unfavourable verdict to Asahara in a property dispute. The gas was released and, aided by the wind, spread quickly through the neighbourhood in which the judges' dormitory was located. Although the targets survived with minor symptoms, seven others died and hundreds more were hospitalized.

Despite the failure to eliminate Asahara's targets, the operation was considered a success and, amazingly, the cult escaped prosecution again.

Asahara could now carry out the large-scale attack he had been planning and so it was that, during an ordinary morning rush hour, the assault took place. The spark for what proved to be his final act of terror came after a former member had reported the kidnap and murder of her brother, who had helped her to escape Aum. Asahara received a tip off and decided to strike first. He gathered together around one hundred cult members and told them that he was likely to be captured as a result of what was to follow, imploring them to sacrifice themselves for the greater good of his corrupt cause – to overthrow the government and to start a world war.

Parcels of liquid sarin were then given to five of the megalomaniac's trusted followers – who were also given antidotes for themselves – and taken onto crowded trains within the government district for maximum devastation. The lethal packages were punctured with umbrellas and the horrific results that ensued were instantaneous. As the fumes spread, frightened commuters began to experience nausea and coughing fits. People began to panic and, within a few minutes, there was a scene of carnage as they began to collapse. In all, a dozen innocent commuters were killed and around 5,500 were choked and blinded.

After a prolonged pursuit, one of Asahara's predictions came true – he was captured, along with over one hundred of his followers. His subsequent trial began in 1996 and, due to the number of charges against him and his uncooperative behaviour as he deliberately delayed proceedings, it lasted eight years. He was finally sentenced to death in February 2004. Two years later, his final appeal was thrown out and he is now awaiting execution.

PART FIVE
TYRANTS

ADOLF HITLER

Ask somebody to name history's true personification of evil and the vast majority will instantly give the name Adolf Hitler without a moment's thought. Accountable for the deaths of millions, among them over six million Jews during the Holocaust, Hitler's legacy is one of brutality, hatred and some of the most heinous acts ever to be experienced by the human race.

UNHAPPY EARLY YEARS

Born in Austria in 1889, Hitler's early years were unhappy at best. His father, Alois, regularly beat him and there was friction between father and son in later years when the former wanted the latter to follow his career path as a customs officer. He left school without any qualifications at the age of sixteen before moving to Vienna where he attempted to make a living as a painter. Rejected twice by the Vienna Academy of Fine Arts, he found himself living in a shelter for the homeless for a while until his inheritance from his father's death in 1903 enabled him to move to Munich in 1913. During his time in

Vienna, where there was a large Jewish community, Hitler became anti-Semitic. After previously being rejected by the Austrian army due to being deemed unfit for service, Hitler eventually served as a volunteer in World War I when he was accepted into Germany's 16th Bavarian Reserve Infantry Regiment. He was a dedicated and enthusiastic soldier during the conflict and was promoted to the rank of Corporal. Despite being shot and gassed, he emerged a decorated hero, being awarded both the Iron Cross Second Class and First Class medals.

JOINING THE NAZI PARTY

In September 1919, Hitler joined the German Workers' Party in Munich. The following year, he was handed the responsibility of propaganda and publicity and soon left the army to concentrate fully on his role within the organisation. The party was then renamed the National-sozialistische Deutsche Arbeiterpartei which, in turn, became abbreviated to 'Nazi Party'. During his first two years within the party, Hitler became a formidable speaker and was well respected by his peers. He chose the swastika – originally a Hindu sign meaning 'good luck' – as the party's logo in 1920 and had become its leader by the following year. He used his new-found power and the party itself as a means of communicating his hatred for other races – Jews in particular. He believed that it was other creeds that were to blame for Germany's humiliation after World War I and the subsequent Treaty of Versailles.

In November 1923, Hitler led an uprising that became known as the Munich Beer Hall Putsch. His attempts to overthrow the government failed and he was sentenced to five years' imprisonment. He only served nine months before being released, during which he wrote his autobiography *Mein Kampf* – My Struggle – outlining his ideology. After his release in 1924, Hitler was forbidden to speak publically and the Nazi Party had slumped in popularity without his leadership. However, in spite of dismal election results throughout Germany in the following years, the Nazis steadily gained new members and grew in the north of the country as a result of an alliance with Gregor Strasser. A key factor in aiding Hitler's rise to power was the Wall Street Crash in 1929 and the Great Depression that followed as a result. The German economy that had been slowly recovering was hit as loans from other countries were withdrawn; production withered and unemployment soared. An election was called for September 1930 and Hitler hit the campaign trail, promising the electorate a way out of the economic misery. The Nazis received more than eighteen percent of the vote, making it the second largest party in the Reichstag. Buoyed by this success, Hitler stood against President Paul von Hindenburg in the 1932 presidential election. After two rounds of voting, the President had retained his position, but support for the Nazis was considerable. Hindenburg was then pressured into appointing Hitler as Chancellor in January 1933. One month later, a fire that gutted the Reichstag – which was almost certainly the Nazis' doing – was blamed on Communists; Hitler used this as an opportunity to suppress the right of free speech to the extreme left and increase what would ultimately become his stranglehold of German politics. The Enabling Act followed next, effectively transferring all legislative power to the Nazis. Within months, it was illegal for rival political parties to exist.

BECOMING FÜHRER AND CHANCELLOR

With the dictatorship now secured, Hitler wasted little time in eliminating those who, he believed, would hinder his progress in any way. On the Night of the Long Knives, several of those who had aided his rise to power were arrested and executed without trial. These included Ernst Röhm – along with several other SA officials – Gregor Strasser and former Chancellor, Kurt von Schleicher. The removal of the SA contingent in particular was welcomed by the German military which, as a result, agreed to Hitler's proposal of merging the roles of Chancellor and President upon the death of Hindenburg in 1934. Hitler became Führer and Chancellor and demanded that soldiers in the German army swore an oath of allegiance to him personally.

The Nazification of Germany was his next objective as he set about releasing the nation from some of the strictures of the Treaty of Versailles. He began preparing Germany for war from an early stage by making alliances with Italy and Japan and militarising the country. He also planned the territorial expansion that would spark World War Two. His plan to invade other countries went hand in hand with that of establishing a New Order, whereby an Aryan race would rule the continent. Meanwhile, all youth organisations were abolished and replaced with the Hitler Youth as he sought to cement his power for generations to come.

The persecution of Jews increased with Hitler decreeing via the Nuremberg Laws of 1935 that they were not German citizens and that they therefore did not have the same rights. Three years later, Hitler's Nazis gave their clearest indication to date of their malevolent intent towards the Jews. 'Kristallnacht' – or 'The Night of Broken Glass' – saw Nazi storm troopers in civilian clothes embark on an outright assault of Jewish people and properties. Synagogues were burned down, while houses were broken into and ransacked throughout Germany and Austria. Men, women and children alike were beaten by the fascist thugs and ninety-one Jews were killed – although other reports suggest that there were many more fatalities than this – while 20,000 were arrested and taken to labour camps. The Jewish community was then ordered to pay the sum of one billion Reichsmarks for the damage.

EXTERMINATION CAMPS AND THE HOLOCAUST

On 1 September 1939, Hitler ordered the German invasion of Poland, prompting the start of World War Two. Two days later, both Britain and France declared war on Germany. After military successes in Scandinavia and Western Europe – but after failing to defeat Britain – in 1941, Hitler ordered an attack on the Soviet Union. In the same year, the true evil of the dictator became explicit with the start of the mass killings of the Holocaust. The existing concentration camps, where persecuted Jews had previously been sent as part of the Führer's initial plans to expel them from Europe, were expanded to incorporate extermination camps as he aimed to completely eradicate the Jewish race. Between eleven and seventeen million people were exterminated, around six million of them Jews. Other victims included around two million ethnic Poles, while four million others deemed unworthy to live by the Nazis – including Romani, Soviet prisoners of war, Catholics, Jehovah's witnesses, homosexuals, the disabled and the mentally ill – were also either brutally murdered or worked to death.

A large proportion of those killed in the death camps were executed in gas chambers immediately after their arrival. Prisoners were ordered to strip and go into what they were told were communal shower facilities. Once inside, hydrogen cyanide was released, killing everyone inside within twenty minutes. After their bodies were removed for burial or, later on, incineration, their teeth were examined for gold fillings; any that were found were removed. Shooting was also commonplace while medical experiments – including castration and sterilisation – were also carried out as part of Hitler's evil regime of ethnic cleansing. In addition to the millions slaughtered in the extermination camps, the German army was followed into the territories of countries it invaded by an SS death squad which executed the resident Jewish populations.

HITLER'S DOWNFALL

Hitler's increasing megalomania would ultimately be the cause of his downfall. With his armies fighting on more fronts than the nation's dwindling resources could afford, the Allies were presented with the opportunity to exploit the Germans' increasingly vulnerable position. On 6 June 1944 the D-Day landings, in which British and American forces stormed the northern beaches of Nazi-occupied France, proved a crucial turning point in the war. From this moment on, the odds were stacked heavily against the Nazis; Hitler, ailing after an assassination attempt left him with superficial wounds, fled to his bunker in Berlin in January 1945 where he stayed for the remainder of his life and, indeed, the war. Accepting the inevitability of defeat, he married his long-term mistress Eva Braun on 29 April before saying farewell to his deputies and handing over power. On 30 April and with Soviet forces closing in on his Berlin bunker, Hitler shot himself and his bride took poison. At his command, their bodies were burned.

Although Hitler was dead and the war over, the aftermath of his empire of pure evil left Germany in crisis for many years to come. To this day, the mere mention of his name and the image of the swastika inspire feelings of revulsion, anger and fear underlining his status as the most despised and corrupt man in the history of the world.

ATTILA THE HUN

One of history's most ferocious leaders, Attila the Hun's ruthless reign of terror in the first century was characterized by barbaric violence, looting and pillaging with his army essentially sweeping westwards destroying everything in its path.

THE SCOURGE OF GOD

He was so notorious, in fact, that even the Romans feared him; referring to him as 'The Scourge of God' and paying him an annual weight of 700 pounds of gold to keep him from attacking the eastern half of its own massive empire.

Attila's empire – which covered large expanses of what are now Russia, Germany and Poland among a great many others – was centred in what we now know as Hungary, although the Huns, a group of nomadic herdsmen, originally came from central Asia. By the time he died in 453 AD at the age of around forty-seven, the mass of land taken by the Huns stretched from Baltic Sea in the north to the River Danube in the south and from Ural River in the east to the river Rhine in the west. The wealth he accumulated along the way from pillaging and extortion fed his power and influence, making his armies increasingly intimidating.

IN THE BEGINNINING

Little is known about Attila's early years, although it was said that he was taught to ride a horse before he could walk, fire a bow and arrow by the time he was three and wield a sabre at five. At around the age of twelve, he was sent as an exchanged hostage to secure peace terms with the Romans. This occurred after the prominent Roman Flavius Aëtius had spent time with the Huns for the same reason, befriending Attila in the process; years later, the two would meet again, although this time as foes. Attila learned much about his future enemies during his time as a hostage; not only did he acquire their language and military secrets, but he was also witness to their extravagant wealth and culture. He was disgusted by the self-indulgent lifestyle of the Romans and although he remained friends with Aëtius – who, as a result of his time with the Huns, believed that they would be better as allies than enemies – he vowed to return to Rome one day only not as a hostage, but as its conqueror.

Along with his older brother, Bleda, Attila

succeeded his uncle, Rua, who died in 433 AD. The two brothers shared power for a few years until Attila had Bleda murdered so that he could unite and rule the Huns – who were made up of several different ethnic backgrounds, possibly even including dissatisfied Romans – on his own. As soon as Attila assumed power, he began attacking territories belonging to Germanic tribes including the Goths and Vandals with the overall goal of expanding his empire westwards into the eastern portion of that of the Romans. Theodosius II – the Eastern Roman Emperor – agreed to make tribute payments on two separate occasions; first between 441 and 443 AD after a Roman Bishop had been caught stealing from a Hunnic tomb and again between 447 and 449 AD, bringing the Roman city of Constantinople – modern day Istanbul – to its knees, although stopping short of invading it. In the vicious attacks that first prompted Theodosius to negotiate terms with Attila, the Huns took many of the major Balkan cities in what are now Bulgaria, Greece and the former Yugoslavia.

INVINCIBLE IN WAR
One of the many legends about Attila's power and reputation concerns his weapon of choice, a sword.

A secondary account from the sixth-century Roman historian, Jordanes, states that Attila was presented a blade that had been unearthed on grazing land and believed that it came from a war god and that it was a sign that he was invincible in war and had been divinely chosen as ruler of the entire world. The belief it inspired in Attila was reflected on battlefields all over western Europe. An often-proffered explanation for the Huns' success in conflicts is the use of stirrups – although this may seem a trivial detail, stirrups would have provided a vitally important part of the Huns' attacks as they enabled warriors to ride at faster speeds and make more powerful attacks with weapons. It is worth noting that the Romans did not use them. Historians also often allude to the fact that the awesome reputation of these fearless mounted warriors preceded them and the subsequent fear of their enemies would have contributed to the overwhelming success of these marauders from the east.

THE WESTERN EMPIRE

Towards the end of his life, Attila's ambition to further increase his territories saw him move further west. His motive for this may have been as a result of an unlikely request from an important Roman

woman in 450 AD. Justa Grata Honoria was the
sister of Valentinian III, the Emperor of the Western
Roman Empire and, against her will, she had been
betrothed to a Roman senator at her brother's
orders. Seeking help, she wrote to Attila, sending
her engagement ring. The leader thought this to
be a proposal of marriage and demanded half of
the Western Empire as dowry. Eager to rebuff this
unwanted advance but equally keen to avoid conflict
with their dangerous enemy, the Romans tried
to appease Attila with delegation after delegation
visiting him with lavish gifts. Ultimately, Honoria
was exiled by her brother and never married Attila
and this event may have been enough to persuade
him to attack the Western Empire. His vast army
marched across the Rhine and into Gaul – which
the Romans still considered as their territory –
destroying and plundering towns and villages along
the way. However, after they arrived in Orléans, a
combined force of Romans and Visigoths turned
them back. The Huns retreated to Châlons where a
defining battle – not only to Attila's legacy but also
to that of Europe as a whole – ensued. Both sides
suffered heavy losses, but the Huns were defeated
by an allied force led by Attila's childhood friend,
Flavius Aëtius – by now a powerful general and one

of the most influential men in the Western Roman Empire – and the Visigoth King, Theodoric.

It seems that Attila was unperturbed by this loss as he then turned his attentions to Italy, destroying much of the northern part of the country and reducing Vicenza, Verona, Padua Brescia and Milan among other cities. A notable example of the destruction that his depleted army was still nevertheless capable of was the complete obliteration of Aquileia. Legend has it that Attila demanded that a castle be built on top of a hill north of the city so that he could watch it burn to the ground. Another legend tells how the survivors of attacks on this area of Italy fled to the Venetian Lagoon ultimately founding Venice upon its waters in order to defend better against future attacks. Rome was Attila's next target, but the invasion of the Italian capital never took place; some records suggest that he was persuaded to withdraw by Pope Leo I, although others report that the true reason for his decision not to was due to a lack of supplies and widespread disease among his troops.

THE HUNNIC EMPIRE COLLAPSES

Attila returned to his homeland where he began making plans for a new assault on the Eastern Roman Empire. His death only a year after his withdrawal from Italy was at great odds with the image that his aggressive reign conjures up; he died in his sleep on the last of his many wedding nights. Some accounts report that Attila drank heavily to mark the occasion and succumbed to a nosebleed while he slept, choking to death on his own blood. After his death, the Hunnic Empire collapsed in a matter of years as his sons fought over who would succeed him, apparently unable to inspire the diverse armies at their disposal. As the dialect of the Huns died with their empire, the story of Attila the Hun was left in the hands of those he persecuted and, although accounts of his great leadership survived, it is the barbarism of his tenure with which his name has become synonymous.

CALIGULA

The third of the Roman Emperors, Caligula has become a byword for cruelty and perversion. Although he started out as a noble and generous emperor – who lavished upon Rome games and great gladiatorial spectacles, as well as establishing himself as a liberal and compassionate leader – mental illness robbed him of his sanity by the end of his reign and he was loathed by his subjects who regarded him as a megalomaniac, murderer and deviant.

LITTLE BOOTS

Caligula was born Gaius Caesar in 12 AD in the army camp in Germany where his father was commander. He was brought up with the regular troops who called him 'Caligula' which means 'Little Boots' – the military boots he wore as a child were known as *caligae*. This would be the name he would be known by throughout history, despite the fact the Emperor disliked the moniker as he found it belittling.

THE CULLING OF HIS FAMILY

Caligula suffered a profoundly sad childhood where he lost all but a few of his closest family members.

He was part of the imperial hierarchy as he was the son of Tiberius' nephew, the general Germanicus, and Agrippina the Elder, granddaughter of the first Emperor Augustus. As such, his parents were objects of envy to Augustus' successor, the Emperor Tiberius, who, it is thought, had Germanicus killed. After this tragedy, Caligula lived with his mother until Tiberius' paranoia got the better of him and, fearing that Agrippina would remarry and threaten his position as leader, banished her and Caligula's brother, Nero, on charges of treason. A year later in 30 AD, Caligula's other brother, Drusus, was also imprisoned on charges of treason and it was discovered that Nero had died of starvation. The teenage Caligula managed to survive the apparent culling of his family and, a year later, was remanded into the custody of Tiberius at his imperial household on Capri. Seeing what had befallen his family, Caligula shrewdly hid all of his anger towards Tiberius and, to the amazement of many, his life was spared and he stayed on the island for six years until the Emperor's death.

The ruler observed that, 'There was never a better slave, nor a worse master than Caligula.'

The unpopular and cruel Tiberius died in March 37 AD, possibly helped by Caligula: it was said that

Tiberius fell into a coma and the court officials began to congratulate Caligula, only to see Tiberius wake up, so Caligula's chamberlain Macro smothered him with his bedclothes.

Tiberius' will named Caligula and his cousin, Tiberius Gemellus, joint heirs to his estate. In an indication of the evil that was to come, Caligula had Tiberius' will nullified on the grounds of insanity and had Gemellus killed so it was he alone who succeeded as the head of the huge and powerful Roman Empire. Initially, the twenty-four-year-old Emperor was very popular. Being the son of the beloved Germanicus stood him in good stead; people also warmed to him for the simple fact that he wasn't Tiberius. To gain the support of his subjects, he started out by recalling all those who Tiberius had exiled, burning police files and abolishing treason trials. He also gave bonuses to the army and provided entertainment for the public in the form of gladiator battles.

THE REIGN OF TERROR BEGAN

This early promise proved to be a false dawn, however, as his head was turned by the unlimited power that he wielded and he indulged in great brutality, underlined by latent paranoia. He is known to have inherited epilepsy and was seriously ill in October 37 AD: the Roman historian Suetonius suggested that this could have seriously unbalanced his mind. Modern medical experts suggest that it could have been encephalitis, which can cause symptoms similar to schizophrenia. To highlight his mental instability, Caligula soon exhausted the treasury and began a reign of terror. He indulged in reckless extravagance, putting on spectacular games, in which he sometimes appeared as a gladiator. He enjoyed prolonging punishments, an example of which came when a supervisor of games and beast-fights was flogged with chains for days on end and he was only put to death when Caligula announced that he was offended by the smell of gangrene in the man's brain. On another occasion there were not enough condemned criminals to fight the lions and tigers in the arena, so Caligula ordered that some of the innocent spectators should be dragged into the arena to replace them.

One of his most famous eccentricities was the building of a bridge made of boats for miles across the Bay of Naples, which he rode across on his favourite horse, Incitatus. Some sources say that his reason for this was to prove false a prediction made by Tiberius' astrologer, Thrasyllus, that Caligula had no more chance of becoming Emperor than of crossing the bay of Baiae on horseback. Others say it was to show his solidarity with the sea god Neptune. Other quirks included housing Incitatus in a beautiful stall made from marble and ivory with its own staff of servants, presenting the animal with a jewelled necklace and threatening to make him a senator. He also built a temple to himself and forced people to worship him as a god on an equal footing with Jupiter. He asked the actor Apelles who was greater, Caligula or Jupiter, Apelles hesitated, so Caligula had him cut to pieces. His justification was significant: 'Remember that I have the power to do anything to anyone.'

THE DEATH OF DRUSILLA

One of the more disturbing facets of Caligula's personality was that of his sexual proclivities. There were strong rumours of an unhealthy relationship with one, if not all, of his three sisters, Drusilla being his favourite. When Drusilla suddenly died in 38 AD, Caligula was devastated, he was at her side when she died and wouldn't let anyone take her body away. It is not known how she passed away; some say it was due to a fever which had taken the lives of many at the time; other, more sensational, reports suggest that she was carrying Caligula's baby but that he could not wait for the birth, so he had her disembowelled, to pluck the unborn baby from her. Whatever the cause, it is said that Caligula never recovered from the loss. Drusilla was buried with the title of Augusta – a title of great prestige, usually bestowed in life upon the wives or relatives of Roman Emperors. Caligula also had her deified and worshipped as the representation of the goddess Venus and named his only recorded daughter, Julia Drusilla, in her honour. Along with the incestuous affairs he is supposed to have had, it is also suggested that Caligula had several homosexual relationships as well as many extra-marital affairs with numerous women, including the wife of his chamberlain, Marco, before the demise of Tiberius. He also opened a brothel in his palace, where Roman matrons, their daughters and freeborn youths could be hired for money.

THE DEMISE OF CALIGULA

To recover his depleted revenues, Caligula introduced a great deal of taxation and encouraged the rich to bequeath their property to him, after which they soon died. One such unfortunate was killed and when Caligula discovered that he had

no money, he quipped: 'Oh dear! He died in vain.'
He also reneged on his promise to abolish treason
trials which returned in 39 AD. Caligula had heard
about several conspiracies against him from within
the senate and duly had those responsible brutally
executed. Though the Roman Empire was vast,
Caligula thought about extending it to take in Britain.
He assembled a large army in Boulogne but then
apparently lost interest in the project. Instead, he
got his soldiers to pick up sea shells from the shore,
to show his victory over Neptune. To lessen their
humiliation, he awarded all legionaries an extra four
gold pieces. Caligula was not an impressive sight.
He was tall and spindly and dressed in effeminate
gaudy silks, with jewellery and gold. His premature
baldness made him insanely jealous of anyone with
a good head of hair and, on a bad day, he could
order them to be shaved. He even enacted a law
which made it a capital crime for anyone to look
down from a high place as he passed by.

Upon leaving the theatre on 24 January 41 AD,
Caligula, along with his fourth wife, was assassinated.
The historian Tacitus states that they were both
stabbed to death by a number of assassins including
a colonel, whom Caligula had made a practice of
insulting. Others among the conspirators included

a man whose wife the Emperor had debauched and another whose high-pitched voice he had mocked relentlessly. He was succeeded as ruler by his bookish and until then undistinguished uncle, Claudius. After Caligula's assassination, the Senate decreed that his portraits should be dragged through the streets of Rome and thrown into the Tiber, the fate accorded to executed criminals.

IDI AMIN DADA

Even the briefest acquaintance with the life and times
of Amin Dada must surely provoke in the reader,
alongside the inevitable feelings of utter revulsion and
horror, jarring thoughts of absurdity and surrealism.
How could anyone possibly reconcile the image of
an amiable buffoon or a charming clown with the
nightmare of a Hitler-admiring,
cold-blooded slaughterer?

BUTCHER OF UGANDA

Coincidentally and highly ironically, the name 'Dada' – meaning a hobbyhorse or child's toy – was also chosen from the dictionary in 1916 to describe the Dadaists' anti-war art movement, a peaceful collaboration between the artists of several warring nations and including Germany, France and Switzerland. Using confrontational and often amusingly arresting techniques – like Marcel Duchamp's Mona Lisa sporting a moustache – artists such as Paul Klee, Sophie Täuber and Pablo Picasso challenged established ideas and beliefs, giving rise to, among others, the Surrealist movement. How ironic, then, that the 'Butcher of Uganda', bearing that same name, Dada, should have achieved notoriety and fortune by pursuing the ends of precisely the opposite camp: war in all its most hideous forms – terror, torture, mutilation, executions and massacres, revoltingly free of remorse and justified in the name of nationalism and personal destiny.

Idi Amin Dada was reportedly born in 1925 near Koboko, in the West Nile Province of today's Republic of Uganda. His parents separated soon after his birth, so he was brought up by his mother, who through subsequent relationships gave birth to a further five children – a figure that pales into insignificance compared to the 40-plus Amin would go on to father with his – at least – six wives and more than 30 mistresses. Significantly, he was a member of the Kakwa ethnic group, a small Islamic tribe that was settled in the region – his father had converted from Roman Catholicism to Islam in 1910, a fact that would prove pivotal in Amin's future political decisions. His education was basic and short-lived, paving the way, no doubt, for all the anecdotes about his bone-headed simplicity; gifted boxer, swimmer and rugby player though he was, the 6ft 4in man-mountain, according to at least one British army officer, needed to have things explained to him 'in words of one syllable'. Chillingly, however, the same officer also described him as a 'splendid type'.

AN APPETITE FOR BRUTALITY

As soon as he joined the KAR (King's African Rifles), Britain's colonial African force, in 1946, the champion pugilist was on home turf, ready to punch above and below his weight, whenever duty called. His appetite for up-close-and-personal brutality was frequently whetted, not least when he was called upon to assist in the suppression of the Mau Mau freedom fighters of Kenya, themselves no strangers to ritualistic brutality and slaughter. He rose rapidly through the ranks, reaching sergeant-major before finally being made an effendi – warrant officer – the highest rank possible for a black African serving in the British army.

As Uganda approached independence from Britain in 1962, Milton Obote, leader of the Uganda People's Congress (UPC), attained the office of Prime Minister. Obote appointed his close ally, Amin, First Lieutenant of the Ugandan army. Once again, assigned the duty of ending cattle stealing in the north, Amin perpetrated such atrocities – torture, fatal beatings and burials alive – that the British government demanded his prosecution.

Instead Obote merely reprimanded him for his 'over-zealousness' and sent him for further military training in the UK.

Having served the British army with brutal distinction, Amin was promoted to major, in 1964, and ordered to quell mutiny in the Ugandan army – nothing that a severe dose of torture, mutilation and glorious slaughter in the name of national harmony couldn't solve. His reward for blood-dripping success was further promotion to colonel.

AMIN, THE VILLAGE TYRANT

The events of the following year set Uganda on the path to economic and social ruin. The thoroughly corrupt and ruthless allies, Obote and Amin, were exposed for their involvement in smuggling gold and ivory out of the neighbouring Democratic Republic of the Congo, allegedly to raise funds for troops loyal to the murdered DRC Prime Minister Patrice Lumumba. When the funds 'mysteriously' failed to materialize, the popular President, Edward Mutebi Mutesa II, King of Buganda, also known as 'King Freddie', called for a parliamentary investigation. Stung into decisive action, Obote promoted Amin to general and made him Chief-of-Staff, had five ministers arrested, suspended the 1962 constitution and declared himself president. King Freddie fled to Britain, in 1966, when Amin's forces stormed the royal palace.

Ironically, Obote, in elevating and trusting Amin, the 'village tyrant', had sown the seeds of his own downfall. Voracious, dissolute and brazenly barbaric as he was, Amin was also shrewd enough to recognize human weakness and susceptibility. He turned the immense funds he amassed, from smuggling and from gun-running to Israeli-backed rebels in southern Sudan, to highly effective, tactical use: he kept his own troops sweet and loyal with regular bribes, not least through the weekly flights he commissioned to Stansted airport, in England, where his lackeys would stock up with forty tonnes of treats, especially abundant supplies of whisky. Despite Obote's attempts to sideline him by first putting him under house arrest and then demoting him, Amin staged a *coup d'état* on 25 January 1971, installing himself as president, whilst Obote attended a Commonwealth meeting in Singapore.

Ugandans were overjoyed at the overthrow of the corrupt Obote by Amin, a man of considerable presence, charm and stature who also had a decidedly common touch. Nevertheless, it was astonishing to note that Britain also approved of his administration. What price moral foreign policy when a former colonial power, fully aware of the sadistic proclivities of a known killer, gun-runner and smuggler stands by and welcomes his illegal seizure of power in a still emerging, independent state?

True, he was cunning enough to promise free and fair democratic elections to allay Ugandans' suspicions and fears. He also disbanded Obote's secret police and granted amnesty to political prisoners, as well as permitting the return of the body of the popular King Freddie for a state funeral, following his death in exile. However, Obote's secret police simply transmuted into Amin's State Research Bureau, while the whisky-fuelled killer squads systematically eliminated Obote's followers and other ethnic groups, leading dissidents and political foes, along with anyone foolhardy enough to investigate Amin's crimes, such as the two Americans, Nicholas Stroh and Robert Siedle, murdered for inquiring into massacres that had occurred at Mbarara barracks in Western Uganda.

His capacity for political expediency above faith and loyalty was exposed for all to see just one year after the coup, in 1972. His former close allies, Britain and Israel, stopped selling him arms with which to continue his killing sprees. The offer of help from Colonel Muammar Qaddafi of Libya no doubt reminded Amin of his Muslim roots, and he turned his unbridled rage on his ex-allies: he expelled Israeli ambassadors and military advisors and up to 80,000 Asians holding British passports, expropriating all of their property, businesses and wealth in the process. This proved to be an early turning point - Amin's ruinous spending on the armed forces at the expense of the country as a whole and the departure of the Asian community, effectively the backbone of the Ugandan economy, began to reveal to the international community the enormity of the Ugandan situation and Amin's gross mismanagement.

BRITAIN SEVERES DIPLOMATIC TIES

In June 1976, Amin allowed an Air France airliner hijacked by members of the PLO (Palestine Liberation Organisation) hoping to have freed hundreds of Palestinian political prisoners held in Israel, to land at Entebbe Airport. In total, 156 non-Jewish hostages were released, while eighty-three Jews and Israeli citizens, as well as twenty others who refused to leave, remained captive on board. Three hostages died during the Israeli rescue operation, while seven hijackers, forty-five Ugandan soldiers, and one Israeli soldier were killed. Jewish passenger Dora Bloch, hospitalized prior to the rescue operation, was subsequently murdered in reprisal. Britain severed diplomatic ties with Uganda and Uganda's international relations were critically damaged.

Nevertheless, Amin clung on to power by constantly reorganising the army, to prevent any group or individual from mounting a challenge to him, especially when he was abroad. He frequently changed routines, itineraries and even bodyguards, to keep his enemies – both real and supposed – guessing his next move. Despite his continued persecution of ethnic groups, religious denominations and major public opponents, he somehow managed to secure election to the Chair of the OAU (Organization of African Unity) in 1975, a fact which surely had major bearing on the next bewildering event: as late as 1977, African countries, no doubt anxious to continue reversing the trend of external influence and control of black African states, blocked a United Nations resolution which would have condemned Amin for his gross violation of human rights.

Amin's utter neglect of the Ugandan economy and infrastructure ultimately precipitated his downfall. The price of coffee, the country's major export, had fallen by at least sixty per cent and the USA was refusing to buy it from the regime any longer. Even the supportive Arab states baulked at subsidising a leader who not only came up short on converting Uganda to Islam but also killed fellow Muslims, among the estimated victims – up to 500,000 Ugandans – he had despatched from this world. This time Amin's diversionary tactics backfired: the failed invasion of Tanzania in 1978 triggered a successful counter-invasion. In April 1979, Amin fled to Libya, later moving to Jeddah, Saudi Arabia, then Bahrain in the early 1990s.

HIS FINAL FOURTEEN YEARS

So, how did the deposed megalomaniac King of Slaughter live out his final fourteen years? Following a blood-spattered career that saw him graduate from torture and eviscerations to single-handed executions, such as that of the Anglican Archbishop of Uganda, Janani Luwum – with a deft bullet through the mouth and one in the groin – and commissioning of massacres and mass executions, with corpses thrown into the Nile blocking up intake ducts at a nearby dam or providing abundant food for passing crocodiles, did he come to repent and see the error of his ways? Not exactly. He lived a quiet, if not modest life, given the generous subsidy, staff and accommodation he received from his hosts, in return for keeping well away from politics, until he died of multiple organ failure, in 2003. In 1989 he did try to stage a comeback in Uganda, but decided against entering the country when he was warned he would have to answer for his sins.

To return to our opening theme: many of the artists, poets, dramatists and writers in the seven-year Dada period felt impelled to decontaminate early 20th century European art in all its forms and did their best to cleanse it with their healing mockery, against the backdrop of a conflict that threatened to destroy creativity and life itself. For his part, the mocking Idi Amin Dada seized control of Uganda – the Pearl of Africa, according to Winston Churchill, in his 1908 book *My African Journey* – and did his absolute worst during his seven years of terror to obliterate its beauty, its culture and its people. We witnessed his monstrous pursuit of power, glory, wealth and fame in a continent that has had most frequently to endure the worst consequences of power vacuums, corruption and post-colonial dictatorships.

IVAN THE TERRIBLE

Ivan IV or Ivan Grozny is much better known as Ivan the Terrible due to his brutal regime as Tsar of Russia. 'Terrible' is actually something of a mistranslation, as its true meaning in the context it was given means 'awe-inspiring', although his vicious actions as ruler make this misnomer more than justified.

OBSESSION WITH RELIGION AND TORTURE

The oldest son of Vasilij III, Ivan was only three years old when his father died in 1533; his mother, Elena Glinskaya, was elected regent until Ivan was deemed mature enough to assume power, but after just five years she was poisoned leaving the eight-year-old Ivan orphaned. The boyars – nobles – who, historians believe, were behind the murder of his mother seized power but despite his fears that he would be the next to be murdered and the abuse of the boyars, Ivan lived. He was largely ignored, suffered ill health and his education was neglected by his supposed guardians. He believed though that he had been spared by God and found salvation in the Old Testament, becoming both devoutly religious and obsessed with its blood-and-thunder contents. In stark contrast, his other obsession in his early years was with torture and he enjoyed throwing small animals like cats and dogs from great heights and pulling feathers off birds. At the age of thirteen, Ivan demanded the execution of one of the boyars who was consequently torn to pieces by hunting dogs at his command. He assumed power at the age of seventeen in 1547, insisting on being Russia's first Tsar as opposed to Grand Duke of Moscow.

In spite of the violent manner in which one of his enemies had been dispatched four years previously, his reign began peacefully. Along with his happy marriage to Anastasia Romanov, who seemed to have a grounding effect on him, he introduced several reforms and initiated trade links with England. In 1552, Ivan successfully defeated the Tartar Mongols to gain the city of Kazan. To celebrate this victory, St Basil's Cathedral was constructed in Red Square. Legend has it that Ivan had the architect who designed the cathedral, Postnik Yakovlev, blinded, lest he create another such building that could rival it, although Yakovlev was the creative force behind two later constructions in Kazan. His successes continued when, two years after his victory in Kazan, he seized Astrakhan on the Caspian Sea. It seemed that the misery he had endured during his childhood was a distant memory, but his happiness was not to last.

REVENEGE AND VIOLENCE

In 1560, Anastasia suddenly died; Ivan was devastated and the rage that his late wife's calming influence had kept at bay returned with dire consequences for his once-favoured courtiers. Convinced that, like his mother, she had been poisoned, he blamed them for her death and set about getting his revenge. At his insistence, entire families were wiped out. As well as the tragic loss of his wife, his health declined due to a bone disease that caused the vertebrae that formed his spine to fuse together. To remedy this, Ivan took mercury – and became addicted to it – which made him volatile and fed his violent urges.

In what seemed to be a manipulative ploy to gain more power, Ivan threatened to abdicate in 1565. When the clergy begged him to reconsider, he stipulated that he would only return to power if he could purge the nation without any interference. His plan worked and he now had total control over Russia and could carry out what he perceived to be God's will. He founded a 6,000-strong secret police force known as the oprichniki which arrested, tortured, raped and executed up to 10,000 victims. This force reported directly to Ivan and were used to remove anybody he perceived as a threat. Torture sessions were a daily event in the 'monastery' that Ivan and three hundred of the oprichniki lived in. The bloodthirsty leader insisted on Biblical punishments, apparently trying to justify his cruelty to himself. He was an avid spectator and also meted out the agony himself on occasion, taking pleasure in doing so. With his fearsome reputation preceding him, few challenged his authority although when the head of the Russian Orthodox Church pleaded with Ivan to relent, he was arrested, charged with sorcery and murdered.

In 1569, Ivan and his oprichniki embarked on a five-week assault on the city of Novgorod. After hearing rumours that senior figures were plotting to side with Poland, the madman led the attack which saw a reported 15,000 innocent citizens tortured and mutilated for simply living in the place he suspected of treason. He took a sadistic delight in watching the bloodshed and returned home triumphant and satisfied. However, even those living in Moscow were not safe from his impulsive and furious temper and he soon established trials to weed out those he suspected of sympathising with the people of

Novgorod. Those who were found guilty were executed in Red Square with 300 killed on one day. One victim was suspended by his feet while soldiers hacked off body parts, while others succumbed to the gallows and a massive cauldron in the bloodbath that Ivan demanded.

MENTAL DECLINE AND SELF PUNISHMENT

In 1581, Ivan accidentally killed his own son and heir, Ivan Ivanovich, in a fit of rage. The Tsar, it was said, was unhappy with the way his pregnant daughter-in-law was dressed and beat her for not changing into something he deemed more appropriate. His son took issue over this and found himself on the receiving end of Ivan's pointed staff. The head wound inflicted by the blow became infected and he died a few days later. Ivan was devastated by what he had done and, according to one account, hit his own head repeatedly against the floor. He spent the remaining four years of his life in mourning and self-punishment. His mental decline seemed to gather pace and he made several desperate pleas to Queen Elizabeth I of England for asylum. Ivan had killed countless people himself and it seems that the death of a loved one at his own hands caused him to finally be repentant for the desolation he had caused. He made lists of all the victims he could remember killing and sent them to monasteries for prayers; one listed 3,148 while another accounted for 3,750. In a final desperate attempt to gain redemption, Ivan had himself rechristened as a monk and after he died playing chess in 1584, he was interred in his monk's habit. His reign of terror was over but the consequences of it left Russia in a bleak condition.

JOSEF STALIN

*Remembered as one of the most brutal and murderous
dictators in history, Josef Stalin remained supreme
leader of the Soviet Union for over a quarter of a
century, during which time he was responsible for
the deaths of tens of millions of people. His series of
Five Year Plans caused wide-spread famine, Ethnic
deportation removed millions of unwanted races from
his country and the Great Purge resulted in the murders
of opponents within his government and consolidated
his absolute power.*

BORN IOSEF DZHUGASHVILI

According to his original birth certificate, Iosef
Dzhugashvili was born 6 December 1878, in Gori,
Georgia, though Stalin had his records and those
of his family altered to confuse those trying to
investigate him. These included his official birthday,
which was changed to 18 December 1879. The
only survivor of four children born in four years,
the young Stalin grew up sickly and in poverty.
His mother, a peasant, worshipped him but his
father, a cobbler, was frequently drunk and beat

him regularly. The hero worship he received from his mother deteriorated over the years to the point where they didn't speak. His mother is quoted as saying that it was a pity that he didn't become a priest and Stalin would often refer to her as an old whore in the presence of colleagues. The antipathy towards his mother seemed to exist because she knew the real Stalin and wasn't taken in by all of his political spin and when she died, having only visited her once in the last forty years of her life, he didn't even attend her funeral.

The ten-year-old Stalin was sent to a church school and he later won a scholarship to study at a seminary, where it is thought that he discovered Marxism. He only lasted three years there as he had no interest in the teachings and was ultimately expelled for not turning up to his exams – although he would later claim that it was because he was discovered reading banned Communist material and had formed a Socialist circle; thirty years after attending the seminary, his anti-church stance would see him ordering the destruction of churches and the removal of all religious icons that hung on the walls of every Orthodox household. Stalin museums became the new place of worship and his image replaced icons of the Orthodox Church.

After leaving the seminary, Stalin had several jobs but devoted most of his time to the Russian Social Democrat Party which he joined in 1903. The young revolutionary wanted an end to the 300 year rule of the Romanovs and as a member of the party organized strikes and demonstrations, spread propaganda and raised money by robbing banks. In 1906, he married his first wife, Ekaterina Svanidze, a tailor. Their marriage was cut short the following year, however, when she died of typhus, which is thought to have been exacerbated by the fact that all of Stalin's money went to his party and not on her care. At her funeral, he is said to have stated that with her died any human feeling in him. In their brief union they had a son, Yakov, who, after the death of his mother, was raised by his aunt as he and Stalin never got on.

MAN OF STEEL

Marked by the Tsar's secret police as a trouble maker, Stalin spent almost a decade being arrested, imprisoned or exiled from the country. It was during his time in prison that, feeling it would be good for his image, he changed his surname to Stalin, meaning 'man of steel'. After Tsar Nikolas was overthrown, Alexander Karensky, the new

Prime Minister, allowed all of the political prisoners to come home. Stalin retuned to St. Petersburg and worked on Pravda, a socialist political newspaper.

Although not one of the main players in the Bolshevik seizure of power in 1917, he still rose through the ranks of the party despite Lenin's mistrust of him. Stalin became General Secretary in 1922, a position that allowed him to build up a support base and gave him control over appointments to government positions, all of whom would be carefully chosen allies. Lenin, well aware of Stalin's brutal character, was also wary of how much power the post of General Secretary afforded him. Lenin distanced himself from Stalin and, following semi-retirement after a stroke, recommended in his testimony that Stalin be removed from central soviet power. Through the forging of various alliances, notably with Lev Kamenev and Grigory Zinoviev, Stalin managed to make sure that the testimony was never made public and thus Lenin's warnings were never heeded. Lenin died of a heart attack on 21 January 1924 and Stalin, using his power as General Secretary, consolidated his power base and gradually rid himself of his opponents on his way to becoming leader of the Soviet Republic.

In 1927, the first of Stalin's 'Five Year Plans' was

put into action. This started off with the massive industrialisation of the Soviet Union. His forced collectivisation of agriculture cost millions of lives, while his programme of rapid industrialisation achieved huge increases in Soviet productivity and economic growth but at great cost. Food wasn't being supplied in the scale that was needed and peasants' smallholdings were turned into state-controlled farms. This collectivisation was a disaster; five million people died of starvation as a direct result and, when the estimates weren't met, Stalin had the people he blamed for the underachievement executed, put into the gulag system of slave labour camps or deported.

To truly consolidate his power, Stalin instigated the Great Terror, during which he purged the party of 'enemies of the people', resulting in the execution and exile of thousands. Colleagues were removed from office; some simply lost their jobs but others were moved to the labour camps or put on trial for treason. Stalin then moved on to members of the military; a large-scale purge of the Red Army followed, with high ranking officers shot or put on trial. His next target was immigrants. It is estimated that 350,000 people from countries including Poland, Germany and America were arrested, two thirds of whom were thought to have been executed.

At the beginning of the 1930s Stalin's personal life suffered another, very public blow. His second wife was Nadezhda, whom he married in 1917 after bonding over their mutual love of Communism. Very little was heard of their private life; they had two children, Wasilly and Svetlana, during fifteen years of marriage but Nadezhda kept out of her husband's limelight. While she was studying to become an engineer, students approached her and told her about the starvation and poverty facing their villages. She later spoke to her husband about this issue and the students were never seen again. Rows broke out as Stalin didn't like his wife interfering in his business or having a different opinion to his. After a heated row between the two at a dinner to celebrate the 15th anniversary of the Bolshevik revolution, Nadezhda dramatically left the room. A shot rang out after Stalin had left to follow her and, to this day, no-one knows whether Stalin shot her or she killed herself. The official announcement was that the great leader had lost his wife to appendicitis.

The 1930s was a decade that saw Stalin's paranoia worsen to the point where anyone displaying anything other than absolute loyalty would be murdered. Colleagues who had once been close to him, including Lev Kamenev and Grigory Zinoviev who were instrumental in getting Stalin to the top, were killed. Sergei Kirov, his protégé who he treated as a son, was assassinated after he had opposed one of Stalin's policies the same fate befell Leon Trotsky who was famously killed by a Soviet agent with an ice pick while in exile in Mexico. By the end of the decade, Russia was at war and Stalin had a new enemy; Adolf Hitler. After Germany reneged on a treaty by invading a Soviet area and then advanced on Moscow, Stalin forged a new alliance with the Allies who agreed to provide assistance and aid. By the end of the war, Hitler's Germany had just under two million soldiers fighting against a Red army of six million in the east and had a force of just one million in battle against four million allied fighters in the west. In 1945, the war was won by the Allies and Stalin was hailed as a hero; Time magazine twice voted him 'Man of the Year' during the war and there were rumours that he was considered among nominees for the Nobel Peace Prize. The Soviet losses, however, amounted to an estimated thirty-five million soldiers and twenty million civilians or one in every four people.

Eventually, Stalin once again became paranoid about an attack from the west and pre-empted such an attack by setting up a 'buffer zone' comprised of friendly subservient states in which he installed Communist governments. The Iron Curtain, a name made famous by Winston Churchill, was interpreted by the Western powers as Stalin trying to impose communism on the whole of Europe. This prompted the North Atlantic Treaty Organisation, NATO, to be set up and thus commenced the period now known as the Cold War.

Josef Stalin died from a stroke on 5 March 1953. Most attributed his death to natural causes, but there are some who argue that he was poisoned with warfarin, a rat poison which inhibits the coagulation of the blood and is known to cause haemorrhagic strokes. Despite the countless millions of dead, the man who had himself celebrated as the father of the Soviet Union and the one who made Russia into a super power once said, 'One death is a tragedy; one million deaths is a statistic'. This disdain for human life would mark Stalin out as one of the most evil men in the history of world politics.

POL POT

Described by one of his brothers as a gentle and kind child, Pol Pot would grow up to oversee one of the worst genocides of the twentitth century. His obsession with the Maoist ideology of a 'year zero' society made him responsible for the deaths of more than a million people.

Pol Pot was born Saloth Sar on 19 May 1925 in the Kompong Thom province of Cambodia into a family of affluent farmers. He was the second son of eight children and enjoyed a happy and privileged childhood. As a young boy, he was sent to Phnom Penh to experience the capital and further his education; with his family's connection with the royal family, he was able to experience regal life first hand. Through his education he learned how majestic and important ancient Cambodia had been and how it had been steadily destroyed by foreign invaders; he became disillusioned with the royal family after seeing them as mere puppets of the French rulers and would one day vow to restore Cambodia to its former greatness. He spent a year being taught the fundamentals of Buddhism but also went to a French Catholic school where he was taught by nuns and these conflicting cultures would have a huge impact on the young, idealistic Saloth.

Despite not being a natural academic, Saloth won a scholarship in 1949 and went to study radio electronics in Paris. It was during this time that he became interested in politics and was lured by the Communist ideology. He would spend hours debating with his fellow nationals about how to free Cambodia from its colonialist shackles; the answer to which seemed to lie in Karl Marx's theories.

SEEDS OF KHMER ROUGE

In 1951, he joined a secret branch of the French Communist party known as the Cercle Marxiste – the Marxist Circle. In joining this group, he would make acquaintances with Ieng Sary, Khieu Samphan, Khieu Ponnary and Song Sen – the men who would ultimately join him to become the leaders of the Khmer Rouge. This group, which had originally been the Khmer Students' Association, transformed into a nationalist, left-wing group which challenged the ideas of the Sihanouk government. In a leaflet entitled *Monarchy or Democracy*, he wrote, '[The monarchy] is a vile pustule living on the blood and sweat of the peasants. Only the National Assembly and democratic rights give the Cambodian people some breathing space...

The democracy which will replace the monarchy is a matchless institution, pure as a diamond.'

Saloth ultimately lost his scholarship due to under-achievement and was required to return to Cambodia. Back at home in 1956, he got a job teaching history and French literature at a private school where he was respected and well liked. In the same year, he married Khieu Ponnary, with whom he was at school. He spent most of his spare time, however, working for the Kampuchean People's Revolutionary Party, or the Khmer Rouge as it was later named, the Cambodian unit of the reorganized Indo-Chinese Communist party. It was about this time that Saloth changed his name to Pol Pot, which came from the French Politique Potentielle, or potential politics which was an extreme form of Communism that he believed fervently in. As a ruthlessly determined and dedicated revolutionary, Saloth rose through the ranks and was first elected to the number three position in the party's central committee, a position where he could exert a considerable amount of power and build up a base of supporters.

Then, in 1962, he was chosen as leader and was given the title 'Brother number one'. In the next year, Prince Sihanouk's secret police stepped up their efforts to round up all of those who were thought to be Communists. Saloth was forced to flee to the Vietnamese jungle as his name was published among those suspected of leftist leanings. Living among the hill tribes there, he changed his ideas about the revolution and saw simple village life as Communism in its purest form and began to convert the tribes people into revolutionaries.

During the Vietnam War, the North Vietnamese troops were positioned near to where Pol Pot was in hiding. They took him under their wing and this eventually led to a life-changing trip to Beijing. Seeing how Mao's Chinese government's Cultural Revolution controlled the country, Pol Pot returned home with the idea of bringing Cambodia up to the 'year zero' ideology – a utopian concept of a peasant economy without any class or money struggles. From there he started to plan an extreme social experiment: to eliminate the modern world, rid Cambodia of its 'evil' cities and move their residents to the countryside where he would create an agrarian society.

In 1970, the National Assembly voted Sihanouk out as head of state. The North Vietnamese offered their resources to Pol Pot for his insurgency against the Cambodian government. Backed by Sihanouk, who pleaded with the Cambodian people to revolt, the people started to distrust the government and the U.S which was their supposed ally and moved towards Pol Pot's party. Before long, the Khmer Rouge and their army had taken the capital and Pol Pot became the country's ruler.

YEAR ZERO

The Khmer Rouge started its reign by evacuating the citizens of Phnom Penh to the countryside to begin the realisation of its 'year zero' utopia. These urban dwellers were forced to work on collective farms and slave labour projects and it is estimated that through his experiments to 'cleanse' the country, he was responsible for the deaths of somewhere between 1.7 and three million people. One of the main policies was social engineering, including agricultural reform, which resulted in a widespread famine. The insistence on self-sufficiency and a ban on the supply of medicine resulted in the deaths of thousands through treatable diseases such as malaria. Eventually the country fell into depression and repression. Vietnam eventually overthrew Pol Pot and the Khmer Rouge in 1979. Pol Pot and various members of the Khmer Rouge fled and operated from the border region of Cambodia and Thailand where they clung to power. Pol Pot eventually retired as head of the Khumer Rouge at the end of the 1980s.

After a power struggle within the Khmer Rouge in July 1997, Pol Pot was arrested by his former colleagues and charged with treason. After a sentence of life under house arrest was passed by a 'people's tribunal', he gave an interview where he boldly stated: 'My conscience is clear'. As the combined effects of the slave labour, malnutrition, poor medical care and executions initiated by him resulted in the deaths of over twenty per cent of the population, this statement was not well received.

THE FINAL ESCAPE

Pol Pot died in 1998. It has not been proven as to whether he died of natural causes, committed suicide or was murdered. Despite his death heralding a new era for Cambodia, there are some survivors of his brutal regime who would have preferred to see him brought to trial for the atrocities that he committed. His legacy remains to this day with Cambodia being one of the world's poorest countries; burdened with decades of conflict, unexploded mines continue to kill and maim its inhabitants, around seventy per cent of the population are still working in subsistence farming and only now are the men responsible for the genocide being brought to trial.

SADDAM HUSSEIN

From the start of his despotic reign as president of Iraq in 1979 to his execution in 2006, the public life of Saddam Hussein will be indelibly imprinted on people's minds due to the invasions, wars and the countless deaths that he was responsible for in his two decades of power.

A date of birth may not seem that significant to some, but even this was subject to Saddam's notorious spin-doctoring. There is some debate as to when he was actually born; his official birthday, which is also a national holiday in Iraq, is 28 April, and the official year, 1937. However, as Saddam was born in an exceptionally poor area of Iraq at a time where the process of registering of births, marriages and deaths was rather primitive, the exact date is all but unknown. It was customary for all children from provincial parts of the country to be registered as being born on 1 July; the real debate, however, is the year in which he was born. It is thought that Saddam could be a few years younger than he proclaimed and took his official birth date from a friend of his, who came from a rich family and therefore had a birth certificate; it is also speculated that he chose 1937 as it would make him look older and wiser in the eyes of his people during his rise to the top, and because it was the same year as his wife's birth – marrying an older woman was frowned upon in Arab society.

THE ONE WHO CONFRONTS

Saddam, whose name means 'the one who confronts', grew up in the impoverished village of Al-Ouja, lying on the bend of the Tigris River on the outskirts of the town of Tikrit, Iraq. It had no electricity or running water and had become a haven for bandits who would steal from the boats bringing supplies to the major towns. Saddam was born in a mud hut which was owned by his uncle, a Nazi sympathizer, and it was this man, Khairallah Talfah, who would provide a huge source of inspiration to the young Saddam. He never knew his father as he is thought to have left his mother before Saddam was born. Unable to support him, his mother sent him to live with his uncle until the age of three. Saddam then returned home after his mother had remarried and sent for him. He suffered beatings from his stepfather, who was known as Hassan the

Liar and, rather than being sent to school, Saddam was put to work around the house and forced to steal livestock and food from local farms. This brutal upbringing would convince him that the world was an unrelentingly harsh place and he eventually ran away to live with his uncle. Here he enjoyed a much better quality of life and was enrolled in a school in Baghdad. As he was illiterate and ill-educated, Saddam suffered bullying and to protect himself, bought an iron bar with him which he would heat up and stab animals with to show his power over life. As he was a bright child and a fast learner, he managed to graduate and went to Baghdad to further his education. Iraq was a hive of political activity in the 1950s as the British had withdrawn from the area after the end of the World War Two and there was a feeling that Iraq could finally free itself from the shackles of colonialist control enforced after World War One. This nationalistic feeling, coupled with Khairallah's vehement anti-British, pro-Nazi views, prompted Saddam to join the Baath Party, an Arab nationalist organisation.

RETURN OF A QUIET, MODEST MAN

After various coups and the end of the British-backed monarchy in Iraq, the Baath Party took its place once more as the country's leading party. After a failed attempt on the previous president's life, which had forced him to flee the country, and a brief spell in prison due to his participation in an attempted coup d'etat, Saddam returned to the free world, married to his cousin, Sajida, and ready to work his way to the top. Prior to his incarceration, Saddam had been given the title of Deputy Secretary General and now back in active government, he bided his time and presented himself as a quiet and modest man who would lay down his life for the present leader, the ailing President Ahmed Hassan Bakr. Gradually, he made sure that the army was subordinate to the government, thus ensuring the protection of the party and making sure that any attempt to overthrow the Baath party would end in failure.

As the power behind the president, Saddam brought about much change in Iraq. Through the seizure of control over oil, he boosted the economy and set about improving Iraq's infrastructure with the development of industry and the building of new roads and, in a nod to his birthplace, nearly all areas in Iraq now had electricity. He also implemented plans to make life better for the people; these included a campaign to make education free, including an anti-illiteracy campaign; hospitalisation was made free, money was given to the families of soldiers, farming was subsidized and the unskilled were trained. These gifts to the nation made Saddam hugely popular and he was credited with the rapid growth of Iraq's development.

In 1979, after forcing the resignation of President Bakr, Saddam took his place as leader. Fearing that few could be trusted, the most important positions in Saddam's government went to members of his own family and very close friends and to further strengthen his position, one of his first acts was to put to death many of his political rivals and after this, there was no stopping him.

CULT OF SADDAM

Many have attributed Saddam's success to loyalty through terror; even as deputy, he had any enemies of the regime executed and his revolutionary tribunals gave the death penalty to hundreds of victims on phoney charges. In the early days of his rule, much like Josef Stalin, a man he looked up to, Saddam set about creating an image for his people to worship; his portraits adorned every house and street, showing the President as a father figure, military leader as well as a humble, traditional

Iraqi. He also had huge statues of himself erected and great monuments, bordering on the religious, dedicated to him.

Behind this façade, Saddam also matched Stalin in his ruthlessness and sheer brutality. One of the few constants during his time in power was Saddam's persecution of the Kurdish people. In the early 1980s, as part of the anti-Kurdish policies the government had implemented, 8,000 men from the Kurdish Barzani tribe were arrested and supposedly deported to Southern Iraq, although no trace of them was ever found. His genocidal crusade against this race continued during the Al-Anfal campaign in 1988 which resulted in huge death tolls. Designed to depopulate the Kurdish areas in the north of the country, the campaign was responsible for the deaths of over 180,000 people; many were killed but the majority were left to starve as their villages were razed to the ground. In the same year, under the command of General Ali Hassan al-Majid, 5,000 people were killed through the use of chemical weaponry in an attack on the Kurdish village of Hallabja; this attack earned the cruel General the nickname 'Chemical Ali'. Saddam's torture of the Kurds continued in the aftermath of the Gulf War where uprisings by the Kurds in the north, as well as Shias in the south were suppressed and once again, villages were razed, and thousands of their inhabitants killed. This contempt for human life was the norm throughout his dictatorship.

THE FIGHT FOR OIL

One of his other constants was his desire to have control over more oil supplies. Seeing the opportunity for glory in 1980, Saddam instigated an attack on Iran in order to capture the Shatt al Arab waterway, which leads to the Gulf. A few years into the campaign and Iraq was on the defensive; Saddam asked for advice from his ministers and it was suggested that he temporarily step down to promote peace talks. Saddam took this advice on board but a few weeks later Dr Riyadh Ibrahim, the health secretary who had suggested the plan, was sacked. Speaking publically about it later, he said that he was lucky to escape with his life; his dismembered remains were sent to his wife shortly afterwards. The Iranian army eventually proved to be a much stronger opponent than Saddam had realized, and only after eight years of fighting, hundreds of thousands injured and a suspected one million people dead, did he agree to a cease-fire.

Ten years later Saddam's greed concerning oil

would once again blind his common sense as he ordered an attack on Kuwait. The US had given billions of dollars to Iraq during the Iraq-Iran war and had also donated a substantial amount to Saddam to prevent him from forming an alliance with the Soviet Union. Thinking that he could count on American aid once more, Saddam complained to the US that Kuwait had been stealing from Iraqi oil wells on the disputed border between the two countries. Saddam sent his troops to this border as a threat and, after relations between the US and Iraq deteriorated, he agreed a deal with Mikhail Gorbachev that the Soviet Union would provide arms and aid to the Iraqi cause. Iraq duly invaded and captured Kuwait, and in doing so, broke its treaty with the US which, backed by the United Nations, drove the Iraqi troops from Kuwait in 1991 in what was known as Operation Desert Storm. After the invasion of Iraq, Saddam had hundreds of Kuwaiti civilians rounded up, tortured and then brought back to Iraq as hostages. To show anger at the situation, hundreds of oil wells were set alight, thus polluting huge areas of the Gulf.

THE BEGINNING OF THE END

In 1991, following the end of the crisis in Kuwait,

the United Nations demanded that Iraq destroy its weapons of mass destruction and consent to have UN inspectors monitor the disarmament; by 1996, the UN was convinced that Iraq was hiding information about biological and chemical weaponry and, after this, Iraq stopped cooperating. Two years later, British and American troops, as part of Operation Desert Fox, started bombing Iraqi command centres, airfields and missile factories and these airstrikes continued on for years.

Soon after becoming President of the USA in 2001, in his state of the union address, George W Bush labelled Iraq, Iran and North Korea as 'the axis of evil' and in March 2003, as part of his war on terrorism and with the full support of British Prime Minister Tony Blair, launched an invasion of Iraq. The government of Iraq and its military collapsed within three weeks of the invasion, but Saddam was nowhere to be found. After a tip-off from an intelligence source, US troops found Saddam hiding in an underground bolt hole on a farm near Tikrit. He was taken to a US prison base in Baghdad before he was officially handed over to the interim Iraqi government where he was put on trial for crimes against humanity. On 5 November 2006, he was found guilty and sentenced to death by hanging, which took place on 30 December of the same year.

During his time as President of Iraq, Saddam divided opinion; some saw him as a great leader, trying to restore Iraq to its former glory; others viewed him as a brutal despot whose vicious dictatorship threatened the safety of the whole of the Gulf region. He was responsible for the deaths of millions of people; whole communities, revolutionaries and fellow politicians were destroyed so that Saddam could remain at the height of his power. Upon his capture, people throughout the world rejoiced and the pulling down of his statues in Iraq will be one of the enduring images of this generation.

TOMAS DE TORQUEMADA

One of his contemporaries described Tomas de Torquemada as 'the hammer of heretics, the light of Spain, the saviour of his country, the honour of his order', however, with his penchant for book burning, twisted vision of a 'pure-blooded' Spain and his attempted eradication of the Jews, it could be argued that he was the Hitler of his time. His legacy is one of zealous fanaticism, single-minded dedication to his faith and to the attempted obliteration of all those he believed to threaten it.

Through the persecution of non-conformists, he was responsible for the deaths of thousands, most of whom were burned at the stake. Among his victims were Jews, Moors, Protestants, Freemasons, criminals and people accused of sorcery, including priests within the Catholic Church.

Born in 1420 in Valladolid, Spain, Tomas de Torquemada was the nephew of a noted theologian and Cardinal and, as a young man, entered into Holy Orders at a Dominican friary. He was later appointed prior at the Monastery of Santa Cruz at

Segovia, a position he held for twenty-two years and it was during this time that he was chosen by Queen Isabella as her confessor. This relationship would later see the xenophobic Torquemada rise to a position of great influence in the heart of the monarchy.

THE SPANISH INQUISITION

In 1478, the Catholic Monarchs Isabella I of Castile and Ferdinand II of Aragon were granted permission by the Pope to set up the Tribunal of the Holy Office of the Inquisition or, as it is more commonly known today, The Spanish Inquisition. Under the control of the monarchy, rather than the Pope, the reigning couple were allowed to appoint their own inquisitors, whose chief responsibility it was to protect Catholicism, which was at the very the core of Spanish society at the time.

Fundamental to the protection of Christianity in Spain was monitoring the conversos – Jews and Moorish Muslims who, due to persecution, had been forced to convert to Christianity. The Catholics believed their faith to be under threat from these pseudo-converts and many suspected that they were continuing to practise their own true faith. It was even suggested that they were holding secret ceremonies which mocked the Catholic Church, thus making them guilty of blasphemy. As members of the Church despaired at the lack of understanding of the Christian mass from their own congregation, there was the overriding worry that the conversos would attempt to convert Catholics to Judaism or Islam.

The animosity towards the Moors had been present for the best part of 800 years; in the early eighth century, most of the Iberian Peninsula, other than the north west, was under the control of the Moors – had the Muslim leaders controlled all of land, modern-day Spain may have looked very different, but in 718 AD, a band of Christians secured their first victory over the Moors, thus starting years of warfare to reclaim Spain. The hostility towards the Jews, however, came because they were a race of powerful businessmen; in particular, they were money lenders. Successive councils of the Christian Church forbade the lending of money for profit, condemning the usurers to hell – as this didn't apply to the Jews, they suffered massive unpopularity as they became wealthy by lending money with interest.

THE GRAND INQUISITOR

The early days of the Inquisition were considered a period of failure, as it was felt that the Inquisitors had not achieved their main task of protecting the Church from those perceived as heretics. In 1483 Torquemada was bestowed with the title of Grand Inquisitor. He had been an assistant inquisitor prior to this but the title gave him supreme power over all of the tribunal members throughout Spain. On receiving the title, Torquemada got to work immediately and a council of inquisitors was created, the main purpose of which was to help with the hearing of appeals.

It was awaiting these appeals where the worst of the Spanish Inquisition's heinous acts were committed; even before the prisoners were tortured, the guards were encouraged to whip anyone who spoke. Outside the prisons, the Inquisitors, under the fierce authority of the cruel Torquemada, visited every district in Spain to weed out any enemies of the desired status quo. Torquemada is thought to have instigated a series of non-Christian book-burning events throughout the nation and tall tales of evil Jews kidnapping Christian children were propagated. This all established a state of suspicion, paranoia and fear where few could be trusted. Anyone could be taken at any time and subjected to questioning and torture from as little as an anonymous tip-off. The minimum age of those who were accountable to the inquisition was twelve years for girls and fourteen for boys. Once the arrest order had been made, the condemned would be taken by armed guard, bound and gagged and locked up in a dark, inquisitorial torture chamber. The prisoners were given the opportunity to confess before any torture began, but the captives were often oblivious as to why they had been arrested, therefore finding it impossible to defend themselves. The torture was many and varied; many of those who resisted arrest had a metal implement inserted into their mouths which, by using a small crank, opened up to such an extent that the victim's teeth and jaw would invariably break. Another favourite of the master torturer was the 'Inquisition Chair', a large wooden seat covered in metal spikes where a wooden board would be tightened over the victim's thighs and shins and a belt could be tightened round the chest to inflict varying degrees of concentrated agony. The torturers also used branding while in the stocks, subjection to the pulley device and near-drowning to extract confessions. The accused weren't allowed any legal representation and, after days, months or sometimes years of torture, had to take an oath before they stood before the jury – refusal to take this oath resulted in immediate incarceration and further torture.

PUBLIC BURNINGS AND PAPAL WARNINGS

The punishment for those found guilty of heresy was the *auto da fé* – literally 'act of faith' – a public ceremony in which the judgement from the authorities would be read out. This usually ended in the victim being burned at the stake; the spectacle was very popular with devout Catholics who flocked to watch in the great public squares where the events took place. It also served as a warning what woe betide those who were disloyal to the Catholic faith.

As his hateful orders were carried out, an increasingly ruthless Torquemada finally invoked the wrath of the Pope in Rome, but as it was the monarchy and not the Pope in charge of the inquisition, the papal warnings were ignored. Finally, no doubt with the words of Torquemada ringing in their ears, the King and Queen decided that Spain must be rid of all non-Christians and, as the Inquisition had no jurisdiction over the Jews, an order was put out expelling them from the country in 1492. According to legend, this order provoked a number of Jewish families to attempt to bribe the King, offering 30,000 ducats to take back the expulsion order. This prompted Torquemada to challenge the King's integrity by likening him to

Judas Iscariot. He appeared before him bearing a crucifix aloft, and exclaimed: 'Judas Iscariot sold Christ for thirty pieces of silver; Your Highness is about to sell him for 30,000 ducats. Here He is; take Him and sell Him.' The King weakened in the presence of the evangelical friar and the order for the expulsion of the Jews continued. This proved to be of great benefit to the countries to which they went, though that was not part of the Spanish plan. In the same year, the King and Queen drove the Moors out of their last foothold in Spain, the kingdom of Granada, so the Inquisition under Torquemada then had a completely free hand to impose its brand of Christianity on the whole country.

Torquemada continued as Grand Inquisitor until his death in 1498 at Ávila, Spain. He left behind a name that has become synonymous with cruelty and attempted genocide. He is remembered as a man who was loathed by his nation and was responsible for the torture of innocents and the deaths of between 2,000 and 6,000 people. Somewhat ironically, given his evil obsession with 'pure-bloods', some historians have argued that he actually descended from a converso, one of those who, in his view, most threatened his faith and purity of his country.

VLAD TEPES

Nearly half a century before Bram Stoker used him as inspiration for the 1897 novel Dracula, Vlad Tepes was notorious throughout Europe for his cruelty and rabid resolve for revenge upon the people who murdered his father and brother. Over the course of almost three decades, Vlad would cement his place in the history books as an indiscriminate killer with a lust for blood that overshadowed even that of Stoker's titular terror, and was responsible for the deaths of between 40,000 and 100,000 people.

Vlad the Impaler, the moniker by which he would later be known, was born into a noble family in Sighisoara, Transylvania in 1431. His father, Vlad II, was a revered military governor and a respected member of the Order of the Dragon, a secret fraternity for selected nobility, created to defend Christian Europe against the Ottoman Empire – Vlad III was sworn into the order at the age of five. It was this secret society where his father adopted the name Dracul. From the Latin *draco*, Dracul means 'dragon'; it can also translated as 'devil'. Vlad

III added *ula* meaning 'son of'. After his father, Vlad II, took over the throne of Wallachia through the assassination of the previous incumbent, his family took up residence at the palace of Tirgoviste and enjoyed a very lavish lifestyle. A few years later, Vlad II betrayed the Order by forming an alliance with the Turks in return for retaining his position on the throne of Wallachia, even going as far as handing over his two younger sons, Vlad III and Radu the Handsome, as insurance against any future uprisings.

During his time as Sultan Murad's hostage, Vlad became increasingly hateful towards the Ottoman Turks. His brother Radu toed the line and became friends with the Sultan's son, Mehmet; he converted to Islam and was rewarded by becoming commander of the Janissary. Vlad, however, was insubordinate and was frequently beaten for his abuse towards his teachers. He was eventually sent away to be educated in the teachings of the Quran as well as Turkish language and literature and warfare.

BLOODY RETRIBUTION

In 1448, at the age of seventeen, Vlad Dracula became Vlad III, viovode of Wallachia, after his father and elder brother Mircea were killed in battle by John Hunyadi, a relative who was opposed to Vlad Dracul's alliance with the Turks. The news that his father had been assassinated and that his brother had been buried alive, set the teenaged Vlad on the path of retribution. His original tenure as *viovode*, or leader, of Wallachia was short lived as he was deposed by Hunyadi after only a few months. Succession to the throne was hereditary, but not by the laws governing at the time. The boyars, the land owning nobles, had the right to elect the prince of Wallachia from various eligible members of the royalty and this often meant that assassination and violence would run riot in overthrowing the current leader. For Vlad, this deposition would start a lifetime's dedication to regaining his father's seat and, as a member of the Order of the Dragon, exacting revenge upon the enemies of Christianity, namely the Ottoman Turks.

Having shrewdly offered his loyalty to Hunyari, Vlad was given a duchy in Transylvania to oversee and, upon Hunyari's death eight years after he was deposed, Vlad resumed his tenure at the throne of Wallachia where he was in charge for six years from 1456 to 1462.

After years of warfare, Wallachia was in a bad state. Vlad needed to boost the country's economy and concentrated on trade and strengthening the agricultural output. This problem would highlight his ambivalence towards his subjects – the building of new villages and the strengthening of trade eventually gave way to the obliteration to those he saw as being surplus to his vision of a prosperous society.

EXTERMINATION OF BEGGARS AND VAGRANTS

He noticed that his country was beginning to have numerous poor people, vagrants, beggars and cripples. He therefore issued an invitation to all the poor and sick in Wallachia to come to Tirgoviste for a great feast, claiming that no-one should go hungry in his realm. When they arrived, they were ushered into a great hall where they were presented with a wonderful feast. The guests ate and drank late into the night. Then Vlad appeared and asked them: 'What else do you desire? Do you want to be without cares, lacking nothing in the world?' The poor and crippled responded positively, so Vlad had the hall boarded up and set on fire, so that no-one escaped the flames. Vlad told the boyars that he did this 'in order that they represent no further burden to other men, and that no one will be poor in the realm.'

It was during this time that Vlad would commit the atrocities for which he would gain his infamy. Early in his reign, he gave a feast for his boyars and their families to celebrate Easter, knowing that many had been involved in the deaths of his father and elder brother. All the nobles were arrested and those who were lame or elderly were impaled on the spot. The younger ones and those in good health were sent north to rebuild Poenari Castle, his home on the Arges River, which lay in ruins: many were forced to work naked as their clothes had disintegrated due to excessive wear. Vlad enjoyed torturing and punishing his workers and few survived. He continued to eradicate the boyar class and replace them with free peasants and the middle classes who would be loyal to him.

THE IMPALER EMERGES

Vlad's propensity for impaling his enemies on stakes in the ground and leaving them to bleed to death earned him the nickname Tepes meaning 'impaler' in Romanian. This would become his calling card; a horse would be attached to each of the victim's legs and a sharpened stake was gradually inserted into the body. The end of the stake was usually oiled and care was taken that it should not be too sharp in case it caused the victim die too quickly of shock. Usually, the stake went up through the buttocks, often up to the mouth. In case this got boring, he sometimes used other orifices, or impaled his victims upside down. Infants might be impaled on the stake forced through their mothers' chests. In 1459 he had 30,000 merchants and boyars of Brasov impaled: when one boyar held his nose to alleviate the terrible smell of the clotting blood and emptied bowels, Vlad solved his problem by having him impaled on a stake higher than all the rest so that he might be above the smell.

The stakes were often arranged in geometric patterns, particularly in concentric rings in the outskirts of a city he was targeting. The height of the spear indicated the rank of the victim. The decaying corpses were often left in place for months. In 1461, Sultan Mehmet II returned to Constantinople after being sickened by the sight of 20,000 impaled Turkish prisoners outside Tirgoviste: this became known as the 'Forest of the Impaled'. A year later Vlad carried out a daring raid by crossing the Danube on horseback into Mehmet's camp, where he and his army had assembled to attack Wallachia. Vlad killed several thousand Turkish soldiers and caused the rest to retreat.

There is no denying that impalement was very much Vlad's favourite form of torture, but he did deploy others; along with impalement, he enjoyed cutting off limbs, blinding, strangulation, burning victims alive, cutting off noses and ears, scalping, skinning and exposing people to the elements or to wild animals. One story goes that Vlad was visited by two ambassadors who refused to remove their hats in his presence; in this instance Vlad recognized the importance of their headwear and nailed them to their heads so that they should never have to remove them again. The mutilation of sexual organs, particularly women's, was another proclivity. He was concerned with female chastity and exacted terrible punishment on female transgressors; one such victim was, rather hypocritically, Vlad's own mistress. She loved him to distraction and always wanted to please him. When Vlad was moody, she tried to lighten his load and on one occasion tried to cheer him up by telling him she was pregnant. Vlad asked the bath matrons to examine her and when they proved that she was lying, Vlad drew his knife and cut her open from the groin to the breast, leaving her to die in agony.

He attacked women and children, lords and peasants, ambassadors from foreign powers and merchants. His savage penalties against thieves meant that there was little stealing in his domains. He tested this by putting a golden cup on display in the central square of Tirgoviste which remained throughout his entire reign.

LEGEND OF THE ESCAPE

Vlad was eventually defeated and killed in battle near Bucharest in 1476 after attempting to regain his seat as the leader of Wallachia once more. His head was sent to Constantinople where it was displayed on a stake to prove that the cruel prince was dead. His body was buried at Snagov, an island monastery near Bucharest, to which he had donated a lot of money in memory of his father and brother. According to Eastern European legends, however, the body and head that were presented were not those of Vlad and he still walks the dark streets of Transylvania to this day.

PART SIX

CHILDREN
OF EVIL

BRYAN AND DAVID FREEMAN

*Irked by the ascetic code of their parents' religion, two
skinhead siblings from Pennsylvania slaughtered their
faithful family in what was the ultimate
act of rebellion.*

FILIAL FRICTION

Sixty miles north-east of Philadelphia on the
outskirts of Allentown, Dennis and Brenda Freeman
led a devout existence. Their distinctive chocolate-
coloured house in the tranquil community of
Salisbury Township was also home to their three
sons whom they raised according to their deep
religious beliefs. Belonging to the evangelical
Christian denomination known as the Jehovah's
Witnesses, Dennis and Brenda had no problem
instructing their youngest son Erik in the ways of
their church, but with his elder two brothers they
met considerable resistance.

Brian Freeman along with David, his younger

brother by two years, had always fought against the family's devotion to this often strict religious doctrine. Its austere code forbade the celebration of birthdays and national holidays. Followers declined to bear arms and considered drunken behaviour, smoking and drug abuse as inherently sinful. Rebelling against these beliefs any chance they could find, the two brothers became a true test of their parents' faith.

As the brothers reached adolescence, they quickly developed into large, imposing figures. Bryan grew to six foot and weighed 215 pounds while David stood three inches taller and tipped the scales at close to 250 pounds. The pair refused to conform, smoking in the driveway, rolling home drunk late at night, dressed in long black coats and army boots, far from the modest attire considered fit for a Jehovah's Witness. Yet their insubordinate behaviour was about to get much worse.

A NEW FAMILY

At some point in 1991 both brothers stopped attending church services. Their father then resigned from his position as an elder and concentrated his efforts on rehabilitating his sons. His endeavours failed spectacularly and after a series of violent incidents at school, Brenda decided to take action. The soft-spoken housewife contacted rehab facilities for her sons in an attempt to bring them into line but by the following year both Bryan and David showed no signs of improvement.

David soon developed a drug habit and spent time inside a hospital where doctors evaluated his state of mind. While the psychiatric report found him of above average intelligence, he was also diagnosed with an antisocial personality disorder and was recommended to attend a care home for juvenile delinquents. Meanwhile, his older brother was receiving help for his own substance abuse at a therapy centre and had struck up a friendship with a fellow resident.

His new friend introduced him to the world of white supremacy. Persuaded to become a skinhead, Bryan began to decorate his room with Swastika symbols and posters of Hitler. On his release he returned home and immediately convinced his younger brother to join his Neo-Nazi family. Together with Nelson 'Benny' Birdwell III, their eighteen-year-old cousin, the brothers started attending Hitler Youth festivals prevalent around Pennsylvania, shaving their heads and tattooing their bodies. Immersing themselves in the barbaric subculture, it seemed Bryan and David had found themselves a new family to which they felt a real affinity.

FOREHEADS FOREWARN

This bond gave the brothers an identity which only served to fuel their anger and escalate the rebellion. The pair became more and more threatening, bragging in school about their exploits, including cutting off the head of a cat and worshipping its decapitated corpse. As the arguments inside the Freeman house intensified verbal assaults turned physical. They once tried to smother their mother with a pillow and, after a separate altercation, even pinned her to the floor whilst wielding a hatchet.

Following these attacks, Brenda sought help from the Anti-Defamation League of B'Nai Brith who suggested she contact a local anti-prejudice organization. When she did so, they informed her they had no legal grounds to remove her children. It was at this time that Dennis began to keep a baseball bat next to the bed as protection from his own two sons.

On 4 February 1995, in an attempt to discipline her unruly children, Brenda sold her sons' cars. Refusing to surrender to their parents' will, Bryan and David retaliated the following day by tattooing their foreheads with neo-Nazi slogans. With 'Sieg Heil' and 'Beserker' inked just above their eyebrows the pair of brutes looked even more menacing. Yet fearing only God, Dennis and Brenda continued to lay down the law, stripping their bedroom walls and confiscating their offensive paraphernalia. It was after this seizure that the brothers began to speak openly about killing their parents.

EVIL ON EHRETS LANE

February 1995 was ending in typical fashion for the Freemans. Tension between the religious and the rebellious mounted in the house on Ehrets Lane, made worse by Bryan's recent five-day suspension for verbally assaulting his school principal. Now, late on Sunday 26 February, Bryan, David and cousin Benny sneaked in through a basement window, having violated an imposed curfew. Hearing the noise below, Brenda marched downstairs and ordered her nephew to go home and her children to go to bed.

When the three skinheads refused to comply, Brenda locked horns with her eldest and a slanging match ensued. Bryan then grabbed a steak knife and stabbed his mother in the back. Pulling the five-inch blade from the wound, she came at her son, whereupon Bryan stole back the knife and stabbed her again, this time up to the hilt. He then stuffed a pair of shorts into her mouth to muffle her screams. Soon there was silence.

They knew then they had to finish off the rest of the family. As Brenda's lifeless body bled out on the basement floor, Ben and David moved upstairs wielding a pick axe handle and aluminium baseball bat. Visiting the master bedroom first, they bludgeoned David Freeman to death, slitting his throat before moving on to Erik whose skull they cracked so hard his eye popped out of his head. Dropping the murder weapons and lifting $200 in cash from their dead father's wallet, the brothers quickly changed clothes and fled the scene in the family's Pontiac Sunbird convertible.

CATCH OF THE DAY
Valerie Freeman, Brenda's sister, was the first to find the dead. Puzzled why Dennis' truck was still on the driveway, she had entered the house via a side door to discover it was bitterly cold and eerily quiet inside. On seeing the bludgeoned bodies upstairs, she ran to a neighbour and alerted the police. Subsequent autopsy reports revealed the true brutality of the

attacks. Both Dennis and Erik had been beaten so savagely their brains had come through their skulls. Brenda had also been struck about the head but had died of her stab wounds, one had gone through her lung and pierced her heart.

Detectives focused on the remaining members of the Freeman family. Due to their belligerent reputation and known affiliation with a white supremacist movement, Bryan and David became instant prime suspects. A tip from a truck driver alerted police as to their whereabouts: the Truck World Motor Inn in Hubbard, Ohio just over the border. Here investigators traced calls made from their motel room to a residence in Hope, Michigan.

The three Musketeers, as they had long been known, had fled over 600 miles to the home of one Frank Hesse, another skinhead whom Bryan had met at a concert in Detroit. Keeping quiet about their triple homicide, the threesome joined their host ice fishing. Returning to the house later that evening the fascist fishermen found themselves surrounded by a Michigan SWAT team and were swiftly apprehended.

EVIL EXTRADITED

All four were taken into custody though Frank Hesse

was soon released insisting he had no knowledge of the crimes. Meanwhile the remaining neo-Nazis had devised a plan. Believing they would be tried as juveniles, the Freemans chose to take the wrap for all three murders to save their eighteen-year-old cousin from receiving a death sentence. On 6 March, the same day their parents and little brother were buried in an Allentown cemetery, the brothers began their confessions.

Waiving their right to counsel, Bryan and David gave their versions of what happened that dark night at home. Conflicting stories helped cloud the truth but all three boys were ultimately charged before a Michigan judge and their extradition to Pennsylvania approved. Back in their home state, individual appeals for their cases to be heard before a juvenile court were withdrawn and, according to state law, both brothers stood trial as adults.

On 7 December 1995, Bryan Freeman brought a hushed silence to the courtroom. Before the judge and jury, the seventeen-year-old skinhead testified to murdering his mother. This unprompted admission of guilt was part of a deal ensuring he avoided the death penalty. David soon followed suit, pleading guilty to the slaying of his father. Each received a life sentence without possibility of parole. In April

1996, Ben Birdwell was found similarly guilty of his part in the death of Dennis Freeman and was given the same punishment. Despite all three being found criminally culpable nobody was ever convicted of killing eleven-year-old Erik.

EDMUND KEMPER

As a fifteen-year-old this mild-mannered man mountain gunned down his grandparents before embarking on a murder spree of California, acquiring the nickname The Coed Killer after slaying six students in under a year.

KEMPER KILLED THE CAT

Edmund Emil Kemper III was born in Burbank, California on 8 December 1948. Bookended by two sisters, he grew up the middle child in a family home filled with tension until the age of nine when his parents divorced. Despite living in such a strained atmosphere he was inconsolable at their separation. On moving to Montana with his mother and sisters, life deteriorated for the sad son. Subjected to ritual beatings and habitual humiliation by his mother, young Edmund began to seethe. Forced to sleep in a locked basement, in the dark corners of his mind and the pit of his stomach a violent rage began to boil.

His first living victim was the house cat, burying the pet alive before digging it up, cutting off its head with a machete, and sticking it on the end of a stick. His sisters would find Edmund acting out bizarre sexual scenarios with their dolls and even asked his siblings to help stage his own mock execution where he played a death row inmate in the gas chamber. The fledgling sociopath began to harbour fantasies of killing and mutilating those around him, however these desires he kept hidden behind a benign public façade.

By the age of fourteen, life in Helena, Montana had grown so unbearable he chose to run away and seek out his father in California. When he arrived in the Golden State in the summer of 1963, the teen found his father was not as keen to see him; Edmund Kemper II had remarried and was now raising a new son. Feeling rejected and unloved by both parents, the unwanted visitor was then palmed off into the care of his paternal grandparents who lived on a seventeen-acre ranch in the North Fork mountains of California.

KEMPER TANTRUM

Life on the ranch was every bit as bad as living with his belittling mother. Maude Kemper consistently made Edmund feel small and worthless, and soon the rage began to rise up inside the big, friendly giant. On 27 August 1964 yet another argument broke out between grandmother and grandson.

The fifteen-year-old felt the urge to react with more than words on this occasion, grabbed a .22 calibre rifle, placed it to the head of the sixty-six-year-old woman and pulled the trigger. He then unloaded two more rounds at close-range into her lifeless body then went at the corpse with a kitchen knife.

Built like an outhouse, Kemper dragged his dead grandma to the bedroom with ease. Any further acts against her person were interrupted when his grandfather returned home from the grocery store. The rookie killer made a quick decision to kill the old man too, purely to save him from finding his murdered wife. Aiming the rifle – a Christmas gift from his grandad – out of the window, he shot his relative dead, then hid his body in the garage.

Alone in the ranch-house, he called his mother to tell her what he had done. She advised him to contact the police. When the authorities arrived, they found the huge frame of Edmund Kemper calmly waiting on the porch. During the interview process, detectives asked him why he had committed the crime. He just wanted to see what it felt like to kill Grandma, came the cold reply.

CLEVER BUT CRAZY
Kemper was detained in Juvenile Hall while a series

of psychological tests ascertained his mental state. A diagnosis of paranoid schizophrenia saw him transferred to Atascadero State Hospital for the Criminally Insane that December. For the next five years he underwent treatment for his condition while also learning how to appear sane. His high IQ of 136 allowed him to memorize twenty-eight separate assessment techniques that would enable him to fake his behaviour and fool his doctors.

Remaining under the supervision of the California Youth Authority, Kemper gained his release in 1969. The powers that be placed him back into his mother's care, ignoring his doctors' recommendations. Edmund was now back in the lion's den and soon mother and son were at each other's throats once again, constantly bickering inside the Ord Drive duplex.

To begin with, the 'rehabilitated' Edmund showed signs of normality. He attended a community college, performing well in all areas, and worked a series of menial jobs until landing a post at the Highways Division of the Department of Public Works. Endeavouring to become an ordinary and upstanding member of society, he fostered hopes of joining the police academy but was informed he was too tall. As a poor substitute he started to hang out in the jury room and listen to officers' tales of law and order. He soon became known as Big Ed to the cops; a big, friendly giant with a softly spoken voice. But they had no idea what Edmund Kemper was plotting inside that clever yet crazy mind.

SANTA CRUZ-ING FOR GIRLS

Despite managing to save enough money to relocate to an apartment of his own, away from his abusive mother, Kemper was unable to escape his dark thoughts of violence. Soon he was filling the trunk of his yellow Ford Galaxy with a kill kit consisting of plastic bags, knives, handcuffs and blankets and cruising the campuses for coed students.

Thanks to a college ID sticker in his windscreen provided by his mother, a university employee at the time, he was able to move freely without suspicion around the campuses. He picked up around one hundred and fifty hitch-hikers before finally succumbing to what he called the little zapples – the sexual urges to kill.

Between May 1972 and February 1973 Edmund embarked on a killing spree, strangling and shooting six female students. He then took their bodies to his mother's house where he would sexually abuse the corpses before decapitating, dismembering and finally dumping the remains. The day after he murdered dance student Aiko Koo, he appeared before a psychiatric panel to determine his mental state. They passed him mentally fit and suitably reformed while Koo's head lay in the trunk of his car outside.

MUM'S THE WORD

Having successfully pulled the wool over the eyes of his evaluators, Kemper now focused his rage on the individual he truly blamed for his behaviour: Clarnell Strandberg, his mother. On Good Friday, Edmund took a claw hammer and bludgeoned to death the source of his rage while she slept. He then severed her head and used it for oral sex then placed it on the mantelpiece and used it for dart practice. As he vented his anger towards her decapitated head, Edmund savoured the moment; it was the first time in a long time that his mother did not argue back.

Once he had said his piece, he cut out his mother's tongue and vocal cords and shoved them down the garbage disposal. Unable to break down the tough tissue, the machine spat her tongue back out. It seemed Edmund couldn't silence his mother completely. His anger still not sated, he called his mother's best friend, one Sara Sally Hallett, over for dinner. On entering the house, Kemper choked her to death, removed her head and stuffed both bodies into closets.

Fleeing the duplex in Hallet's car, Edmund drove eastwards, heading out of California. Popping caffeine pills, he travelled 1,500 miles, aiming to distance himself from his crimes. Thinking the nation would now know all, he turned on the radio, expecting to catch a news flash. But there was nothing. Disappointed, Kemper pulled over in Pueblo, Colorado to telephone the Santa Cruz police. Each time he tried to confess his misdeeds, the officer on the other end treated it like a crank call. When the authorities finally realized his disclosure was genuine, they found Edmund Kemper waiting in the car for them with three guns and 200 rounds of ammunition.

A CALL FOR TORTURE

In custody, Kemper described his crimes in full gory detail, confessing to eight murders. He then took detectives on a tour of his burial and dump sites in Carmel, Boulder Creek and Eden Canyon near San Francisco. Following his arraignment on eight counts of first-degree murder in May 1973, Big Ed attempted suicide on two occasions, failing both times. He underwent a thorough psychiatric evaluation and was deemed fit to stand trial.

On 23 October, his case came to court. While three separate prosecution psychiatrists found him sane, Kemper pleaded insanity and did all he could to persuade the jury of his unstable mental state. He admitted to necrophilia, cannibalism and called for the judge to issue a sentence of death by torture. When asked what he thought when he saw a pretty girl walking down the street, the six men and six women of the jury heard his disturbing reply: that he wondered how her head would look on a stick.

Despite Kemper's admission, his peers took five hours to find him sane and then guilty on all eight counts. With a moratorium on capital punishment in the United States at that time, the defendant did not get his wish for death but received life imprisonment. He now resides at the Vacaville Medical Facility in Solano County, California and his next scheduled parole hearing is due in 2012.

ERIC SMITH

*In a small farming community in up-state New York,
a freckle-faced fiend lured a younger child to his death,
violating his body with a savagery exceeding his
thirteen years.*

EXPLOSIVE ERIC

By the time Eric Smith came into the world on
22 January 1980 significant damage had already
been done. His mother Tammy had taken Tridione
during the pregnancy to combat her epilepsy; a
drug known to cause birth defects. Born small in
size and with low-set protruding ears, Eric threw
regular temper tantrums as a toddler, banging his
head on the floor when he failed to get his own way.
His parents quickly discovered their little boy also
possessed learning difficulties. Struggling in class, he
was forced to repeat a year but being held back was
the least of his worries.

School for Eric became a living hell. Not only did
his deformed ears and weak frame make him an easy
target for bullies, but his bright red hair singled him
out from the crowd as a sure-fire scapegoat. Beaten

over the head with books to being the sitting duck for spit balls, the endless abuse he received turned Eric into an outcast. With no friends to speak of in this rural village of Savona, New York, he went to his great-grandmother for emotional support but when she died in 1989 he was alone once more.

Constantly being told he was nothing, his anger began to bubble up inside. With nobody else to talk to he approached his hot-tempered stepfather, Ted Smith, for help. Downplaying the problem, he told him to take out the frustration on something inanimate. But bloodying his knuckles on a bag or the trunk of a tree only served as a short term solution.

By now, Eric was suffering from intermittent explosive disorder. Unable to control his emotional responses, he would often fly off into a rage and soon needed more than a punch bag to cool his temper. Next, he focused his attention on living things and the first to feel his wrath was the neighbour's cat which he strangled. He also drowned birds and shot at dogs with his BB gun in a bid to quell the fire within him. It did not take long before this ticking time bomb progressed to something larger.

DERRICK ROBIE DUPED

In the summer of 1993, Derrick Robie, a blonde-haired, blithe-spirited boy just four years of age woke up every morning eager to play ball; the excitable infant loved baseball, often donning the outfit of his favourite team. Thankfully, a youth summer camp, a locally-run recreation program in the nearby park, provided the necessary focus for his boundless energy. However, on the morning of 2 August, Derrick's mother, Doreen, was running late.

Keen to attend camp, little Derrick refused to wait to be taken by his mother and said he would go on his own. With no roads to cross and the park less than a block away, Doreen saw no danger in letting him walk unaccompanied, even if it was the first time he would do so. Sending her son off with a kiss, Doreen watched Eric step out into the big bad world. She would have no idea that in less than ten minutes he would be dead.

Walking down the street on his first solo journey, Derrick was just 400 yards from his destination when Eric Smith entered his life. The angry redhead was riding his bike when he saw the four-year-old heading for the park. He did not know his name but knew he was defenceless. When Eric called out, Derrick stopped and turned around. The older boy then suggested they take a short-cut to the summer camp, coaxing Derrick to follow him with the assurance that nothing bad would happen. This was a lie.

VICTIM BECOMES VILLAIN

Eric led his victim through a wooded area adjacent to the park. Once out of plain sight, the heinous redhead began to choke him. Derrick thrashed and flailed, fighting for his life, while Eric squeezed his tiny neck, picturing the faces of the bullies that had abused him at school. Once his prey was out cold, the freckle-faced strangler grabbed two rocks from the dirt and used them to bash in the boy's head. Eleven blows later and there was silence.

Sadly, the ordeal was not over for Derrick Robie. Despite having choked the boy unconscious and striking him repeatedly over the head, Eric was still unsure whether the boy was dead. Unable to run the risk of him surviving and telling tales, Smith resolved to stop his heart. He found a stick and began poking the body, but could not puncture the skin. Eric then sodomised Derrick with the tree limb, enjoying the power he wielded over another – a new and pleasurable experience as for once Eric was not the victim.

The pushover turned persecutor then ripped open the boy's canvas bag and found his lunch box. Inside was a banana, which he squashed, and a flask of Kool Aid which he proceeded to pour over the lifeless, violated body. Finally, he took a plastic sandwich bag and stuffed it down Derrick's throat. After returning several times to the murder site to check there were no signs of life, Eric headed home, washing his hands of blood and dumping his stained clothes into the laundry basket.

POSED FOR POLICE

Later on that morning at approximately eleven o'clock, Doreen Robie went to pick up her son from the day camp. To her dismay, she was informed he had never arrived. Following a missing persons report made to police, a massive search of the surrounding area got under way. Four hours into the hunt for Derrick they found his body in a small patch of brush under a copse of trees.

The four-year-old had suffered multiple skull fractures, severe cerebral swelling, his intestinal wall had been perforated and there were haemorrhages on his neck and face consistent with strangulation. While asphyxia had been a contributing factor to his death, an autopsy revealed the primary cause was blunt force trauma. His body had also been posed with his left shoe by his right hand and his right shoe by his left hand. Due to the nature of his injuries, police believed they were looking for an adult and possibly a paedophile in the local area. As part of the investigation, around five hundred witnesses were interviewed including young Eric.

On Thursday 5 August Tammy Smith accompanied her son to the police command post to help with enquiries. Following the interview, detectives felt compelled to pay a visit to the Smith household. There had been some discrepancies in Eric's story that needed to be resolved.

STORY SWITCH

The young teen had stated during the first interview that he had not seen Derrick on the day of his murder, but when investigating officers spoke with him at his home later that night, Eric quickly changed his story. He now admitted seeing the Robie child early that morning and proceeded to describe Derrick's clothing and bag in great detail. While the about-turn was suspicious there was something else that concerned the detectives. Eric had recently broken his glasses meaning his myopia prevented him from making such an accurate description from the other side of the street.

The next day Eric was asked to show officers

where he was when he saw Derrick. Riding his bike, reliving the experience, the thirteen-year-old was anything but solemn. Instead, he seemed upbeat, enjoying the attention he was getting from his new-found 'playmates'. But hiding his terrible secret was too much for Eric and on 8th August, two days after Derrick Robie's funeral, he broke down in front of his mother and confessed to murdering the little boy.

DIAMOND FOR DERRICK

As news of the killing sent shock waves through this tiny, rural village in upstate New York, Eric Smith underwent a thorough psychiatric testing. While no brain abnormalities were discovered, his intermittent explosive disorder along with ADHD was detected, providing some small clue as to why Eric had acted in such a violent, cold-blooded manner.

His trial began in the summer of 1994 at which the hot-tempered teen pleaded not guilty by reason of insanity. The jury, however, sided with the prosecution who believed Derrick Robie's murderer understood right from wrong and knew he was about to commit a crime when he coaxed the boy into the woods, away from prying eyes. On 16 August, Eric Smith was convicted of second-degree murder and sentenced to the maximum term possible for juvenile criminals: nine years to life in prison. While the child convict sat behind bars at the Brookwood Juvenile Detention Center, volunteers bulldozed the murder site and, in memory of the boy who loved baseball, created a new diamond.

A statue was also erected, showing Derrick Robie kitted out in his team's outfit. As the inscription stated, this was, 'a gentle reminder of what childhood is meant to be'.

In April 2010, Eric Smith had his fifth parole appeal rejected since his transfer to Clinton Correctional Facility, a maximum security prison in Dannemora, New York. His next hearing is scheduled for April 2012, when he hopes he will gain his freedom and return to Savona, much to the fear of the Robies and the other residents.

THE JASON SWEENEY MURDER

With a promise of sex, a juvenile jezebel lures her date to a remote spot where a thrill-seeking threesome execute a murder plot turning a romantic rendezvous into a brutal bloodbath.

BAD COMPANY

At odds with its nickname, the City of Brotherly Love, Philadelphia has long held a reputation for violence and crime. And in 2003 – despite its murder rate dropping faster than any other metropolis in the United States – an evil act in a north-east district proved to be a shocking example of such vice. Once a centre of the shad fishing industry, Fishtown had grown into a solid blue-collar neighbourhood of working-class immigrant communities. And it was here that the Sweeney family lived on East Susquehanna Avenue.

Paul Sweeney owned a local construction company and had recently joined forces with his sixteen-year-old son who had dropped out of eleventh grade to follow his father into the family business. Jason Sweeney was an easy-going teenager who dreamed of becoming a Navy SEAL and planned to join the Navy when he turned seventeen. Sadly, Jason would never reach that age.

The young construction worker was a popular boy, but in recent years had fallen in with the wrong crowd. His parents had become increasingly concerned about his association with an old friend. Edward Batzig had been a close companion since the fourth grade and had even accompanied the Sweeneys on holiday in Florida. But it was during this outing that Paul and Dawn noticed a change in Batzig and soon after returning home, they suggested Jason limit the time he spent in his company.

ROMANTIC RENDEZVOUS

In contrast to Batzig, his parents could not be happier about the development of a more recent relationship. Around the middle of May, Jason had started seeing a girl, his first by all accounts. Her name was Justina Morley, a pale yet pretty dark-haired fifteen-year-old and, although they had yet to meet the sweetheart, it was clear their son was enamoured with eighth grader.

On Friday 30 May 2003, Jason finished work earlier than normal. It was a special day. He had a date to keep with his new girlfriend. At around four o'clock, with a cashed pay cheque in his pocket, he left Fishtown to go pick up Justina from her home on East Palmer Street. The young lovers met up then visited a corner store where Jason bought his date a soda. Next Justina suggested they take a stroll through The Trails; an isolated industrial area overgrown with weeds along the Delaware River.

Once inside the secluded wood, the young girl made amorous advances towards her companion, insisting they had sex there and then in the bushes. She began to strip, seductively shedding her clothes. Keen to notch up an early sexual experience, the teenage boy eagerly followed suit. He hastily removed his shoes and unzipped his trousers. It was at this moment that they attacked.

As if from nowhere, three teenagers Jason knew well burst from the brush, brandishing weapons and started to attack him. Among his assailants was Edward Batzig, the boy his parents deemed a bad influence. And as the blows rained down upon him, Jason glanced over at his date. He now realised young Justina Morley had lured him into a trap.

411

THE PLOT THICKENS

This unprovoked attack had been over a week in the making. The two boys assisting Eddie Batzig were Dominic and Nicholas Coia, aged seventeen and sixteen respectively, renowned troublemakers and junkies about town. Far from the good Catholic schoolgirl the Sweeneys believed, Justina Morley was in cahoots with all three, often having sex with the brothers in exchange for drugs.

As chronic abusers they were keen to find new ways of paying for their next hit. The previous Sunday they had managed to persuade Jason to give them ten dollars in order to buy a bag of weed. This only served to expand their collective greed as they prepared for a bigger score.

The initial plan was to raid the safe inside the Sweeney home. A party was planned at Jason's house for the Thursday night where Justina would seduce her new beau and the boys would beat him up, however their victim was unable to organise the party due to work commitments. A revised plan had to be forged and the cabal chose to lure the gullible Sweeney into 'The Trails' using Justina as bait.

Finalizing their strategy that Friday afternoon at the home of eighteen-year-old Joshua Staab, the gang of four conspirators listened to The Beatles' song *Helter Skelter* some forty-two times. This tune enjoyed a previous deadly connection to violence. Back in 1969, it had been the inspirational anthem of the Manson Family as the cult-created spree killers brought murder to Los Angeles. Fuelled by such notoriety, the boys donned latex gloves, grabbed their weapons and secreted themselves in the undergrowth, waiting for their prey to walk by.

AN EVIL EMBRACE

Lured into the trap by his complicit date, the boys quickly pounced on the poor victim. The first blow came from his erstwhile best friend, Eddie Batzig. Raising a hatchet above his head, the honour student struck downwards with all his might, striking Jason's head. Feeling a nasty gash, the duped teen staggered away as further swings made contact. Then Dominic Coia joined in. Armed with a hammer, the eldest child lashed out, striking Jason so hard the tool lodged in his skull. Undeterred by the inexplicable violence, his younger brother stepped up and began beating him with a brick.

As blood gushed and spattered, Justina Morley stood no more than eight feet away. Providing no help to her new boyfriend, she simply stood and watched the violence play out. Following the relentless assault, poor Jason Sweeney choked on his own blood. Once his killers knew he was dead, they rifled through his pockets and found the $500 in cash. Then the partners in crime came together in a group hug, celebrating their evil, savouring the rush.

Leaving Jason dead in the weeds, Justina and the three boys returned to Joshua Staab's place. Their host ran their bloodstained clothes through the washing machine, while the four divided up their ill-gotten gains. Now each accomplice had $125 and, with no remorse nor fear of the consequences, they partied hard, spending the money on marijuana, heroin and cocaine.

BEYOND RECOGNITION

When Jason's father filed a missing persons report on his son, police began a search for the sixteen-year-old. Local residents also volunteered their time to help find the boy including one Justina Morley who knew exactly where he was. At around two o'clock the following day, a group of children riding their bikes through The Trails stumbled across the horrifically battered remains of Jason Sweeney.

The subsequent autopsy revealed the extent of his injuries. Anything up to forty blows had broken every bone in his face save the left cheekbone, rendering him unrecognisable. In fact, investigators on the scene had been unable to tell whether the corpse was young or old. With no identification on the body, Paul Sweeney came to the county morgue on Monday morning and told police the John Doe was his son.

Retracing the dead boy's steps, detectives brought in Justina Morley and the three boys to help shed some light on what had happened. Potential witnesses soon became prime suspects. Confessions to Jason's murder were forthcoming from Batzig and the Coia brothers but none of them showed any compunction for the crime. All they seemed to care about was when they could return home.

DEAL WITH THE DEVIL

On 17 June 2003, Judge Seamus McCaffery presided over the preliminary court hearing. Having reviewed the shocking photographs of the Sweeney corpse, the official equated the crime akin to something from the Dark Ages. The six-day trial of the three teenage boys culminated in guilty verdicts, charged as adults on four separate counts: first-degree murder, conspiracy to murder, robbery and possession of an instrument of crime. The threesome were later sentenced to life without parole.

Next came the trial of Justina Morley. Too young to receive the death penalty, she also managed to avoid a charge of first-degree murder. Following what prosecution lawyer Jude Conroy termed his deal with the Devil, Morley's charge was reduced to murder in the third degree in exchange for her testimony during the hearing of her fellow collaborators. This commutation, however, did not prevent the court from learning the evil ways of this enchantress.

She freely admitted in court of her ability to manipulate the gullible, persuading the weak-minded to do her bidding. Prosecution counsel used a series of love letters written behind bars to her accomplices to reveal how wicked this juvenile jezebel truly was. The disturbing and often sexually explicit correspondence told how she claimed to enjoy the flashbacks of the murder, that they gave her pleasure. She even described herself as a cold-hearted devil-worshipping bitch. The jury seemed to agree and on 21 March 2005 Justina Morley received her sentence: seventeen-and-a-half to thirty-five years in jail.

JESSE POMEROY

*Dubbed 'The Boston Boy Fiend', this milky-eyed
monster tricked the trusting, enticing young children
away to be savagely assaulted, mutilated and,
on two occasions, murdered.*

SICK AND UNSIGHTLY

Jesse Harding Pomeroy had a face only a mother
could love. But when Ruth Ann gave birth to her
second son on 29 November 1859, even she could
be forgiven for recoiling from what was placed in her
arms. He was born with a cleft lip that highlighted a
mouth too wide for his head, quite a feat as his head
was considered too large for his body. To top it all
off, two large ears jutted from the deformed head to
create this distinctly disturbing profile.

Not only was Jesse an unsightly child but a sickly
one too. When still just months old, he suffered a
brain fever causing three whole days of delirium
during which he exhibited convulsive seizures. From
then on he experienced regular bouts of dizziness
and violent head pains. As if this was not enough,

the infant had a disturbing reaction to a smallpox vaccination. Losing sight in his right eye, it turned an eerie milky-white, further adding to his grotesque visage. It was said even his own father could barely look at him.

Thomas Pomeroy may not have enjoyed laying eyes on his son but the same could not be said about his hands. Jesse would often be taken behind the outside privy by his father for a whipping across his bare back. The beatings became so severe that one evening Ruth Ann intervened, chasing her husband out of the house with a kitchen knife. Thomas never came back, though his method of punishment would return in years to come.

OUTHOUSE OF PAINE

Unsurprisingly, young Jessie developed into a maladjusted child. Intelligent but antisocial, he refrained from joining in with other children and as he grew older took to stealing from his mother's purse and playing truant. Cutting class and lifting the odd penny gave way to more violent impulses. He tortured the neighbour's cat and twisted the heads off his mother's prize canaries before even animal torture became banal for the Boston boy.

Jesse quickly turned his attention to other boys.

On 22 December 1871, he lured four-year-old Billy Paine to a ramshackle outhouse on Powder Horn Hill in Chelsea. Lashing his wrists to a roof beam, he brought out his father's brand of violence, whipping the boy within an inch of his life. When passersby discovered him, they found his pale white back covered in deep welts. He was sadly unable to provide a description of his attacker.

This allowed Jesse to repeat his crime, coaxing one Tracy Hayden to the same abandoned barn with a promise of going to see the soldiers. Stripping and stringing up the seven-year-old, Jesse proceeded to flog his victim, then knocked out his two front teeth, broke his nose and threatened to castrate him before running away, leaving him to an uncertain rescue.

When help did come, Tracy could tell police nothing to help identify his attacker and paranoid rumours began to circulate that a devilish man with a pointy red beard was to blame for the attacks. Two more victims met the same fate while police questioned hundreds of boys in the area. A $500 reward was offered to capture the 'Boy Torturer', bringing vigilante groups out onto the street to hunt for the sadist. In just a few months Jesse Pomeroy had succeeded in bringing panic and fear to the streets of Chelsea, Massachusetts.

NEEDLES TO KNIVES

Following the four vicious beatings, Ruth Ann and her two boys moved across the Chelsea Creek to South Boston. Jesse's mother needed to find a lower rent apartment although, in the back of her mind, she suspected her youngest had something to do with the attacks. Her suspicions gained weight when young children from South Boston were assaulted in the same sick manner.

In fact, Jesse's routine was changing. He still stuck with his trademark whipping, but now the young sadist elevated the level of violence, introducing needles which he would stick into various parts of his victim's body. Needles gave way to knives and, in the case of Joseph Kennedy, he slashed at the face then dragged his prey to the shoreline and washed the wounds with salt water. His savagery seemed to know no limits, biting chunks of flesh from the face and buttocks of one child to trying to sever the penis of another.

With the violence escalating, police were relieved when Jesse's eighth victim, five-year-old Robert Gould, managed to give a workable description of his assailant: a big bad boy with a funny eye. A tour of local schools failed to locate the culprit, until Jesse inexplicably wandered by the police station.

He was spotted and hauled inside for questioning. One threat-induced confession later and Jesse was brought before a magistrate. Not even his mother's testimony could save him from a guilty verdict and, at a mere twelve years of age, he was sent to undergo the harsh discipline of a reform school in Westborough.

THE KILLING OF KATIE CURRAN

Due to remain within this house of reformation until his twenty-first birthday, Jesse worked the system, behaving like a model prisoner. His exemplary conduct earned him a shock release and on 24 January 1874, after just a year-and-a-half inside, Jesse Pomeroy was paroled back to his mother in South Boston. To aid his rehabilitation, he was put to work in his mother's dressmaking store, but the dark urges within him quickly came to the fore and demanded to be sated.

On the morning of 18 March 1874, while Jesse was opening up his mother's shop, ten-year-old Katie Curran walked in hoping to buy a new notebook for school. Suggesting there might be stock downstairs, the milky-eyed miscreant lured the young girl into into the basement. As she reached the last step, Jesse placed his hand over her mouth and slit her throat with a knife. He then dragged her body further into the darkness and proceeded to hack away at her lower body. Dumping Katie's corpse in an ash heap, he washed his hands and went back to work as if nothing had happened.

Katie's mother searched the streets for her missing daughter and, on discovering she had last been seen entering Pomeroy's store, she feared the worst; she knew of Jesse's past. A detective was dispatched to check out the shop but found nothing amiss. And when a credible witness insisted seeing Katie being lured into a car, the police declared the child a victim of kidnapping. Once more, Jesse Pomeroy was in the clear.

BURIED IN THE BASEMENT

Feeling invincible, Pomeroy continued to coax children from the streets but found none naive enough to fall for his tricks until one day in late April. Permitted to visit a bakery on his own, four-year-old Horace Millen had the misfortune of bumping into Jesse who persuaded the blond-haired child to come see a steamship at the harbour. Taking a rest from their journey, Jesse took out his pocket knife and slashed the boy's throat with its three-inch blade. When the boy's body was discovered on Savin Hill

Beach, it had been savagely mutilated. More than a dozen stab wounds had pierced his flesh and the right eye had been punctured.

Police immediately linked Pomeroy to the crime and ordered his arrest without delay. Forced to look at Millen's corpse at the morgue, Jesse broke down and confessed. News of this teenage killer swept across both state and nation and the resultant infamy forced Ruth Ann Pomeroy to close her dressmaking store. When the building was taken over by a local grocer's, workmen renovating the space noticed a foul smell emanating from the cellar. Closer inspection revealed the decomposed body of Katie Curran.

His reign of terror now over, Jesse Pomeroy stood trial early that December where a packed court recorded his plea of not guilty by reason of insanity. The jury took five hours to disagree, pronouncing him guilty of first-degree murder. While they recommended clemency on account of his age, Massachusetts law imposed mandatory execution and in February 1875 Judge Horace Gray handed down the sentence: death by hanging.

EXECUTION TO SECLUSION

As a clamour for clemency clashed with the hard-line call for the full force of the law, Governor William Gaston agonised over the signing of Jesse's death warrant. He set up an executive council to decide how Pomeroy should be punished. Following two voting sessions upholding the death sentence, Gaston's replacement, Alexander Rice, revisited the case. In August 1876, the council officially commuted his sentence to life imprisonment.

Due to the severity of his crimes, Jesse was ordered to spend his life term in solitary confinement. On 7 September 1876, aged just sixteen, he was transferred to Charlestown State Prison where he spent the next fifty-three years of his life. In 1917, the state commuted his sentence, allowing him to join general population. He had spent forty-one years alone and, aside from Robert Stroud, the infamous Birdman of Alcatraz, had become the longest serving American prisoner held in isolation.

In 1929, an elderly Pomeroy was transferred to Bridgewater Hospital for the Criminally Insane where he spent the last three years of his life. Two months before his seventy-third birthday, the murderer with the milky eye took his last breath, his body cremated, his ashes scattered to the four winds.

JON VENABLES AND ROBERT THOMPSON

Described as evil freaks of nature, these two truants were captured on camera abducting a blue-eyed baby before leading him on a two-and-a-half mile trip of torture and torment that ended in murder.

BEFORE BULGER

The two ten-year-olds who stole James Bulger had more than just murder in common. Both August-born boys suffered a difficult childhood. Robert Thompson was the fifth of six brothers abandoned by their father and left to fend for themselves by a neglectful alcoholic of a mother. His siblings were little better. Ranging from career thief to arsonist, sex offender to repeat suicide attempter, they often bullied Robert at home. When he came of age he began to replicate the treatment he received, once abandoning his younger brother Ryan at a canal – a shocking premonition of what was to come.

Jon Venables also lived in an unstable family atmosphere. Though separated, his mother and father had an on-off relationship that would deeply affect their three children. Jon was the middle child. His older brother and younger sister both received special education leaving Jon to feel unnoticed. This led to attention-seeking acts of self-harm – banging his head and cutting himself with scissors – that quickly developed into violence towards others. When he attempted to choke a fellow classmate with a wooden ruler, it was decided he needed a fresh start elsewhere.

Jon Venables was transferred to St Mary's Primary School. Unable to cope with the advanced levels of a new year, he was held back and soon made a connection with another difficult pupil forced to repeat a year; Robert Thompson. Both past targets for bullies, together they formed a formidable bond, emboldening one another. Tough as a two they then became bullies themselves, bringing out the worst in each other, choosing to skip school and make mischief beyond their bedtime.

STEALING CANDY AND A BABY

Friday 12 February 1993 was just another typical school day for the terrible twosome. With no intention of going to class, Jon Venables ditched his bag and joined Robert Thompson to play truant.

Wandering about town, they were drawn to the bright lights of The Strand Shopping Centre, a two-storey retail complex in Bootle, just north of Liverpool City Centre. Dipping into random stores to steal sweets, batteries, and a can of blue enamel paint, the pair of shoplifters soon grew restless for a new challenge. Bored of playing with inanimate objects, the petty thieves turned their minds to kidnapping.

Searching the walkways and shop-fronts, the hookey-playing child hunters tried to snatch a number of potential victims without success. Then at around 3.40 pm they spotted two-year-old James Patrick Bulger outside a butcher's shop. While his distracted mother sorted out a mix-up with her order inside, the two boys approached the toddler and lured him away. Seconds later, all three boys were lost in the crowd of shoppers, and Denise Bulger found her blue-eyed baby had vanished.

Denise quickly reported her son missing to the centre security but, by the time his name was called over the public address system, all three boys had left the shopping precinct. Leading little James by the hand, Jon Venables and Robert Thompson had now embarked on an aimless walk around the streets of Liverpool that would culminate in the death of their innocent captive.

IDLE EYEWITNESSES

With no plan in mind, the kid kidnappers meandered their way along Stanley Road and eventually ended up at a canal where the pair considered pushing the boy into the water. Instead, they dropped him on his head leaving a nasty gash which they covered up with his anorak hood. Following this first violent assault, the partners in crime continued to torture their victim, punching and shaking him as they roamed the streets.

Along their vagrant and violent ramble across busy intersections, passing shops, houses and pedestrians on the street, the two schoolboys and their charge were spotted on a number of occasions. Many witnesses, who later became known as the Liverpool 38, merely assumed the three were brothers, never suspecting the toddler had been abducted. A handful, however, did make enquiries, having spotted the fresh wound to James' head, but their concerns were too easily mollified by the kidnappers' lies.

After endless blind eyes had been turned, James Bulger came within a whisker of rescue when they stopped inside a shop. One woman, sensing not all was right between the boys, wanted to take the teary-eyed tyke to the nearby police station. However, when she asked another woman with a dog to watch over her little girl while she made the short trip, the pet owner refused. This lack of community spirit allowed poor James to be escorted to meet his end.

THE RAILWAY CHILDREN

Following a series of sporadic highlights, including a visit to a pet shop, an altercation with some older boys and gazing at a fire that had broken out in a street, captors and captive arrived at the entrance of the disused Walton and Anfield railway station; the final stop on their eventful two-and-a-half mile journey. Two hours had passed since the abduction from the shopping centre, and now darkness was descending on this late winter day.

As the sky turned black so did the thoughts of the kidnappers. Crawling through a hole in the fence, Venables and Thompson began to conceive further acts of cruelty as they led little James across the white shale towards the railway lines. In a subconscious move to dehumanise their victim, the two boys threw the stolen blue paint into James' face before pelting him with bricks and stones. They then struck him repeatedly with a two-foot-long iron bar until the tiny body stopped moving.

Some reports have stated the boys then removed his trousers and underwear to molest the toddler before deciding to leave the lifeless body on the tracks, weighing his head down with rubble. The two boys then left James Bulger and made their journey home. Two days passed before their discarded plaything was discovered. The corpse had been run over by a train and severed in two. Medical examiners were quick to confirm the cause of death was unrelated to the impact.

THE BLAME GAME

Detective Superintendent Albert Kirby led the police investigation into the murder. After analysis of the surveillance cameras at the shopping centre revealed indistinct images of two young boys with little James, officers questioned over sixty youngsters. When news broke that the suspects were boys, amateur-sleuthing went into overdrive leading many parents to report their own children as the killers.

Acting on an anonymous tip, detectives visited the homes of Jon Venables and Robert Thompson and on Thursday 18 February invited them to make statements at their local police stations. Despite the paint-marked coats and blood-spattered shoes, investigators did not immediately believe they had murdered James Bulger. They looked too young to be killers. However, following a week of gruelling interviews in which the pair denied, lied and blamed each other for the crimes, police had sufficient evidence to prosecute. On Saturday 20 February, Jon Venables and Robert Thompson were charged with abduction and murder. Detained in secure units until their day in court, both boys underwent rigorous psychiatric evaluation and were deemed fit to stand trial. Three months later, as blood-baying protesters rioted outside the Liverpool courthouse, the two killers entered their pleas of not-guilty.

UNLAWFUL ACT

The trial got under way on 1 November 1993 amidst a media frenzy at Preston Crown Court. Given the pseudonyms Child A and Child B to protect their identities, the two defendants were adversely placed on a raised platform affording all those in attendance a good look at their faces. Neither child was called to give testimony throughout the entire three weeks of court proceedings. Their confessions together with some twenty tapes of CCTV footage provided the judge and jury with sufficient evidence to decide on the fate of these young offenders.

While there was little question that the boys had killed James Bulger, the focus of the opposing counsels was to deduce whether their clients knew right from wrong. Expert testimonies from psychiatrists verified the boys were not insane and had understood their actions were criminal. These findings led to guilty verdicts for both children making them the youngest convicted murderers in modern British history.

Their subsequent sentencing to eight years detention was met with public indignation and in July 1994 the then Home Secretary Michael Howard extended the tariff to fifteen years. This ruling, however, was deemed unlawful by the European Convention for the Protection of Human Rights and the original sentence was reinstated. In the summer of 2001, following a six-month parole review, Jon Venables and Robert Thompson were deemed no threat to society and released.

Granted a lifetime of immunity to protect them from reprisals, the pair began their new lives with new identities. Though, while Robert Thompson appears to have turned over a new leaf, Venables has since shown to have been unable to shake his criminal behaviour. Arrested twice in 2008 on charges of affray and possession of cocaine, in June 2010 the child killer was handed a two-year prison sentence for downloading and distributing indecent images of young children.

JOSHUA PHILLIPS

When a young girl goes missing from a quiet suburban
street in north Florida, only one teenager knows the
truth behind her disappearance, remaining silent
until a shocking discovery is made.

MADDIE GOES MISSING

Nothing out of the ordinary ever happened in
Lakewood. It was just your everyday stereotype of
American suburbia on the outskirts of Jacksonville in
North Florida. Station wagons parked on driveways
and children played in the backyards of the 1950s
homes without fear. Yet on Tuesday 3 November
1998, this picture of suburban serenity was forever
destroyed when little Maddie Clifton went missing.

It had been Election Day across the United States,
where citizens voted for their preferred public
officials, but as dusk set in on this average autumnal
evening Sheila Clifton was more concerned with
preparing dinner for her family. At six-thirty she
called for her two young daughters to come inside.
Jessie, her eldest, promptly returned but when eight-

year-old Maddie failed to appear her mother grew anxious.

As dusk turned into night the distraught Cliftons called 911 and reported their daughter missing. Maddie had last been seen around five o'clock that afternoon, dressed in a red YMCA shirt, blue shorts and black tennis shoes. Next-door neighbours helped them to search the local area with torches but to no avail. It was as if their little tomboy had simply vanished into thin air.

PRIME SUSPECT

Straight-away the local police focused their attention on one man: Larry Grisham. This prime suspect was a Lakewood neighbour who had two previous arrests for sexual battery to his name. The fact that these accusations were over fifteen years old and charges in both cases were eventually dropped did not assuage the authorities who, at this stage, had no alternative leads.

Bringing the suspect in for questioning, detectives soon had reason to feel more confident they had the man who stole Maddie when Grisham failed a lie detector test. Such faith in his guilt, however, was swiftly destroyed when he provided an air-tight alibi for the time-frame in question. Grisham was cleared of all wrongdoing and the police returned to the drawing board for clues, focusing their efforts on finding the missing little girl.

A massive citywide search for Maddie Clifton brought together over four hundred volunteers to scour the woods, dump sites and local parks of Lakewood and the surrounding areas. A reward of $50,000, later doubled, was offered for information leading to Maddie's safe return, and even the FBI were contacted to bring a successful end to a case growing colder by the hour.

Little did they know there was somebody in Lakewood who had vital information on Maddie's whereabouts. One of the helpful neighbours involved in the extensive search and who also had handed out flyers within the community knew exactly where Maddie was. His dark secret would soon be revealed in the most shocking manner.

CLEANING UP AFTER A KILLER

On Tuesday 10 November, a week after Maddie's disappearance, Melissa 'Missy' Phillips opened the door to her fourteen-year-old son's bedroom. A typical teenager's domain, the carpet was barely visible for clutter; it was like a bomb had gone off inside. Missy and her husband, Steve, had been on at their Joshua to tidy his space for weeks. With a few hours to spare before she was due at her job as a typesetter, the despairing mother decided to make a start on the mess.

The room was in dire need of a clean. There was also a strange smell emanating from somewhere amid the jumble of books, dirty laundry and other junk. Missy then spotted a water mark on the floor at the corner of her son's water-bed. Thinking it had sprung a leak, she moved closer to investigate. Studying the bedframe, she noticed a dirty white sock protruding from under the mattress. She tugged at it but it wouldn't move. Loosening the baseboard, she stuck her hand into the gap to retrieve the sock. It was then she touched something cold.

Peering into the dark hole she had created, she received the shock of her life. Staring back at her was the dead corpse of Maddie Clifton. Missy's first thought was to call her husband. Unable to reach him directly, she left a panicked voice-mail message to contact her immediately. When no call came she was forced to go against her protective role as a mother and raise the alarm, thus implicating her son.

Walking down the block, she approached a detective engaged in the ongoing search. Unable to bring herself to inform him of what she had found, she merely pointed back at her house. In next to no time, authorities descended on the Phillips home and discovered the body of Maddie Clifton. With yellow crime scene tape circling the property, reporters clamouring for information, and neighbours eager to learn the news, Sheriff Nat Glover declared on camera that Maddie had been found and that she was dead.

NINE STRIKES AND OUT

Joshua Phillips was a ninth grader at A. Philip Randolph Academies of Technology. A normal student with a C average, this unassuming fourteen-year-old was in the middle of a geography class when he was summoned to the principal's office. There, two detectives read him his rights and took him into custody. Inside an interrogation room with his father at his side, Joshua answered questions regarding his involvement in Maddie's disappearance and death. Here, he gave his version of events that early November day.

According to Joshua, Maddie had come over to the other side of the street to ask to play with him. The older boy knew he had chores to complete and was also aware of his strict father's rule of no playing outside while alone at the house. But Maddie's pleas for playtime continued and he soon gave in to the girl's persistence. Outside in the backyard they started to play ball. At approximately five-fifteen, Maddie pitched to Joshua who swung his bat, connected with the baseball which then struck Maddie in the eye.

The wounded girl began to cry and, on seeing the nasty gash he had caused, Joshua began to panic. Fearing punishment from his father for breaking house rules, he dragged Maddie into his bedroom and attempted to suppress her screams, hitting her as many as nine times with the baseball bat. When this failed to bring silence he grabbed a penknife and stabbed her in the neck. Joshua then shoved her lifeless form into the hollow bed-frame and went to clean up the blood.

The nightmare had yet to end. After his father returned from work, Joshua heard faint moans coming from his bedroom. Not wanting to incur the wrath of his domineering dad, he rushed to his room and stabbed her again until all was quiet. For the next seven days, Joshua pretended nothing had happened, burying his nose in books, forcing himself to believe it was all just a bad dream. Meanwhile, the mutilated cadaver of Maddie Clifton lay beneath him, decomposing as he slept.

TAKEN LIKE A MAN

The case was brought before the Grand Jury which voted for adult sanctions. Joshua remained in a maximum security facility, held in isolation for nine months before his trial date came around. During this time he underwent a series of psychological and neurological tests which showed the presence of bilateral frontal lobe lesions. These were known to directly impair a person's ability to comprehend the consequences of their actions. Unfortunately for Joshua, these findings were deemed inadmissible in court and played no part in his defence.

His trial, moved from Jacksonville to Polk County some two hundred miles away due to huge media interest, lasted a mere two days during the summer of 1999. His lawyer chose not to bring any witnesses to the stand nor submit any evidence that may have helped his case. Consequently, the decision for the jury was an easy one. Facing such overwhelming evidence as the blood-covered bat and knife together with his own confession, Joshua Earl Patrick Phillips was unsurprisingly found guilty of first-degree murder.

When it came to sentencing, his fifteen years prevented Joshua from receiving the death penalty, however in all other respects he was punished as an adult. The judge handed down a sentence of life imprisonment with no possibility of parole. The skinny, spectacled teenager was then delivered to Sumter Correctional Institute before being transferred to a facility in Wakulla County following threats to his life.

A series of appeals fell on deaf ears during the succeeding years, however to this day neither Missy Phillips nor Joshua himself has given up hope of a retrial. Even officials involved in his prosecution have had second thoughts as to whether the sentence given to such a young man was correct.

Despite facing a life and death behind bars, Joshua has achieved his high school diploma and even works as a legal clerk, helping fellow prisoners with their own appeals. When asked by successive reporters and interviewers why he did what he did, to this day the inmate – now in his mid-twenties – remains unable to provide an explanation for his actions.

KIP KINKEL

Having put down his parents, this gun-toting teenager paid a visit to his high school and unloaded an entire clip into a cafeteria full of students before being brought down by the heroics of one of his peers.

IN HIS SISTER'S SHADOW

Six years after their first-born, William and Faith Kinkel of Springfield, Oregon welcomed their second child into the world on 30 August 1982. They hoped Kipland Philip would follow in the footsteps of his older sister; Kristin had already proved to be a popular young girl and was excelling at school. But when the family chose to spend a year in Spain during Kip's preschool, his optimistic parents realised raising their son would be more of a test.

Finding the transition difficult, Kip struggled at the non-English-speaking school and on the family's return to Oregon, his teachers at Walterville Elementary grew increasingly concerned with his development. Feeling his maturity was below that of his peers, the school called for Kip to repeat his first year. By the time he reached fourth grade, the young pupil had been diagnosed with dyslexia and was attending special education classes.

Sensing he had become a disappointment to his parents, in contrast to his perfect cheer-leading sibling, Kip's self-worth began to take a nosedive. He started to fraternise with friends his parents considered a bad influence. While this concerned them, they would have been more troubled by another development kept hidden by their son. Since the sixth grade Kip had begun to hear voices inside his head.

DEPRESSED DELINQUENT

Outside school, the maladjusted youth developed a disturbing fascination with firearms and explosives. Believing this adult hobby would help his son to mature, his father supported the interest, enrolling him in gun safety courses and even buying him his first gun, a .22 calibre rifle. Sadly, this recreation did not bring responsibility. By the eighth grade, Kip had turned to petty theft, shoplifting compact discs from a local store and was later arrested for throwing rocks off a highway overpass.

Subsequently referred to Youth Services, the teenager underwent a series of counselling sessions to assess his behavioural problems. His psychiatrist, Dr Jeffrey Hicks, diagnosed Major Depressive Disorder, highlighting a need for anger management. Following the completion of thirty-two hours community service for the rock-throwing incident, Kip's temper went from bad to worse. In the spring of 1997, he received two school suspensions for violence and by the summer had been placed on a course of anti-depressants.

The daily dose of Prozac seemed to have a positive effect on Kip Kinkel. His depression appeared less acute and the tantrums had abated, just in time for his transition to high school. His freshman year at Thurston High began with promise. There were no signs of his temper to speak of and Kip had even been invited to join the school's football team. It looked as if the young tearaway had turned a corner. Unfortunately, the dark depression had not vanished but was merely hiding, waiting to explode.

LOCKERED AND LOADED

Kip had become adept at hiding things. As well as keeping his rage under wraps, he had also started to stockpile a secret cache of guns and explosives. Dipping into his armoury, the delinquent would later claim he had tested his materiel on animals, blowing up cats and even a cow. Always eager to add to his magazine, Kip stirred when a fellow student called him with news of a new gun. This potential purchase would set in motion a series of events that would shock Oregonians and Americans alike.

The amateur arms sale began with a telephone call on 19 May 1998. Korey Ewert had stolen a Beretta handgun from Scott Keeney, a friend's father and, knowing Kip's passion for pistols, offered it to him for a price. The next day, Kinkel brought $110 to school and following the exchange stashed the firearm in his locker. When the owner found his gun missing he reported it to the police, giving them a list of possible suspects who might have taken it. While Kip's name was not yet involved, further investigation led authorities to the troublesome teen and he was pulled from study hall.

Kinkel was searched and after a brief interrogation admitted the loaded weapon was in his locker. Promptly suspended from school for a third time pending an expulsion hearing, he was placed in police custody and charged with possession and receiving stolen goods. Driven home by an angry father, Kip knew he was in big trouble and began to consider his options. Nobody could have guessed the decision he would make.

KILL BILL

Back at home later that afternoon, Bill Kinkel

scolded his son, threatening him with boarding school if he did not start to behave. The frustrated father was all out of answers. At around three-thirty, Kip entered his parents' bedroom to retrieve his .22 Ruger rifle, loaded a full cartridge and returned downstairs where his father was sat drinking coffee at the kitchen table. Aiming the shotgun at the back of his head, Kip pulled the trigger instantly killing his father. For the next three hours, Kinkel waited at home, taking calls from concerned students at Lane Com-munity College who wondered why their Spanish teacher had not come in. Kip calmly explained his father would not be working that day due to family problems. A conference call with friends revealed something was wrong. His mind spiralling out of control, Kip cryptically told them everything was over.

At around six-thirty, Faith Kinkel arrived home from work. Her gun-wielding son met her on the garage stairs and, after telling his mother he loved her, shot her twice in the back of the head. Not yet finished, he then fired three times into her face and once through the heart. The parricidal psychopath then dragged his mother's body back into the garage, pulled his father into the bathroom and covered both with a white sheet.

HIGH SCHOOL HEROICS

The following morning, Kip woke as normal and readied himself for school while his parents lay dead below their makeshift shrouds. He drove his mother's Ford Explorer to school, parked on North 61st Street and walked into Thurston High. Hidden under his tan trench coat he carried a 9mm Glock, a Ruger semi-automatic rifle and a .22 pistol, his pockets filled with ammo.

Armed to the teeth, Kinkel entered the patio area and fired off two shots, one fatally wounding Ben Walker. He then marched into the cafeteria where nearly four hundred students congregated, awaiting the start of first period. When the gunfire began, many of those inside thought it was the sound of fireworks, a joker's juvenile prank. But when students began dropping to the floor in agony, it became clear this was more than just horseplay.

Kip Kinkel let rip the remaining forty-eight rounds from his rifle, wounding twenty-four students and killing sixteen-year-old Mikael Nicholauson. When the hollow click of the empty chamber forced him to reload, one injured teen saw a chance to end the madness. Despite sustaining a shot to the chest, puncturing his right lung, Jacob Ryker wrestled the gunman to the ground. As six more students rushed to pin him down, Kinkel managed to draw his Glock, firing one shot striking Ryker in the hand, but the shooter was unable to wriggle free and remained restrained until police arrived on the scene.

LOCKED UP FOR LIFE

Around nine o'clock, Kinkel arrived at the police station and was placed in an interview room. As Officer Al Warthen entered to begin questioning, the boy lunged at him with a hunting knife he had taped to his leg. Screaming for the policeman to shoot him, Kinkel received only a defensive shot of pepper spray to the face. Suitably subduing the prisoner, police then found two bullets taped to his bare chest; it appeared the final act to his terrible plan was to have been suicide.

When detectives discovered the shooting spree had not been his first murderous move, Lane County sheriffs visited the Kinkel home. In addition to the two covered corpses, they discovered ammunition strewn about the living room floor and five home-made bombs about the house, the fifth hidden beneath his mother's dead body.

Admitting to ending the lives of his parents to spare them the shame of his imminent expulsion, Kip Kinkel was ultimately charged with four counts of aggravated murder and twenty-six counts of attempted murder. Pleading guilty at his trial in the autumn of 1999, Judge Jack Mattison sentenced the defendant to 111 years in prison without the possibility of parole.

Nearly eight years later, Kinkel appealed for a retrial, citing ineffective counsel. He insisted his previous lawyers should have advised him to plead insane, however in August 2007 a Marion County judge denied him another day in court. A further appeal was rejected in January 2011 and, as of writing, Kip Kinkel remains locked up for life in Oregon State Correctional Institution.